Opposition by Imitation

Diverse Economies and Livable Worlds

Series Editors: J. K. Gibson-Graham, Maliha Safri,
Kevin St. Martin, Stephen Healy

OPPOSITION BY IMITATION

The Economics of Italian Anti-Mafia Activism

Christina Jerne

Diverse Economies and Livable Worlds

University of Minnesota Press
Minneapolis
London

Portions of the introduction, chapter 1, chapter 2, and chapter 4 are adapted from "Performativity and Grassroots Politics: On the Practice of Reshuffling Mafia Power," *Journal of Cultural Economy* 9, no. 6 (2016): 541–54; copyright 2016 Informa UK Limited, trading as Taylor & Francis Group. Reprinted by the permission of Taylor & Francis Ltd, http://www.tandfonline.com. Portions of the introduction, chapter 1, and the conclusion are adapted from "Anti-Mafia Enterprise: Italian Strategies to Counter Violent Economies," in *The Handbook of Diverse Economies,* ed. J. K. Gibson-Graham and Kelly Dombroski (Cheltenham, UK: Edward Elgar, 2020), 82–89. Copyright J. K. Gibson-Graham and Kelly Dombroski 2020. Reproduced with permission of Edward Elgar Publishing Limited through PLSclear. Portions of chapter 1 are adapted from "From Marching for Change to Producing the Change: Reconstructions of the Italian Anti-Mafia Movement," *Interface: A Journal for and About Social Movements* 7, no. 1 (2015): 185–213; copyright 2015. https://www.interfacejournal.net. Portions of chapters 3 and 5 are adapted from "The Syntax of Social Movement: Jam, Boxes and Other Anti-Mafia Assemblages," *Social Movement Studies* 17, no. 3 (2018): 282–98; copyright 2018 Informa UK Limited, trading as Taylor & Francis Group, reprinted by permission of Taylor & Francis Ltd.

Published by the University of Minnesota Press
111 Third Avenue South, Suite 290
Minneapolis, MN 55401-2520
http://www.upress.umn.edu

ISBN 978-1-5179-1605-3 (hc)
ISBN 978-1-5179-1606-0 (pb)

A Cataloging-in-Publication record for this book is available from the Library of Congress.

Printed in the United States of America on acid-free paper

The University of Minnesota is an equal-opportunity educator and employer.

UMP BmB 2025

To Elio, who waited for me.

Contents

Acknowledgments

My first thank you undoubtably goes to Britta Timm Knudsen. You believed in this project before you even knew me. You have profoundly disturbed my conceptions of the world and have opened eclectic avenues of thought that are now impossible to close. Thank you also to Christian Borch for directly and indirectly inspiring coherence, clarity, and rigor. To the teachers and students at the Experience Economy program, Aarhus University, for stimulating me to broaden my horizons. To Ivana Asta and Isabel Jerne for your precious help with transcription. To Henry Fording Eddins and Tom Hoctor for your editorial assistance; to Alice Campo, Arianna Vitale, Gabriele Fantoni, Mauro Pagnano, Pasquale Corvino, and Zenyse Miller for your help with images; and to Robert Parkin for your excellent and incredibly fast copywriting work. Thanks to Christoffer Kølvraa, Esra Erdem, and Kevin McDonald for engaging with this work in its doctoral format, and for pushing me to refine it into a book.

It was the editors of the Diverse Economies and Livable Worlds, however, that dragged me through the dirty work of making this happen. Thank you Maliha Safri, Stephen Healy, J. K. Gibson-Graham, and Kevin St. Martin for your clarity, precious insights, and kindness. I am continuously awestruck by the intellectual dedication, energy, and generosity you, and the larger CERN network, infuse in the world. It is largely thanks to this kind of scholarship that I continue to work within academia. Thank you also to the University of Minnesota Press for supporting this project and for ensuring the best possible quality of your publications. To my two reviewers, one anonymous and the other Ceren Özselçuk, for your hard work, patience, and at times obsessively intricate critiques. Without your scholarly input this book would have been substantially less mature and far easier to write. Thank you for repeatedly pushing me to my limits.

This work would not have been possible without the support of all Danish taxpayers who make free education a priority, the goodwill of Carlsberg Foundation (CF17–0871), the European Research Council (Grant ID: 725194), and the Independent Research Fund Denmark (Grant no. 1024–00201B). You have sustained me as a worker throughout the years it has taken to complete this book. To the Department of Anthropology and the Centre for Global Criminology at Copenhagen University, headed by Henrik Vigh: thank you for providing a generous and supportive environment to write. To Kasper Tang Vangkilde, Line Vestergaard, and Simon Lex: for reanimating my motivation and helping me rekindle with the intellectual drive that drove me to start this project in the first place. You are a most wonderful group of human beings, and the context of our project, *Re-animate: Designs for Life-Enhancing Economies in Anthropological Perspective,* could not have been a more fitting place to finish this book.

To the anti-mafia forces who have guided me:

Salvatore Lupo e Umberto Santino (per la disponibilitá ad incontrarmi e per i ricchi consigli), Lillo Gangi (che dal primo incontro mi aiuta, mi spinge e si interessa, perché si è fidato), Francesco Citarda (per la sua serietá e la sua profonda dedizione all'antimafia), Elena Ciravolo (per il suo cuore splendente), e Stefano Tringali (perché ha visto, e protetto, l'isola che è in me). Simon Maurano (per avermi tracciato il campo), Gianluca Torelli (per le profonde conversazioni che continuano a voler capire ed ascoltare), Tonio deRosa, Peppe Pecoraro, Ciro Corona (perché siete dei matti e senza la follia non si cambiano le cose), Peppe Ruggiero (perché ha condiviso con me un frammento del suo magico sguardo sul mondo). Pietro Fragrasso (che mi è venuto a prendere di notte e mi ha dato un letto e dei vestiti quando non ne avevo), Manuela Fortunato (che mi ha perdonata per essere scappata), Vito Merra (per la luce che emana), e Nicola Palladino (che mi ha infuso di gioia e musica quando non ne potevo piú). Infine a tutti i volontari, campisti e attivisti per aver condiviso con me questa sfida.

Introduction

Piazza San Giovanni, Rome, July 7, 2020. "We are not bodies to exploit!" proclaimed trade unionist Aboubakar Soumahoro in the wake of the pandemic crisis. Around him, hundreds of masked precarious workers raised their socially distanced voices in a square that rendered the invisible workforce visible; a workforce whose indispensability and vulnerability has been most forcefully revealed worldwide.

#nonsonoinvisibile (I am not invisible) started as a protest campaign for migrant farmworkers who were grieving their conditions in the south of Italy. The closure of borders worldwide made the importance of migrant farmworkers more evident than ever. The Italian government responded in two contrasting ways: on the one hand, they made various attempts at sealing extraordinary international mobility agreements, and on the other, they launched several campaigns to employ the local workforce to save the produce from rotting in the fields.

Aboubakar Soumahoro and a group of workers responded that what was rotting in the fields was not food, but workers' rights. "This is gang mastering, this is mafia!" they proclaimed, asking for basic rights and urging consumers to boycott the exploitative production chains dominating the agricultural sector. Soon, other forms of exploitative labor relations were framed as gang mastering and mafia: cultural industry workers who were forced to work for free to keep their jobs, underpaid educators improvising online teaching, and undocumented foreign care workers being denied their freedom to return to their homes. Even food courier service Uber Eats was accused of gang mastering after an investigation revealed several intermediaries abusing their power

1

and intimidating workers. The message was clear: workers felt exploited across sectors, and Italian activists call this kind of exploitation "mafia."

Why so? The same kind of exploitation, beautifully and tragically explored by Seth Holmes in his ethnography on migrant Mexican and indigenous farmworkers in the United States (Holmes 2013), would, for example, hardly be termed this way. In fact, it would not even be termed in criminal or legal terms, but simply as a form of structural violence, based on a naturalized and unjust ethnic hierarchy. Does the difference lie in the fact that, in Italy, these enterprises are run by mafia organizations?

The answer is both yes and no.

In the Italian context, the term *mafia* refers to more than a network of criminals who make illegal profits. In fact, the popular use of the term is so inflated that it has come to signify almost anything "bad." We shall make amends for this later. For now, it suffices to clarify that what these peasant activists refer to as "mafia" is a paralegal system of power, in this case, composed of gang masters, traffickers, and smugglers. What makes this system mafioso, and not only criminal, is that it derives its social influence and wealth on the parasitic use of dominant and/or legitimate forms of power (Jerne 2024) such as, in this case, the infrastructures of agricultural corporations, international food supply chains and the problematic European immigration legislation. So while "the mafia" refers to a concrete criminal group, say a specific branch of the Cosa Nostra, we could say that "mafia" without the definite article refers to a broader political order where the legal and the illegal intersect, of which "the mafia" organization is but a part.

Mafia, in both declinations, is no new problem for Italy. You will perhaps be unsurprised to hear that in the same period as #nonsonoinvisibile, April 2020, a truck transporting half a million euros in cash was stopped at Italy's eastern border, testifying that the 'Ndrangheta, one of the world's largest and richest mafia groups, had made its own emergency liquidity plan. In the midst of tough European negotiations on EU solidarity mechanisms, the German newspaper *Die Welt* published an article stating that the "Mafia awaits to be showered with money from Bruxelles," initiating diplomatic litigations. Despite the problematic nature of these accusations that conflate *Italy* with *mafia,* there is an underlying truth to them: this is an opportune time for investment for the mafia.

Worldwide, businesses and families are desperate for liquidity, and the institutional gazes are taken up by the urgency of keeping GDPs afloat and maintaining public order. Today, public massacres and bloody mafia wars are less common than tacit financial rivalries and intricate business partnerships, which are progressively globalizing as different criminal organizations are able to communicate and collaborate through extensive trading practices. Indeed, estimates suggest that the total sum for global criminal proceeds amounted to US$2.1 trillion in 2009, or close to 3.6% of global GDP (United Nations Office on Drugs and Crime, 2011). Although these figures are difficult both to collect and to interpret, they suggest that criminal markets represent a large and understudied portion of the world's economic activity (Savona and Calderoni 2015; Savona, Riccardi, and Berlusconi 2016; Hall 2018; Hall and Hudson 2021). The mafia specificity then remains an ever-pressing matter of concern.

What is less known is that for over one hundred and fifty years, Italy has been bubbling with collective action that opposes mafia. Long before Uber Eats and the European Union, the Italian anti-mafia movement, one of Europe's most important, enduring, and yet understudied social movements (dalla Chiesa 2024), has understood that mafias capitalize on social poverty. During the last two decades in particular, anti-mafia activists have started to address this issue by taking a more markedly economic turn. This approach underlines that mafias are not merely a set of criminal actors, but that they are part of a broader exploitative entrepreneurial system. Thereby, in order to fight the mafias, it is not sufficient to put mafia bosses behind bars: it is necessary to compete with their enterprises. Although violent, mafia-type enterprises often provide jobs and protection (Varese 2010); their entrepreneurial talent lies largely and precisely in their ability to create the necessity for these services. Anti-mafia activists have started to react to this business model by competing for social consensus through their own forms of enterprise: cooperatives, consumer unions, social enterprises, critical marketing, and volunteering initiatives that operate against mafias.

This book explores these forms of economic activism. Drawing on the ethnographic fieldwork I carried out in different parts of Italy between 2014 and 2019, it illustrates how ordinary people are organizing to prevent and counter the expansion of mafias, in the hope that others in other contexts might learn from these experiences. More broadly, it illustrates the different subjectivities and forms of agency involved in economic action, and sets out to rethink the scope of cultural and political transformation that economic action can (and already does) bring about.

My analytical focus lies on two central developments in contemporary grassroots struggles against the mafias. The first is the anti-mafia movement's tactic of *mimicking* the mafia. I am interested in the political possibilities afforded by this particular form of opposition, as well as the implications this mimetic relationship might have for broader questions of crime prevention and criminalization. The second development, which is the one I will unpack first, is the fact that this mimetic opposition is articulated in *economic* terms. Not only is this interesting in and of itself, but this shift in repertoire opens broader questions about the forms in which collective action is most commonly conceived of and practiced.

The (Im)possibility of Economic Activism

Anti-mafia activists are not alone in turning to critical economic organization to counter injustices: slow-living movements challenging racial, class, and interspecies oppression inherent in industrial production models (Hersey 2022); fair-trade enterprises improving social equality along supply chains (Naylor 2019); African diasporas organizing alternative forms of banking to contest the exclusion and racism faced in dominant market economies (Hossein 2016, 2018); permaculture and veganism as reactions to environmental degradation. All these movements are expressing their discontent by challenging business-as-usual models by owning up to their own economic agency. Concurrently, and particularly since the 2008 financial crisis, there have been a growing number of public demonstrations manifesting dissent toward structural aspects of "the economy." The antiausterity protests around Europe questioned the power of public and private bodies in relation to national debt. The Occupy Wall Street protests questioned the workings of the financial system and its effects on wealth distribution. Today, people are voicing their desperation at losing their sources of sustainment due to harsh lockdowns and increasing costs of living all over the world. It seems that, particularly in recent decades, "the economy" has increasingly become an object of explicit contestation.

This economic turn led me to seek out literature that would help me explain and make sense of what I was observing in the Italian context. Why were these activists experimenting with economic strategies? Was the shift I was seeing in anti-mafia activism a reaction to shifting forms of mafia action? Or was it a broader trend within contemporary collective action? The most obvious starting point to answer these questions was the field of political economy. However, its prevalently institutional take on politics pushed me to look elsewhere: literature on social movements and collective action. I soon found that although numerous studies were being undertaken on collective action that was manifesting some form of dissent toward economy (e.g., Fominaya and Hayes 2016; Caruso and Cini 2020; Rossi 2022), there seemed to be an essential dualism between the economy and politics. The economy, in other words, is often treated as something outside politics: a monolith that travels on a track parallel to politics.

On the one hand, it is discussed as something that *allows* grassroots politics to happen. In this understanding, *economy* means, for example, the financial resources needed to mobilize activists or to achieve visibility and access to arenas where lobbying activities can occur. We can call this the "instrumental rational action" paradigm, which is a mixed legacy of Habermas[1] (1987) and utilitarianism, in the guise of new institutional economics (Olson 1965). In this case the social movement is envisioned as a rational economic actor, seeking to optimize its marginal utility, implying a broader colonization of politics with utilitarian logics. On the other hand, economy is framed as something that needs to be contested *by* politics. Unequal wealth distribution, privatization, or structural class issues, for example, would be seen as economic questions that need to be tackled by unions and other institutions where political power resides. The social movement is here usually a victim of an inescapable economic system, and its agency is reduced to its capacity to mobilize, to publicly manifest its claims to the true holders of power, usually state institutions. We can call this the "neoliberal diagnosis," which is, not unlike the previous model, particularly prominent in radical leftist scholarship, and is a residue of Marxian essentialism, which conflates "the economy" with a unified, complete, and totalizing capitalist system that must be opposed.

In sum, both approaches separate the two realms, politics and economy, by placing them in a hierarchical position to one another. In neither version is economic action seen as having constitutive effects in its own right: it is either instrumental to politics (below it), or the object of politics (above it). But how can we talk of economic actions that are, in themselves, political without limiting ourselves to either one of these directions? Does the deficiency of alternatives within the literature mirror a scarcity of historical precedents? In other words, does economic contention constitute a new mode of political action per se?

The answers I kept finding within different literatures kept bringing me back to the terms I was dealing with: economy and politics. Both of these words carry a colossal historical and theoretical weight, which I can in no way address here. However, two aspects of their conceptual heritage are of particular relevance for this context, as both of these obscure the possibility of recognizing that economic actions can have political agency. For this reason, they must be shortly addressed before turning to the activism per se.

Economy as a Transcendent Realm

Most economics, business, and social science textbooks will derive the etymology of "economy" from the Greek term *oikonomia* (οἰκονομία): *oikos* is interpreted as household and *nomos* as the management, administration, and ruling of the first. Economy would then be the art of managing the household, while political economy would classify a particular form of management that is dealt with by the government of a nation-state. The adjective "political" would then operate as an extension of the act of manage-ment to a broader realm than the private, namely, the public. This is the classic understanding of the academic discipline of political economy,[2] which has in the nineteenth and twentieth centuries in fact mainly been a prerogative of moral philosophy, and later, political science.[3]

According to much progressive-leftist thought, particularly the kind that draws inspiration from the work of Karl Polanyi,[4] the rea-son for the very development of the subject area "political economy" is in fact a *moral* response to a historical transformation. Indeed, in 1944, Polanyi described the Great Transformation, the emergence of two parallel movements throughout the nineteenth century: the emergence of free-market capitalism, which eroded social ties and raced toward calculated profit making, and its countermovement, connected to social protectionism that, through regulations and taxations, aimed at shielding the weakest members of society from the deleterious effects of capitalism (Polanyi 1957, 138). Under-lying this thought is the view that the market has a disembedding force that, if left to itself, destroys the very fabric of society. This is what Mark Granovetter famously called the *under*socialized con-ception of human action (Granovetter 1985), which does not grant social life any possibility of impacting the market economy, which instead operates in a vacuum, and becomes a force of its own.

The moral concerns proposed by Polanyi did indeed materialize in the development of a subject area. It became the task of political economy to find the best way to manage this force and minimize the collective damage.[5] The political in economy became mascu-line rigor that contains the dangers of feminine hysteria (Berardi 2014). And this rigor would effectively be exercised by the state. In other terms, the idea that "the market economy" had a destruc-tive, feminine force of its own allowed for the enforcement of state-centric and elitist views of political economic action. In the words of Martijn Konings (2015, 10), "the conceptual evacuation of ethics from economy entails an emphasis on the need for external infusions of morality that displace agency from ordinary people to elites."

Paradoxically, economics became a separate discipline focused on the calculative schemes that follow the logic of profit, taking little regard for human relationships (Konings 2015, 43). These disciplinary developments resulted in the economy becoming natural and the political artificial. The consequences of this conceptual divorce become most apparent during the early twentieth century, when the term *economy* became most commonly used as a noun (*the* economy) rather than an adjective (the economic x). That is, during the Great Acceleration where "the economy" became a *thing* that grew from its addiction to fossil fuel (Miller 2019, 16).

Philosophers such as Giorgio Agamben (2009) and Michel Foucault (2008) have convincingly illustrated the depths of this theological and ideological semantic heritage, which grants the term *economy* some metaphysical force to it. Other thinkers have identified the same force in a most recent variant, capitalism, or neoliberalism, whose end is less easy to imagine than the very end of the world (Gibson-Graham 2006b; Jameson 2003; Fisher 2009). At a time dominated by cuts in public spending, financial crises, and widespread ecological destruction, this is a question that many may relate to: Just who is in charge of the neoliberal machine? The Occupy protests were clear carriers of this message. Only the 1 percent have the upper hand; the remaining 99 percent of the world is subjected to economy. While the existence of unequal wealth distributions and social injustices is undeniable, as is the fact that certain actors take advantage of economic regimes to grossly increase their power, I believe that thinking in these terms is problematic. Indeed, the 1/99 ratio in a way indicates that there is one unified system (the 100 percent) of which almost everyone is simply a spectator. The system is in this sense above the people, and therefore it is impossible to think outside it. At best, it can be redistributed (that is, if the 1 percent, whoever they may be, comply). In this understanding, economy is a unified whole that not only transcends actual relationships, it determines them.

But are economic arrangements, on all scales, not also in themselves possible sites for political action? If the economy is "the social site that constrains activities at all other sites, the supreme being whose dictates must unquestioningly be obeyed" (Gibson-Graham 2006b, 94) then it would be impossible for ordinary people to change or contest any economic order. Yet the protagonists of this book demonstrate that there are many people (who are neither enlightened economists nor politicians) who are indeed contesting oppressive economic orders by taking matters into their own hands, recognizing that they too are economic subjects who are indeed capable of changing how they act. But in order to plot these concrete experiences onto a broader historical canvas, it is first necessary to bring "the economy" back down to earth.

To achieve this, I draw inspiration from scholars who work pragmatically and focus on the economic *processes* that make organizations. I am referring in particular to feminist political economists J. K. Gibson-Graham and the diverse economies tradition that followed (see Gibson-Graham and Dombroski 2020 for a recent overview), as well as science and technology scholars concerned with valuation processes such as, among others, Noortje Marres, Fabian Muniesa, Michel Callon, and the late Bruno Latour. Both these scholarships have powerfully challenged the idea of a unified, totalizing, and inescapable whole that we might call "the economy" through the work of deconstruction. Their work illustrates the numerous *practices* that compose different economies, which, as the plural suggests, don't all add up to a single system, and cannot be reduced to one particular logic or rationality (Gibson-Graham et al. 2018). Breaking down "the economic system" is essentially a feminist deconstructive strategy that aims to break down the modern rationalist conception of the (economic) subject as unified and complete (Gibson-Graham 2006a, 2006b). Rather, as the protagonists of this book show, economies and their subjects are works in progress, chains of actions that cite or reinterpret norms to constitute meaning (Butler 1993) and materialize them into organizations.

Following Bruno Latour (2013), politics and economy are not two different realms made up of different "stuff" (e.g., voting booths, parliaments, and armies versus stock markets, factories, and banks), but rather two different but complementary ways of organizing. In antiquity the term *economy* was not primarily used for matters of exchange and production. Instead, it was more of a pragmatic "sphere of life," characterized by the practical realization of a given principle (Konings 2015, 43). It referred to "regimes for governing interdependent systems—the economy of the body, the economy of the farm, or the divine economy of God" (Miller

2019, 15). Thereby, it did not denote a purely calculative exercise that ignored morality (although calculations were included), but, quite the opposite, represented the diversity of ways to realize different norms on Earth (that were, given the time, primarily religious in kind).[6]

My understanding of economy comes close to these more administrative understandings. I would characterize as "economic" all those practices and technologies that aim at sustaining, improving, and caring for our livelihoods and for life on earth. These can of course be expressed in numerous and ethically contrasting ways, from increasing one's individual wealth and prosperity through the illicit sale of human organs, to living in quasi-asceticism to minimize one's impact on even a blade of grass. The overall guiding principle of economic action is the enhancement of life.

While this understanding of economy is broad, I do not see everything as economic, nor do I mean to conflate it with politics (see next section). Examples of economic practices are activities such as treating something as part of a circuit/system, abstracting, regarding something as abundant/scarce, pricing, calculating, administering/allocating, or preparing something for exchange (Muniesa 2014, 39). Concrete examples from the anti-mafia movement include, respectively: creating a consumer union against extortion, making a collective investment in a crime-prone neighborhood, prioritizing certain expenses over others in a social enterprise to facilitate the survival and education of ex-felons, putting a price on "mafia-free" products and services, calculating a fair wage for an undocumented migrant farmworker doing piecework for a cooperative, commoning mafia-expropriated property for the benefit of the community, and developing marketing strategies that benefit "extortion-free" enterprises.

By looking at these types of action, it becomes clear that economy is far from transcendent. Instead, it is a practical order populated with all sorts of very secular things, both human and nonhuman, that take part in its formation. This perspective makes it possible to look at the multiple aggregates that enforce economic systems of power, instead of focusing on who can get the most out of an unquestionable system of power.[7]

State-Centrism and the Preemption of Political Diversity

Of parallel importance to this study is the location of the political. Enlightenment political theory tends to reduce politics to the specific form of collective government that is represented by the state and its institutions. For Thomas Hobbes, for example, the state of nature is "apolitical." Only when the social contract is established—that is, when a state is established—is there the possibility for politics to occur. In light of this, collective action would be understood as a direct confrontation between the contractors and the contract. Because of this relationship, many early social theorists saw collective behavior as a threat to politics (Borch 2012).

Connectedly, since political philosophy has a normative agenda—that is, it seeks to answer the question of what the "best" form of government might be—the quality of political action has often been measured, in both theory and practice, in terms of its relationship with the most legitimate form of politics, the kind that emanates from the modern nation-state. Other attempts to govern lives by setting and performing certain rules of conduct are thereby regarded as alternative, illicit, backward, developing, utopian, conspiratorial, or outright dangerous: "The very *concept* of politics thus becomes a guarantor of security, a tool for policing the borders of ordered social interactions" (Viriasova 2011).

Twentieth-century political theory has challenged this view. The works of numerous feminist and postcolonial thinkers have brought about a less foundationalist view of politics. One important move has been to mark the difference between the terms *politics* and *political* (Mouffe 2005). Politics broadly describes the set of rules and related practices that govern and order a given collective though technologies, institutions, and agents that enforce the distinctions between people's possibilities and limits based on their social position. The political, on the other hand, is a mode of opposition, an agonistic force that is constitutive of politics (Mouffe 2005, 9). It is "an index of the space of disagreement" (Barry 2002, 270), or in other words, the fulcrum of what the public considers to be a *problem* at a given point in time (Lippmann 1993). In this understanding, politics and its driving force, the political, can occur in a variety of sites and can involve a plethora of types of actors, thus allowing us to decenter political analyses from the modern nation-state.

While this is old news to a number of more philosophically inclined disciplines (e.g., cultural studies, geography, political anthropology, and the humanities in general) that work on contentious political activities, this paradigmatic shift has failed to fully enter the field of social movement studies and the more influential social sciences (i.e., the ones that the world's leaders are often educated in). That is, the signifier "collective action" is still indexical to "institutionalized state power," which seems to be the only legitimate site for "real" political action. Although social movements have been widely theorized as operating across scales and sectors, the majority of this scholarship still remains focused on actions that fall into classic representation of politics (Alvarez et al. 1998; Haenfler et al. 2012; Yates 2015a). I am referring to collective actions that cry out for power changes in state institutions that *represent*. In fact, both terms, *politics* and *political*, are most commonly used to refer to institutions and activities that take up a preestablished form (Barnes 2017).

This is problematic for two reasons. The first, more empirical reason is that this focus on the most visible culmination of the political (read, the protest event) leaves little attention for the myriad of contentious arrangements that are, in my view, increasingly more actual, and perhaps even more possible. Although many contemporary waves of protest events around the world demonstrate that this form of political action is far from irrelevant or bypassed, and that the state is even gaining prominence and force, other forms of collective action, which are far more multicentered, fluid, and often with little or no engagement with the state, are marking their presence in space and duration in time.

Second, I believe that loosening up the relationship between collective action and the state is a necessary step to constructing meaningful and effective political projects for the present. While holding signs and demonstrating in front of banks and town halls is of fundamental importance to ensure the upholding of institutional democracy, its many failures and let-downs also suggest a need to diversify strategies. Thus, this reservation regarding readings of collective action that are founded on nineteenth-century

Eurocentric conceptions of politics is more normative in temper. Dignity and voice are finally beginning to be granted to the oppressed, colonized, and hitherto invisible forms of political action. Since the spectrum of colors allowed in the polis is broadening, it is imperative to seize this opening and learn to recognize and navigate diversity in order to shape it.

Luckily, numerous social movement scholars I refer to throughout the book have developed a more hybrid and nonessentialist vision of politics. I join these voices by granting critical economic action the possibility of being considered contentious "enough."

In many ways, this problematization of state-centric views of collective action is inspired by the same critique that economic geographers Julie Graham and Katherine Gibson made of capitalocentric views of economy in the mid 1990s (Gibson-Graham 2006b). The original iceberg that they elaborated to represent this critique is featured in Figure 1a (Community Economies Collective 2019) and illustrates the economy as a whole. The tip of the iceberg shows the main descriptor we use to speak of and envisage economies, that is, capitalism. The submerged part of the iceberg instead represents the diversity of ways in which economy is actually practiced. This illustrates that capitalocentrism, the discursive move of creating a capitalist/noncapitalist binary and conflating economy with capitalism, violently makes less credible a whole swathe of economic activities that has sustained lives around the world for millennia. Thanks to their work, today numerous voices are making visible the multiplicity of economic practices that exist around the world, and that do not require "leaning" on capitalist categories to identify themselves (some recent examples include Diprose 2016; Borowiak et al. 2018; Schram and Pavlovskaya 2017; Dombroski 2018, Gibson-Graham and Dombroski 2020). This is a postcapitalist politics, also called "a politics of possibility" for its dedication to theorize and support emerging political imaginaries of the *here and now* (Gibson-Graham 2006b).

As highlighted in my own elaboration of the iceberg model of economy in Figure 1b, my intent is to explore and bring forth diverse ways of doing collective action. Similarly to capitalism, the protest event has become the dominant imaginary of collective action (the whole iceberg in Figure 1b) and social change.

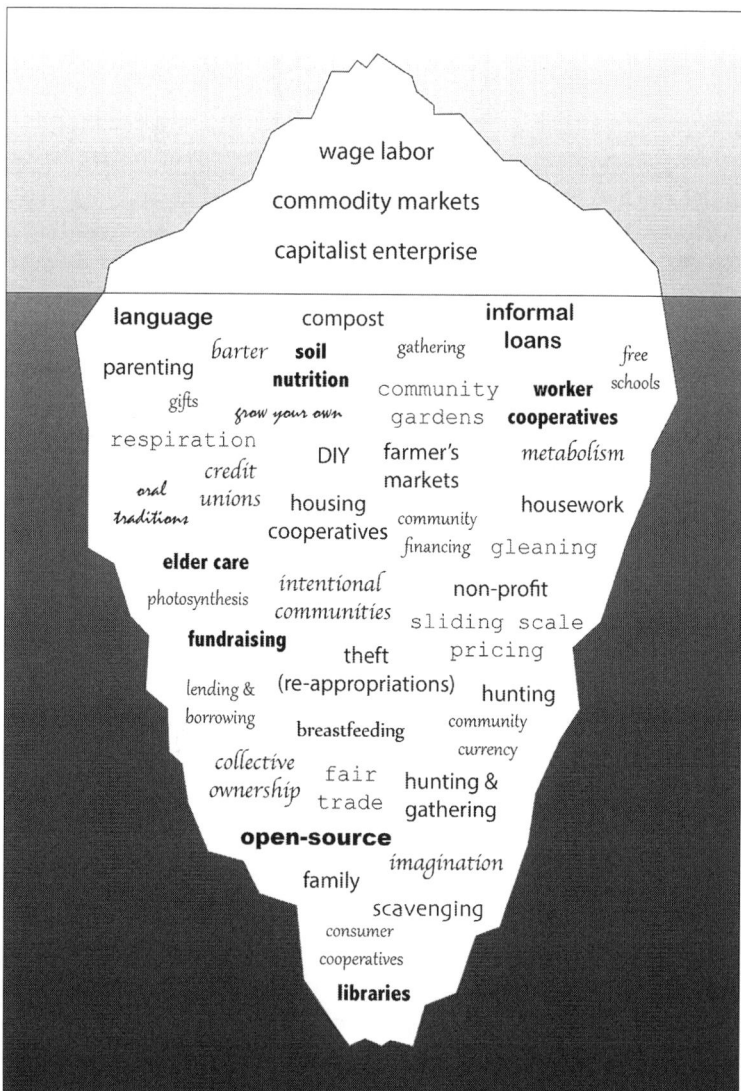

Figure 1a. Iceberg model of diverse economies by Community Economies Collective (CEC). Licensed under a Creative Commons Attribution-ShareAlike 4.0 International License. 2019.

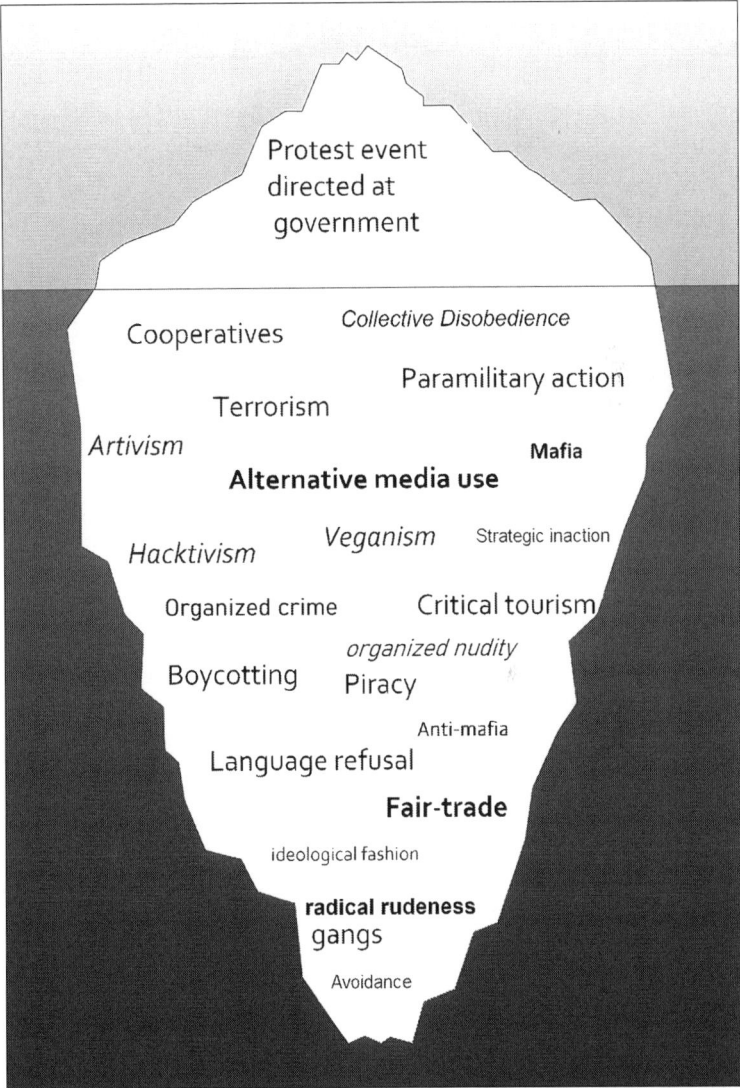

Figure 1b. Iceberg model of diverse collective action. Re-elaboration of the CEC iceberg model by Christina Jerne.

Throughout this book I will illustrate numerous and diverse ways in which anti-mafia activism is currently being practiced. Due to the recent developments I opened with, my particular focus lies on economic forms of activism, but these are but one of many repertoires of the anti-mafia movement. This very diversity testifies to the importance of moving beyond the protest event as the culmination of the political, and beyond the state as a prime keeper of political agency.

There are, of course, numerous examples of collective action that are not a protest event that arguably aim to achieve or succeed in achieving *less* livable worlds. Terrorism, paramilitary action, organized crime, and piracy are in many ways extremely successful and increasingly global ways of critiquing existing power arrangements and counterexerting power over a given territory. Indeed, this theoretical opening could in prospect also be used to reflect on these forms of collective action.

However, my focus lies on tools that *break* social orders that are not respectful of the life of others and are thereby violent and oppressive. My empirical and political attention is one that seeks to highlight ways that challenge and disrupt mafia orders in particular, and thereby encourage and make visible those forms of collective action that are achieving this goal.

Other than illustrating these actions by reconstructing them empirically, my contribution to enforcing a politics of possibility is also conceptual. That is, my deconstructive work is situated in one of the scholarships that is most central to social struggle: social movement studies. Indeed, while postcapitalist politics are broadly understood as "a politics of collective action" (Gibson-Graham 2006b; Roelvink 2016), little work has been carried out to actually discuss the implications of this politics for the way *collective action* is conceptualized. Inspired by the view that language has a constitutive (rather than a merely representative) function, and triggered by the tensions highlighted so far in the sociology and politology of collective action, I have made my particular starting point the relationship between social movements and economy.

Surely, some authors might not see collective action and social movements as synonyms. I have chosen to work with the social movement literature because it has become one of the broadest fields dedicated to the study of "people acting together in pursuit of a common interest" (Tilly 1977), which is my general understanding of collective action. In other words, although a broad range of theories informs social movement studies, together it constitutes a "strong" approach (Sedgewick 2003, 134) to collective action, that is, an approach that "knows where the power lies, it suspects how phenomena line up to consolidate power and it cannot be surprised" (Gibson-Graham and Dombroski 2020, 8). Therefore, it is an important field of study to engage with because of its huge influence on popular understandings of both politics and economy. But also, and no less importantly, because of its rich intellectual repertoire.

Mafia in the Plural

Not unlike capitalism, *mafia* has in many ways become an all-encompassing signifier used to classify the Italian political economy. (Any Sicilian reading this might relate to the first reaction one gets when introducing oneself as such: "Ah! You come from mafia land.") In fact, some common mafia metaphors include the hydra, whose heads continue to proliferate if you cut them off, or the octopus, whose many arms steer and strangle the whole system. To counter this monism, I will make visible many different tools that are already being used to interrupt mafia orders. This demonstrates that mafia is not an inescapable whole.

Not only is the mafia escapable, it is also plural. Although the term *mafia* originally signified a specific criminal organization that descends from Sicily, namely, Cosa Nostra, the term is now commonly used to refer to all Italian organized crime groups (such as Camorra linked with Campania and 'Ndrangheta linked with Calabria). In fact, the word *mafia* is used to describe a broad range of other phenomena: a specific mode of dress, organized crime, illegality, an aggressive attitude, corruption, a synonym for "evil" corporations, or even a leftist "fantasy" (Hess 1973; dalla Chiesa 2017). Deborah Puccio-Den has recently addressed just how semantically slippery the term is in her book *Mafiacraft* (2021). In it she illustrates the performative power of this polysemic term, showing that in different phases of history, mafia itself manifests in the terms through which it is uttered and especially, *not* uttered. Given the political importance of language, particularly in the context of the mafia, which has been defined by silences, absences, denial, and omertà, we must make some clarity, for this type of plurality can be misleading for our purposes.

Most criminologists would agree with the fact that mafia is a specific type of organized crime, that is, in Federico Varese's words "a group that attempts to regulate and control the production and distribution of a given commodity or service unlawfully" (Varese 2010, 4–17). But while "mafia is most certainly organised crime" as Judge Giovanni Falcone rightly noted, "not all organised crime is mafia" (Falcone 2024, 66). Historians and criminologists also point to the need to distinguish between different mafia organizations,[8] as each group has a distinct genealogy and contextual significance (e.g., Tarde 1890; Lupo 2007, 2009; Renda 1984, 1997; Romano 1963; Barbagallo 2010). However, some have chosen to systematize the connection between these (Dickie 2013), pointing to the need to find historical convergences, such as the fact that all these groups emerged in areas of Italy that had been governed by the Spanish and the Bourbon dynasty (Ciconte 2008).

Others have instead focused on the different markets in which these networks invest (Savona 2014; Savona and Calderoni 2015; Savona, Riccardi, and Berlusconi 2016). Indeed, there is an important body of literature focusing on the commercial aspect of mafias (e.g., Smith 1980; Reuter 1983). Studies have emphasized their entrepreneurial aspect (Arlacchi 1983; Catanzaro 1988), analyzing the mafia as an industry whose supply can be found in protection (Gambetta 1996; Varese 2010). Theodoros Rakopoulos's ethnography (2017) has also demonstrated how mafias strive to push out other models of enterprise not only through violence, but also by competing for and winning consent.

Political and sociological studies have instead prioritized the different power dynamics that surround mafias. Some have focused more on their internal dynamics (Hess 1973), while others have stressed their relations with institutions (Della Porta and Vannucci 1999). Alternatively, the gaze has been on the center-periphery power dynamics that have facilitated their emergence, influenced by dependency or world-systems approaches (Blok

1974; Schneider and Schneider 1976). These studies have helped break the idea that the mafia is an isolated phenomenon that has no contact with the "outside," whether this is to be found in national or international institutions and infrastructures.

Others have undermined the possibility of there even being an "outside" to mafia. Here the outside is not intended as a set of relations but rather as a general cultural essence that is seen as inescapable. An early example of this type of thinking is the work of the anthropologist Giuseppe Pitré, who defined mafia not as an organization or a form of crime, but rather as being "the exaggerated conscience of the self" belonging to the Sicilian people, one that led to hatred of others' superiority and arrogance (Pitré [1889] 1978, 292–94).[9] More recent, internationally notorious studies adhere to this line of thought. Edward Banfield (1958), for instance, saw the entire south of Italy plagued by an inherent "amoral familism" that impeded the overall progress of society. Robert Putnam (1993) took this view further, arguing that amoral familism is the most rational way to behave in an "uncivic" context,[10] where arbitrary justice, corruption, fear, and suspicion reign. To Putnam, the south of Italy demonstrates an incapability of association and horizontal cooperation due to its lack of reciprocal trust. Diego Gambetta (1996) too confirms the chronic inability to trust others as a founding essence of the Sicilian people, as well as the reason for an industry of protection, namely, the mafia. Other than being deterministic, essentialist, and somewhat demeaning, these readings lack coherence with the object of study being treated here. As we shall see in the next chapter, it is precisely in the "uncivic" South that the anti-mafia movement, a fervid example of "horizontal solidarity," has its roots.

Moreover, the protagonists of this study require a different level of openness to such interpretations. As will hopefully become clear throughout this book, the anti-mafia movement stands in opposition to a very broad range of phenomena that certainly cannot be limited to specific aspects of the problem as they have been discussed by specialists. In other words, the anti-mafia movement is *uniquely* opposed neither to a specific form of criminal organization nor to one form of enterprise. And it is not solely opposed to a specific network of people or a general culture of distrust, but instead opposes a composite arrangement of aspects that enforce mafia power and culture. Different parts of the movement are concerned with their own contextual specificities.

Building on these emic understandings, I suggest that mafia can more appropriately be defined as a paralegal form of power.[11] I say *paralegal* and not *illegal* or *extralegal* because it is at once *against* the rule of law (it corrupts its principles and agents) and *for* it (it uses its infrastructures to its own advantage and does not seek to replace them). The peculiarity of this type of political entrepreneurship lies in the fact that it takes a parasitic form: it infiltrates, navigates, and exploits a "host," that is, a legitimate form of governance (a kingdom, a republic, a corporation, a fiefdom, a family) to gain social influence, and it uses different forms of violence to ensure it is maintained (see Jerne 2024 for a more detailed account).

This interpretation of the mafia phenomenon is based on a historical study I have carried out with Nando dalla Chiesa on the protagonists of anti-mafia movement since its origins in the nineteenth century (dalla Chiesa and Jerne 2024), as well as the contemporary interpretations of anti-mafia activists I have worked alongside for the past decade. As such, it is based on the concrete historical development of the Italian mafias, but from the perspective of those who have opposed it.

Recognizing that the mafia is more than a network of criminals but instead a peculiar form of governance that many nonaffiliates also partake in enforcing (more or less directly) is thus an important acknowledgment for both analytical and political reasons. It allows for the recognition of the diversity of forces and actors that compose mafia, which implies that it cannot simply be defeated by locking up bosses, the most "visible" part of the mafia. Thus, it makes possible the development of a nuanced counteroffensive that has multiple sites of action and proves that mafia is not an inescapable necessity, an approach that General Carlo Alberto dalla Chiesa called "a global anti-mafia" (dalla Chiesa [1982] 2024).

Today it has also become more common to speak of *mafias* rather than "the mafia." This semantic expansion is not confined to expert scholarly circles but has gained traction within the anti-mafia movement and popular usage more generally (Santino 2006; dalla Chiesa 2014a). This reflects, for one thing, the empirical expansion of Italian mafias (and anti-mafias) (Santino 2007): they have moved to different territories, expanded to new sectors, and started collaborating with other networks and forms of organized crime around the world. The presence of Italian mafias in the world is in fact now well established, as is the presence of Nigerian, Albanian, Chinese, Columbian, Moldovan, and Russian mafias in Italy. This confirms that they are not territorially bound to some cultural essence but that they travel and interact. Indeed, while national identifications can help trace geographical movements, they do not necessarily provide the best lens to read their increasingly hybrid connections (Sausdal and Vigh 2019). Mafias are in themselves processes and trajectories of globalization.

We might describe contemporary mafias as having these three chief characteristics: a composite and hybrid nature (they work across classes, sectors, ethnic groups, and nation-states), a distinctive drive for power and capital (they work across systems of power: formal and informal, state and corporate), and a tendency to rely on violence[12] and intimidation to build consensus (the cultural codes that lie behind this violence draw on corporate, religious, political, and/or popular matrixes).

The pluralization of the term *mafia* also reflects a broader cultural shift. The fact that activists are addressing mafia as a particular form of paralegal power reflects a greater global awareness of the diversity of forms of governance that coexist with the state worldwide (e.g., Comaroff and Comaroff 2006; Nordstrom 2007; Hazen and Rodgers 2014; Hirschfeld 2015; Hall 2018; Barnes 2017; Lessing 2021). This is a most important and positive development. The gradual acknowledgment of the need to address the place and force of illicit political actors in a realpolitik, however, implies abandoning the idea that these actors should be treated with moralizing denials, sensationalist criminalization, or worse—a patronizing myopia that sees these forces as exceptional and as momentary failings of the liberal democratic state. Furthermore, it requires recognizing that illicit and submerged economies are just as real and widespread as capitalism or other types of formal economy that are often considered dominant, natural, and inevitable (McKinnon et al. 2018; Hall and Hudson 2021; Rodgers 2022).

As we shall see, both mafia and anti-mafia economies are incredibly diverse. Given the parasitic relation of mafias to existing and dominant forms of power, both the nation-state and capitalism certainly play an important role in shaping both mafia and anti-mafia economies. But these are but two of many forms of governance that they relate to. By highlighting the diversity of ways of organizing against mafias in Italy, my overall aim is thus also to encourage the abandonment of state-centric and capitalocentric treatments of political economy in other contexts of the world, a shift of attention that is vital to any attempt to contrast entities as complex and multiscalar as mafias.

Mimesis: A Political Tactic

How to defeat such a complex parasite? Criminologists, jurists, statesmen, generals, trade-unionists, and priests have asked themselves this question for more than 160 years.[13] The answers have been numerous and at times conflicting. But if we focus only on the enquiries made by those directly involved in the struggle against the mafias, there is at least one point of agreement: the eradication of the problem does not lie in the removal of deviant individuals.

What was striking and initially counterintuitive to me was the way various activists instead addressed the mafia as a kind of competitor, as a force that they in some way had to shadow and outsmart, or "beat at their own game." Like any other form of power, mafia exerts social control in a variety of ways: for example, by providing employment, sanctioning certain behaviors that threaten its authority, or subsuming or isolating individuals with certain dangerous skill sets. One of the central tactics that grassroots activists have therefore developed is to imitate the mafia's work of social control. The ethical terms of the social control are reversed, though: while mafia uses social control to preserve its power by resorting to different kinds of violence, anti-mafia activists seek to interrupt this type of social control by eradicating violence and empowering the oppressed via, for example, the restoration of economic agency.

Crime and Mimesis

From a criminological perspective, this mimetic relationship reflects a broader insight about the very nature of crime. In particular, it challenges the view of crime as an individual possession, and society as the antonym of crime (Tonkonoff 2014a, 530). This perspective is a residue of classic criminological approaches that developed throughout the nineteenth century in critique of the penal codes that, at the time (and to some extent, still today), were based on the notion of free will.

Various scholars thus sought to conceptualize crime as more than an individual responsibility or a calculated interest. Some, such as Enrico Ferri and his teacher Cesare Lombroso, believed that crime was instead an instinctual act determined by innate psychological or biological traits. This implied that the source of criminal behavior, being intraindividual and more or less determined at birth, lies outside the social realm. Others, influenced by early Durkheimian thinking (Durkheim 1984), saw the criminal as an individual moved to violate rules because of a poor socialization. In this case the criminal is also antisocial, but this time in the sense that she/he operates from a position of failure and/or lack of sociality.

As Sergio Tonkonoff (2014a) usefully reconstructs, cultural approaches[14] developed as a response to these positions and had the intent of rehumanizing (or better, resocializing) the criminal. They demonstrated that crime does not happen in a social vacuum. Gabriel Tarde's work (1886, 1890) was of a particular importance for the development of this paradigm. His sociology was founded on the notion of imitation. In his view, society is the outcome of the mimetic repetitive action that heterogeneous networks engage in over time. Crime, being a particular kind of imitative phenomenon, is likewise founded on social actions that gravitate toward "becoming similar." And this entails that the criminal is actually a hypersocialized individual. "In nobody is society so present as in those who violently oppose it" (Tonkonoff 2014b, 66). To Tarde, the relation between crime and society is thus characterized by excess, rather than lack or deficit. Crime is an exaggerated, extreme (imitative) expression of the very criminalizing culture from which it emerges. In Tonkonoff's words, because "all socio-symbolic order is defined and held up by interdictions that mark its ultimate boundaries" (2014a, 533), crime might be better understood as a radical form of alterity, which illustrates the limits of a given culture.

Crime is thus as constitutive to culture as culture is to crime. Consequentially, crime prevention should be an exercise that *exceeds* the mere denial or prohibition of a given action performed by a group or an individual, for criminal actions are in fact deeply intertwined with culture that they are even an excessive manifestation of.

Anti-mafia activism is a clear example of this realization. Simply removing the tip of the (mafia) iceberg does not eradicate the culture but rather only one of its symptoms. The collective actions that we shall explore in fact operate precisely by *plunging* into the culture that mafia reproduces, and fully recognize themselves as active protagonists of the very same. In other words, criminal culture is not external or parallel to anticriminal culture, but merely one direction of the same social field. As such crime must be opposed from "within."

Mimesis and Repetition

The notion of mimesis resonates strongly with repetition:[15] both invoke some kind of similarity and reiteration. Authors such as Gilles Deleuze, Judith Butler, and Jacques Derrida posit that social orders are made and maintained via the differential repetition of previous norms, structures, and signs (see Moebius 2004 for an in-depth discussion and comparison). These poststructuralist perspectives thus, akin to Tarde, suggest that repetition serves as the foundational principle underlying all social interactions. They, however, also bring us closer to answering the question of what is required to *break* these social orders, and thus to gain a better understanding of the agonistic use of mimesis exemplified by the anti-mafia.

Indeed, all these thinkers have also, in different ways, illustrated that while all social life is fundamentally shaped by repetition, each repetition always entails a difference, as the very act of
repeating something entails a change; be it micro- or macroscopic.
In fact, there are different kinds and degrees of difference, which
are termed differently by each of these authors, and differently
throughout their careers. While the details of these differences
exceed the scope of this book, it is appropriate to remark that the
kind of difference that is of interest to this context is the kind that
makes something else possible. The kind that transforms precedent dominant structures, like mafia. The kind that diffuses, that
is in turn imitated, and brings about broader social change.

In the work of Gabriel Tarde, these kinds of repetitions are
called *inventions.* Inventions are eventful interruptions, "individual revolts against accepted ethics" (Tarde 2000, 86) that bring
about a new kind of imitative series. Importantly, although inventions can be accidental and the results of unconscious imitations,
inventions are ultimately tied to moments of *decision,* of awaken-
ing from the somnambulistic, semiconscious work of mimesis.

Stephan Moebius (2004, 63) poignantly notes that this will-
ful moment, or imitative event, has its parallels in Butler's performative theory of politics (1997). It is comparable to the moment
in which the subject decides precisely how to respond to how it
is being interpellated by others. Indeed, Butler notes that every
repetition entails a choice on the part of the subject: it can either
respond by conforming to norms that the speech act enforces, or it
can choose to rearticulate the structures of calling, thus opening a
space for ethical and political intervention.

Indeed, these mimetic moments[16] are not limited to moments
of individual resubjectivation but can also be found in collective
actions. The tactical work of differential imitation is thereby an
important aspect in the construction of subversive political economies, such as the ones we shall explore.

Mimesis and Opposition

Opposition might seem like an antonym to mimicry: one invokes
difference, the other sameness. This is not the case in Tardean

cosmology. To him opposition is in fact in itself a particular kind of repetition or imitation, "that of similar things ready to destroy each other in virtue of their very similarity" (Tarde 1898, 33). Opposition is thereby a case of two social phenomena conflicting with each other, not due to their fundamental difference, but rather due to their "counter-similarity" (Tonkonoff 2014b, 63). And this very particular kind of sameness is the source of social innovation, or *invention,* as he calls it. His entire sociological universe is in fact structured around a cycle made of microinstances of imitation-opposition-adaptation (Tarde 1898), meaning that mimetic opposition is in no way specific to agonistic political action, but rather an integral dynamic of any aspect of collective life.[17]

Other authors have similarly theorized mimesis as an elementary socio-anthropological dynamic of opposition. The contributions of Michael Taussig and René Girard have been particularly important for moving the mimetic question beyond the more traditional aesthetic problematizations, which have primarily been focused on matters of representation, verisimilitude, truth, and simulation in meaning-making processes (e.g. Halliwell 2002; Isomaa et al. 2012). Drawing on critical theory, Taussig's ethnographic account of the Cuna people illustrates the essential role that mimetic relations play in the production of relations of radical alterity (Taussig 1993). For example, he observed that it is common for people to make or relate to an artifact (e.g., Cuna figurines used for healing purposes) that portrays something (the Western colonizer), with the aim of achieving power over that which is portrayed (the very same colonizer). His homeopathic, sensory investigation of colonial relations illustrates how the mimetic faculty is deeply tied to the desire of becoming *Other.*

A similar observation was made by René Girard, who posited that mimicry is founded on *rivalry,* on the fundamental animal urge to acquire prestige and subordinate the *other* by copying them and/or desiring what they have (Girard 1987, 90). Although this is an unavoidable dynamism that orders society, in his view mimicry is also something that should be avoided, as it is the source of conflict and chaos.[18] This is why societies across the world engage in ceremonies that *simulate* the resolution of mimetic desire, via, for instance, the use of the surrogate victim who is either celebrated (religious rituals) or prohibited (penal justice) (Girard 1987, 48). This mimetic simulation acts a regulating force, one that represents a process of hominization, which is the evolution away from animal instincts.

Although both Girard and Taussig are more concerned with agonism and power than Tarde is, these authors all approach mimesis and opposition as fundamental sociological dynamics, that is, as universal patterns of human interaction. While these views certainly inform this book, my own interest in the imitative-oppositional relation is, however, more specific. As mentioned previously, it relates to the instrumental use of mimesis to subvert a political order. Indeed, whether mimicry may or may not be an inevitable, even fundamental, anthropological dimension of political life is not a question that I seek to answer here. And although the mimetic opposition I am interested in is surely also rivalrous and inevitably produces (and is symptomatic of) a specific type of alterity, it is neither chaotic nor arbitrarily destructive. Rather, it reflects a choice, a process of deep investigation and careful planning, tactically aimed at safeguarding life from entering, in this case, mafia relations. Mimesis is here used to obtain a certain goal; it is a way of articulating an opposition to weaken and defeat a nemesis. I am interested in the kind of agency that is afforded if mimesis is, more or less intentionally, used to subvert a certain form of power. For the oppositional mimicry I will shortly illustrate is a political tactic that seeks to empower the oppressed. My use of mimesis relates more to its instrumental than fundamental nature. And to my knowledge, this is an underexplored aspect of mimesis.

Outline

Although this is not a historical work, I dedicate the first chapter to delineating the history of this social movement, particularly in its Sicilian expressions, to bring readers who are foreign closer to the case. In fact, following pragmatic approaches to the study of politics (Lippmann [1922] 1997; Dewey [1927] 2012), I see the anti-mafia as an issue that follows a trajectory (Marres 2005; Latour 2007). A genealogical approach can ultimately help trace continuities and discontinuities in the anti-mafia discourse and its material expressions. The chapter forms the premise to the core, which is essentially a study of contentious economies in the making.

The study is structured around three different registers of action: the semantic, the syntactical, and the sensory. Put differently, I have arranged the cases around three different *modes* of collective action: meaning, structure, and feeling. This choice is not coincidental. As we shall see in chapter 5, they correspond to the most divisive concepts within social movement scholarship. As one of my aims is to bridge these divisions by demonstrating the deep intersection between these modes of action, my critical reconstructive work begins, not unlike the anti-mafia, in the choice of mimicking a dominant order of things. Further, due to the mimetic nature of the opposition that is under analysis, I have outlined them, respectively, as instances of resignification, rearrangement, and affective reframing.

Chapter 2 explores the semantics, the meaning-making strategies, that shape anti-mafia political economies. Here, discourses— how they are practiced, and what they materially bring to life—are central. This chapter is about confiscated mafia assets, one of the founding sociotechnical arrangements of contemporary anti-mafia activism. In particular, I highlight the recent turn to embodied forms of valuation and experiential design as a fundamental strategy used to effectuate anti-mafia, to give this political project corpus and life. Here contention takes the shape of *resignification,* that is, of giving new meaning to the hybrid and multiple arenas that constitute mafia power, and reclaiming these as sites of opposition and agency.

Chapter 3 focuses on the structures of these political economies. Here I move further away from semantics (the meaning and values represented by the structures) and into syntax (the very arrangement of the structures) (Foucault [1966] 2002). Drawing on assemblage thinking (DeLanda 2006), I trace the web of anti-mafia relations that surround an unruly jar of peach jam. This analytical approach allows me to illustrate different strategies of production and distribution that disrupt Camorra economies in the region of Campania, which capitalize on the trade of illicit waste and cement and have detrimental effects for the ecosystems of the area.

Rearrangement is central to this mode of contention: placing different actors and resources in new configurations that hinder and undermine mafia power.

Chapter 4 explores the centrality that affects and emotions play in shaping anti-mafia politics. With the help of semiotic and communication theories, I bring forward the opportunities that desire offers to cultivate different modes of being. Through the case of Addiopizzo Travel, a tour operator that opposes relationships of extortion, I point to the importance that the elements of seduction and attraction play for mobilizing people to join a political project. Here the anti-mafia mimics the mafia's method of manipulating emotions to gain consensus. In particular, I explore how activists capitalize on immersive experiences of difficult mafia heritage, pointing to the potentials and limitations that the genre of tourism carries for political mobilization. Here the force of affective *reframing* becomes evident in its ability to create novel affective ties between mafia signifiers and the public.

Chapter 5 situates these forms of activism within a broader discussion about the vocabularies that are available to conceptualize collective action. It is the only theoretically driven chapter. I have chosen to place it at the end to allow the stories to speak first. Depending on your reading taste, you can either skip it (if you are here for the anti-mafia action) or start from it (if you like to know the ingredients before you taste the dish).

If you do read it, you will find that the three primary themes that hold *Opposition by Imitation* together are not coincidental. As mentioned earlier; meaning, structure, and feeling correspond to different theoretical perspectives that often times divide social movement scholars and practitioners alike. Assemblage thinking, which inspires this book and is unpacked in this final chapter, does not prioritize any order (meaning, structure or feeling) a priori, and thus grants each of these ingredients a potential role in building, in this case, more livable worlds. It is thus a method that allows for "reading for difference" (Gibson-Graham 2020, 475–85), and thus bringing forth the radical heterogeneity of identities, relationships, and political trajectories that exist in the world. My intent is to thus reconstruct the different and complementary forces that can effectively counter mafias, be they ideals, words, laws, or other nonrepresentational forces such as the material properties of land, the taste of a wine, or the smell of toxic waste. And I do so in this particular order so as to enter and challenge discourses that insist on the importance of preemptive ordering.

My hope is to address those who are interested in grassroots politics and who seek to understand how power arrangements are enforced and how they can be challenged. I especially want to address those who, like me, are concerned with economic practices that are of damage to the collective, and who, unlike me, have lost hope. For economy is a mode of organization through which social struggles can (and already do) take place.

1 Anti-Mafia

A Brief History

Many have been seduced by the idea of an underworld organization that undoes the law. On the one hand, it is a violent force that murders and trades with ruthlessness, and on the other, a political entrepreneur that navigates legal systems, ghettos, and financial markets with almost enviable skill. As the film industry has capably shown us, these activities are accompanied by series of cultural codes, styles of dress, myths, and archaic rites of passage that fortify their alluring presence in our imaginaries. Honor, loyalty, masculinity, family, protection, and respect: these are the words that we may commonly associate with the mafia. While these connotations have spread globally, interest in and knowledge of coordinated efforts to repress mafia are less diffuse. Indeed, the hegemony of these captivating imageries have often been seen as reinforcing mafia organizations: they have promoted the idea that mafia is invincible, that it ridicules attempts at state building, or simply that it is a parallel fantasy world. These ideas have consequently been of hindrance to social forces that are attempting to put an end to this phenomenon.

Nevertheless, institutional efforts in this direction are far from absent. On April 3, 2014, the European Council of Ministers adopted a directive addressing the problem of mafia-type criminal organizations for the first time in the history of European legislation (Arcifa 2014).[1] The text crowns a longer process of steadily growing international awareness of the economic aspect of organized crime, and more specifically on the abundance of illegal money and its reinvestment in the formal economy. Estimates from 2009 suggest that global criminal proceeds amounted to US$2.1 trillion, which is close to 3.6 percent of global GDP (United Nations Office on Drugs and Crime 2011). Although these sorts of estimates are among the most difficult to compile, they are perhaps also one of the most collaborative forms of research that can be undertaken, as they require information that ranges across sectors, jurisdiction, and nations. The mere existence of such reports testifies to a certain level of international awareness, concern, and effort.

The overall expansion of the wealth of organized crime has also brought attention to the diversity of sectors in which it invests, as well as the speed and stealth that characterizes its global network of transactions (Varese 2011). Criminologists themselves have begun to shift their focus from asking questions such as "Who is part of organized crime, and how many organized crime groups are there?" to "What things is organized crime investing in?" (Savona 2014). The traditional markets in drugs, weapons, gambling, and sex work have been supplemented with traffic in renewable energy, toxic waste, and parts of or whole human beings.

These forms of trade are intricately connected to the legal economy through money laundering activities and public procurement. The rise in migrants crossing the Mediterranean is a blatant example of how human lives have become the currency of trade between European and African criminal groups. This also suggests that these issues are not separate from the state, as they are proving to be lucrative business opportunities for, among others, the Libyan authorities, who are using prisons as tax collection points for migrants, and certain Italian politicians feeding off migrant reception centers.

The diversity of sectors and landscapes involved points to the complexity of the mafia phenomenon. Consequently, any form of opposition to it entails a parallel level of intricacy. Although international political and legislative measures have been on the rise,[2] they are also somewhat timid and leave a void in the executive power that is expected to implement them. However, in terms of institutional efforts to fight organized crime, it is on the national level that there has been the most progress. It is in fact Italy that has developed some of the most nuanced laws and criminal trials against mafias, reflecting the fact that this is not a new problem for the country.[3]

But noninstitutional efforts have also been numerous and varied. While there are many historical precedents for anti-mafia activism in Italy (dalla Chiesa and Jerne 2024), the past twenty years represent a particularly experimental moment for grassroots initiatives determined to fight mafias in novel and productive ways. They seem to be taking an increasingly entrepreneurial turn and, just like the mafias, are resorting to economic forms of organization. This challenges the common view of mafias as simply violent, criminal actors that need to be repressed. Instead, it recognizes that they also manage and compete over the control of economic relations that provide livelihoods, mobility, and capital. Therefore, they must be competed with and not only denied and criminalized.

Contemporary mobilizations are particularly worthy of attention for the richness in their political repertoires and their ability to spread. Investigating this richness is my overall intention in this book. The aim of this chapter is to provide some contextual rudiments to situate the contemporary anti-mafia into a broader struggle. While the topic of the mafia has historically attracted a lot of attention, interest in the anti-mafia movement has been a lot less widespread (dalla Chiesa 2024). This disparity might be attributed to the typology of the subjects who make up the anti-mafia (dalla Chiesa 2014a): how could farmers, women, the mourning relatives of mafia victims, and young rebels possibly compete with godfathers, drug lords, and political patrons? The coverage of the literature testifies to the gap in allure.

Nevertheless, a few important contributions have granted these grassroots actors the role of protagonist.[4] The most extensive works are Nando dalla Chiesa's *Manifesto dell'Antimafia* (2014b), which is perhaps one of the most engaged attempts to analyze and catalyze the movement nationally, as well as his study on Libera (2014a), the largest network of anti-mafia associations in Italy. Another important and extensive study is activist Umberto Santino's study of the history of the anti-mafia movement (2009). Despite being focused on its Sicilian history, his work is a useful guide to some of the main characteristics of the Italian political developments that situate the anti-mafia struggle. Lastly, the revised and

English edition of *Against the Mafia*[5] (dalla Chiesa and Jerne 2024), provides a unique collection of original writings of anti-mafia activists spanning from 1877 to 2021, making them available to an English readership for the first time.

This chapter takes these works as a starting point. Digging into the past is a precondition for understanding the current transformations of grassroots anti-mafia activism, which I investigate in the second part of the text. Here I incorporate some of my own observations from fieldwork conducted across Sicily, Emilia Romagna, Campania, and Apulia, the details of which are specified at the end of this chapter.

Tracing the Origins

Workers' Movements and Collective Rentals

One of the most crucial questions to emerge when tracing a genealogy is where to begin. Unsurprisingly, there are several disagreements on the specific date that launched the anti-mafia movement. The debate is first of all centered on the question of when we can begin to speak of mafia itself.

Some argue that it is possible to speak of pre-, pseudo- or molecular mafias and dedicate some level of analysis to a period of "incubation" (Ciconte 2008; dalla Chiesa 2014a; Renda 1997; Romano 1963). Historian Salvatore Lupo is skeptical of these terms, noting that to label connections between sociopolitical powers and criminality as being mafiosi in character, it is essential that these operate within modern state institutions. In the ancien régime, it was both praxis and law that established personal ties, unequal rights, and particular privileges regarding the use of force. Such relationships were therefore seen as "physiological rather than pathological and [were not] so scandalous as to require a specific word to define their illicit character" (Lupo 2004, 51). In other words, before modern state institutions were established in Sicily—that is, before the official abolition of the feudal system in 1812 and the process of the "democratization of violence" (Lupo 2004, 51) that saw the progressive legal transfer of the right to use force from the aristocracy to the state—one cannot talk of illegality as mafia. This resonates with the idea that there are indeed many analogies between coercive state making and organized crime (Tilly 1985). It also implies that while mafias operate in a parasitic relation to many types of governance, these must operate within a nation-state context in order for them to qualify as mafiosi. In light of the diversity of modalities that nation-states take up today, the mafia is an increasingly transnational, hybrid, and networked phenomenon. It is a form of globalization in its own right, worthy of anthropological attention and political scrutiny.

However, historically, and for good reasons, the study of mafias remains rooted in Italy. Indeed, despite minor disagreements, the unification of Italy is considered the most important event in the formation of mafias. It is therefore in the postunitary scene, which crowned a longer process of administrative reforms that had started during Bourbon rule in the south and Sicily, that the first instances of resistance to the mafia have been identified. As we shall see shortly, even this initial phase saw anti-mafia sentiments expressed through contentious economic acts. However, the first wave of protest saw the Sicilian Workers' Leagues (*fasci siciliani*) emerge as protagonists (Santino 2009), mainly expressing themselves through demonstrations and petitions. These leagues emerged as a response to an international period of recession that lasted from 1888 to 1894, during which the Sicilian working class was hit particularly hard. Although the region's produce had shown continual growth since 1860, in both quantity of mined sulfur and the size of agricultural markets, the working class suffered from the use of backward technologies, the exploitation of its miners, and an increase in taxation that was disproportionally distributed in the midst of a period marked by protectionism. The workers' leagues therefore emerged as a response to a system of social injustice at a time of increased sensitization to social claims (Santino 2009).

It is on this terrain that one of the first concrete cases of socialist action emerged in Italy, with an estimated 350,000 members, including farmers, building workers, sulfur miners, and artisans (Renda 1977). Although the leagues were heterogeneous in their social composition and political aims,[6] their general objectives were analogous: a larger share of the output, a fixed minimum wage, a worker's minimum age of fourteen, and a reduction in work hours. The content of these claims was directed at the landowners and mine owners, but they were also aimed at the state, which was gaining legitimacy as the rightful holder of executive and legislative power.

Our question here is: Why are these workers' movements also considered expressions of the anti-mafia movement? Although these claims are not explicitly (or at least solely)[7] against mafias, they questioned the labor relationships and power structures of the time that saw the wealthy agrarian class use *gabellotti* or private tenants as their enforcers. *Gabellotti* were in fact rural entrepreneurs who either took payment for the use of their lands or sublet their land to *sotto-gabellotti,* often hiring guards (*campieri*) to police their assets. These lands were managed in a manner that established firm relations of class exploitation, which did not permit farmers to access any surplus that was necessary for the sustainment of their livelihoods and excluded the possibility of social mobility. In fact, several *fasci* were directly aimed at "giving men the necessary conditions for not committing crime . . . for if the people also shunned them, they would commit more crimes" (Rossi [1894] 1988, 74). That is, they had explicit redistributive principles that aimed to include the poorest and *prevent* the most degraded members of society from becoming criminals. In this sense, they were also implicitly against the social conditions upon which mafia-type relations thrive.

Nonetheless, the nature of the ties between *gabellotti* and mafias are historically unclear, and sources even testify that some *fasci* collaborated with mafias in their struggle against the landowners (Dickie 2004; Lupo 2007; Rakopoulos 2017). What this collective upheaval reveals is ultimately that the true force of mafias lies in their ability to resort to any[8] form of alliance to establish their power and wealth. However, in postfeudal Sicily, the *fasci* ultimately represented a threat to the agrarian class and to the emerging middle class, whose enterprise consisted in skillfully mediating between the different sources of local power (rural and urban), as well as administrative relations between the periphery and center of the newly established state. These were the actors who effectively dominated nineteenth-century Sicily and were certainly not willing to let the status quo be questioned easily (Franchetti [1877] 2024; Mosca [1900] 2024). In fact, the Crispi government supported this vision by officially banning the leagues and arresting and prosecuting the leaders of the *fasci*. It is estimated that 108 civilians were killed by Crispi's soldiers and *campieri* from 1891 to 1894 (Santino 2009). This is fundamental to defining the movement: not only were the agrarian mafias and the broader power structures they embodied contested, they also directly *responded* and protected their position by repressing the movement.

"The anti-mafia allows us to see the mafia" (Lupo 2007, 8) and thereby understand the context, which is under contestation. Until around the end of World War II, mafias were closely linked with the agrarian class and their respective political representatives. Even though these forces continued to dominate, thereby acting as push factors in the first wave of Sicilian emigration (Renda 2003), their legitimacy was nonetheless contested on various other occasions.

Although the Sicilian peasant movement was among the largest social movements in Europe at the turn of the twentieth century, the economic forms of contention the movement adopted are not well known. In fact, this is also the period when the first anti-mafia economies emerged. Their first expression was the so-called collective rental (*affittanza collettiva*), a particular form of agrarian cooperative that was aimed at eliminating the intermediation of the *gabellotti* and directly managing the land (Sturzo 1974, 68). As opposed to the *gabellotti*'s enterprise model, this form of economic organization was explicitly antiexploitative and more democratic. It is no coincidence that proto-cooperatives were initiated by both Catholic and socialist[9] figures and tried to tend to two different needs: the desire to put an end to mafia intermediation, and the craving for land (Santino 2009, 127).

Collective rentals emerged in four different regions of Italy: Sicily, Emilia Romagna, Piemonte, and Lombardy. According to Umberto Santino, the appearance of these cooperatives was linked to different contexts and needs, and nowhere but in Sicily was the organization linked to the issue of the large landed estates and mafia. Yet Sicily had the largest number of rentals: 53 in 1906, with 15,900 partners and covering 39,800 hectares of land (Renda 1972, 145). Although these collective rentals replaced the *gabellotti* and were therefore at risk of becoming new subjects through which both old and new client relationships could be channeled (Lupo 1987), the fact that they emerged in such numbers is inconsistent with the idea that Sicily lacks traditions of cooperation and horizontal solidarity (Gunnarson 2014; Putnam 1993).

Another form of solidaristic social entrepreneurship was the Catholic rural credit union. These microcredit agencies aimed at helping poorer members of society who had been forced to resort to loan sharks and fell into debt and bankruptcy as a result. These institutions were born in Veneto in 1896, but they soon reached Sicily, which in just a decade proved to have the highest number of rural credit unions per municipality (La Loggia 1953).

These forms of resistance to mafia continued throughout the early twentieth century and were accompanied by workers' strikes that obtained some victories in terms of work conditions for the farmers, but also resulted in the assassination of prominent activists such as Bernardino Verro in 1915.

World War I increased unrest among the farmers, who were not only promised land and rights that ultimately they did not receive but were also called to the front to fight in a war that tore them away from their land. These conditions led to the rise of bandit groups that refused military conscription and more generally antagonized the established social order, surviving as fugitives by robbing and sacking. Although these groups were an expression of social discontent, they were soon used politically by both mafia and the state to repress the increasingly unpopular agrarian union (Santino 2009).

In this regard, 1947 was an important year: as the threat of fascism faded, the antifascist unity fell apart, and the Christian Democratic Party gradually drifted away from the left and started to shift its alliances toward the conservative classes and mafias. These had been the primary interlocutors with whom the Allied forces collaborated in returning democracy to the south of Italy. However, the first regional elections led to a strong victory for the left and the agrarian movement. This result was certainly not to the taste of the agrarian class, the mafias, or their institutional counterparts, which swiftly showed a firm fist. On a symbolic date, the annual Worker's Day celebration in Portella della Ginestra, the Giuliano Bandits[10] shot into the crowd, killing twelve civilians and injuring thirty (Santino 2009, 203). Although official statements denied there were any political reasons for the massacre, the message was clear: a new political liaison had been formed, and the left was not welcome.

Charismatic Voices

The workers' movements also lost much terrain in their more direct forms of dissent. In fact, although the numbers of cooperatives and collective rentals under administration were high, and the cooperatives (both leftist and Christian Democrat) even held a one-week event dedicated to the movement, there were stronger forces that aimed at supplanting these efforts. Indeed the 1950 regional agrarian reform did not even mention them as subjects (further weakening the farming class, which continued to migrate in search of greener pastures), and the list of trade unionists who had been murdered grew longer.

This period indeed marked one of the final crises of the large landed estates, and thus mafias began selling their properties and finding new avenues in which to invest. As Sicily began progressively industrializing throughout the fifties and the sixties, the mafias followed, and began shifting their interests toward more urban areas, home of the tertiary sector and official political institutions.

Mimicking this shift in interests, the anti-mafia movement began using more formal institutional channels, and consequentially lost its character as a mass movement. The weakening of the cooperatives and the labor unions in fact meant that the Communist Party acquired a central role in representing the farmers against the mafias and the Christian Democrats with whom they devised (Mattoni 2013). However, these institutional efforts, which took place in Palermo and included the newly established Anti-Mafia Commission,[11] did not succeed in stopping mafias from investing heavily in the construction industry, who built entire sections of Palermo in collaboration with large construction companies and the municipal administrators who managed the contracts.

Although the anti-mafia lost its mass character during this

period of transformation, this did not mean that the movement perished. Indeed, there were some singular cases of charismatic activists who stood up to mafias in creative ways, as the more formal paths led to cul-de-sacs. Their activities in fact ensured a continuity in the collective dimensions of anti-mafia action.

One example was Danilo Dolci, a philanthropic pacifist, writer, pedagogue, and activist from the Trieste region, who moved to Sicily in 1952 to explore the poorest part of what he saw as the edge of Europe. In Sicily, he took on the personal mission of educating and empowering the poor using Socratic maieutics. Through these methods, he organized a "reverse strike" based on the idea that if you wanted to achieve something as a worker, you should refuse to work, but if you wanted to achieve something while unemployed, you should work. Dolci gathered a hundred unemployed Sicilians in Partinico, who symbolically started fixing an abandoned public road, but he was soon arrested for obstruction.

Upon being released, he found he had gained so much public attention that he was barely obstructed in his project to construct the Jato dam in 1967. Although his initial aims were not directly mafia related, his attention to the poor and the marginalized soon led him to fight their oppressors (Dolci 1955). The construction of the Jato dam was in fact aimed at breaking the mafias' monopoly of water sources in the area, which suffered from a lack of irrigation that caused poor agricultural yields and contributed to the wave of emigration.

Apart from mobilizing the weaker parts of society and leading various hunger strikes, Dolci carried out an impressive amount of research and collected important declarations by prominent politicians, which led to his arrest for making false claims (Santino 2009; Grasso 1956). Dolci's intellectual engagement, pedagogical interventions, and entrepreneurial activities were thus crucial to mobilizing entire communities against mafias in a time when mass demonstrations had lost their momentum.

Another striking figure is Giuseppe Impastato, who was born into a mafia family. He began showing opposition to his own father in his adolescence and was therefore thrown out of his home. He started engaging politically in 1965 when he joined the far-left section of the Socialist Party and started a political magazine,

L'idea Socialista, in which he published an article entitled "Mafia: A Mountain of Shit," causing threats to all the editors and deeper ruptures with his own family. Nonetheless, Impastato continued his activities through student demonstrations and marches.

One of his most important actions was the organization of protests among small estate owners who were in the process of being expropriated to make way for the construction of a new runway at Palermo Airport. Impastato was extremely perceptive regarding the economic transformations of mafias at that time, as the latter were investing more of their capital in drugs and had been progressively expanding their Atlantic trade routes since the 1950s. The airport would in fact become a cardinal node in the heroin market using the United States–Europe trade route that the FBI would later call "the pizza connection."[12]

Impastato also started the satirical political radio station Radio Aut, where he discussed the relationships between politics, mafia, drugs, and the Badalamenti clan. His voice, however, became too loud, and on May 9, 1978, he was kidnapped, tied to railway tracks, and blown up with TNT. His assassination spurred a demonstration involving up to two thousand participants, a founding event in the anti-mafia's collective memory. The biographical film One Hundred Steps, which came out in 2000, further contributed to making him perhaps the most iconic mafia victim. In fact, his home and radio station are today some of the most frequently visited anti-mafia heritage sites, which masses of activists visit and venerate.

Excellent Cadavers and Mass Protests

Although Impastato's death mobilized the masses across Italy, the fight against the mafias only truly assumed widespread national characteristics in the 1980s. These were some of the bloodiest years in the history of Palermo.[13] The cause of this increase in violence has been linked to the increase of the mafias' capital assets. The two main groups that ran Palermo's drugs traffic (inter alia)—the Corleone families (allied with some historical Palermo families, such as the Greco) and the Palermo families—began fighting for hegemony, particularly because of Salvatore Riina's desire to impose himself as an "absolute monarch" (Santino 2009, 313). The murders also spilled over into the "outside" world, and for the first time[14] since 1893 the violence of the clans was aimed at institutional figures, threatening the political system as a whole (Lupo 2004, 291). Among the more prominent victims were the regional president, the leader of the main opposition party, Pio la Torre, and General-Prefect Carlo Alberto dalla Chiesa, as well as other political figures, key law enforcers, and magistrates.

Although many have interpreted these acts as an attack on the state, it is important to remember that the victims of these murders were individuals who were particularly and passionately involved in the fight not only against the mafias but also the failings of the state, and were therefore considered threats at a *personal* level rather than an institutional level (Santino 2009, 314; Lupo 2009). In fact, in many cases the "state" itself, in the guise of a corrupt public servant, was their main persecutor.

However, these massacres were indeed perceived as an attack on the state and against democracy, justice, and the health of Italian institutions, and not solely as attacks against individuals who were devoted to a cause. These were called "excellent cadavers": they represented a greater stake. The reaction of civil society was therefore also national. The headings of the two main national newspapers after the assassination of Carlo Alberto dalla Chiesa in 1982 both read: "A National Issue" (Santino 2009, 319). Other than the mass participation in his and Pio la Torre's funerals in Palermo, other areas of Italy began mobilizing too.

In 1985, young students in Campania started marching against the Camorra, which was gaining in strength, while new anti-mafia associations begin emerging in northern Italy[15] as well. In 1984, the establishment of the National Anti-mafia Coordination was the first attempt to unite anti-mafia associations; although this organ was short lived because of the many different ideological backgrounds of the thirty-eight member associations, it led to the formation of a new National Coordination in 1986 in which individuals (rather than associations) could participate (Mattoni 2013, 340).

Along with the increased geographical reach of the movement, there was also a change in the forms of protest, especially after the deaths of Giovanni Falcone and Paolo Borsellino in 1992.

These two judges had carried out important investigations that led to the Maxi trial. Their murders incited a series of demonstrations of dissent and solidarity.[16] One woman hung a sheet from her balcony that read "Palermo asks for justice," which was soon imitated by so many that a "sheet committee" was formed whose participants agreed to put their personalized slogans in this common form (Mattoni 2013). Citizens formed a human chain from the Justice Palace to the magnolia tree in front of Falcone's home, which has become a symbolic site of resistance to the Cosa Nostra, covered in flowers, banners, and slogans. Another group of women organized a month-long hunger strike to plea for the removal from office of various law enforcement officers who had been considered responsible for Falcone's safety. In response to and in support of this action, eight deputy prosecutors resigned to "denounce the impossibility of performing their functions against the mafia" (Santino 2009, 374). In July 1992, seventeen-year-old Rita Atria, daughter of a mafioso from Partanna, committed suicide in desperation: she had collaborated with Borsellino and was under protection in Rome. Her funeral was an important moment of collective mourning, at which women from Palermo carried her casket on their shoulders.

Another central theme that began taking root within the movement is the fight against extortion. Extortion is one of the traditional practices employed by the mafia to gain territorial control. Throughout the 1980s and 1990s, a growing number of businessmen began reporting threats and racket-related violence, a trend that received an increasing amount of media coverage and support from trade associations. In January 1991, Libero Grassi, owner of a clothing factory, decided to publicly denounce his extorters in some of the most prominent Italian newspapers. Although he received some sympathetic declarations of solidarity, he was murdered seven months later and portrayed as a "hero" killed by the indifference of the state, of trade associations, of his fellow businessmen, and of the mafias. It was clear that Palermo was not yet ready to oppose this form of economic despotism. His death, however, resonated widely in the media, giving the issue of extortion prominence in the public debate.

His individual action marked a turning point that set an

important precedent for the collective antiextortion initiatives that followed. For example, shortly after his death, the government passed an antiracket law establishing a support fund for victims of extortion. Concurrently, just a year before his death, the first antiracket association emerged in Capo D'Orlando, only 150 kilometers away. Unlike in Palermo, the extorters who pressured businesses in Capo D'Orlando did not have a strong and historical presence in the area, coming instead from Tortorici, a nearby town badly affected by poverty where crime was a key to economic advancement. Capo D'Orlando, by contrast, had been experiencing an economic boom tied to tourism and commerce and was therefore very enticing. After a series of violent acts, the new association successfully brought the extorters before the courts and won their case in 1991. This association would soon set an example for others that slowly emerged nationally (Santino 2009).[17]

Recent Developments: Expansion and Normalization

While the traumatic events of the 1980s and early 1990s effectively spread the movement nationally, they also led to a quantitative growth in grassroots anti-mafia associations (Ramella and Trigilia 1997). From the mid-1990s, the central actors of the movement increasingly became individuals, groups, and associations that are, in rich and diverse ways, furthering the anti-mafia cause.

Yet the preponderance of these types of subjects was also connected to the nature of the mafia's relations with public institutions and the role of the latter in the public sphere. The 1990s were emblematic with regard to these interactions: in 1992, a turgid corruption scandal, dubbed "Tangentopoli" (Bribesville), hit most political parties and led to the imprisonment of many public figures. There was a strong belief that the state's involvement in the market economy was what allowed corruption to take root, resulting in a deregulation policy that aimed at minimizing the state's interventions through a series of liberalization and privatization measures (Tridico 2013). However, these were implemented inefficiently, resulting in the creation of private monopolies, which were not followed by private investments (Consiglio Nazionale dell'Economia e del Lavoro 2007). This period is colloquially referred to as the Second Republic, as the historical national parties (both the Christian Democratic Party and the Communist Party) almost vanished from the political scene, inaugurating the Berlusconi era, which did not end corruption but further mediatized it.

In this scenario, with a growing public awareness around national scandals and judicial hearings, and with the increased recognition of mafia as a truly national problem, civil society increasingly organized itself outside evasive political parties and weakened labor unions. In fact, the growth in popularity of the associative form is not specific to the anti-mafia, but a general trend that swept the entire south of Italy in the same period (Ramella and Triglia 1997). The 1990s were thus a period of the politicization of the everyday, intended as a turn to the collective experimentation in different organizational forms aimed at developing professional, recreational, and also overtly civic spheres of life, regardless of institutional input.

Furthermore, public institutions were increasingly transformed from objects of contestation into potential allies. This does not mean that the movement stopped contesting the state, but rather that it entered into a peculiar dual position in relation to the state; it is both pro- and anti-state, as it seeks to reform the system using principles that belong to the system itself. It is pro-system because it does not aim to radically change the terms of the social contract, but rather to ensure they were maintained. It is anti-system because it questions the quality of the social order by wanting to cleanse the state from criminal power (dalla Chiesa 1983, 58).[18] This is mimetically aligned with the very object of contestation, mafia, which similarly operates by both affirming and negating the rule of law (Jerne 2024).

The role of associations is indeed increasingly important for institutions themselves. Many of my informants talk about the "absence of state," confirming other studies on anti-mafia associations that have shown a particularly low trust in public institutions compared to other organizations (Gunnarson 2014). In a sense, in some cases the role of associations has become one that surrogates and palliates the failings of institutional welfare. As one activist explained when I asked him about the challenges of his work:

> I sometimes find that the state expects us to do their job, and this is because we are so visible and acknowledged, so they trust us to have the "know-how." For instance, we are the ones who point out to the prefects which need more reallocated confiscated land: we know where the mafia is most active, and they lean on us. (personal interview, July 5, 2014)

Not only have associations thereby autonomously sought to fill in gaps in the executive role, they have also won a high level of legitimacy in the eyes of public institutions. This has granted them a novel role in everyday politics, now being called upon as subjects rather than objects of governance.

The activities of the movement are thus gradually becoming daily performances of a worldview that contrasts with that of the mafia, more than immediate reactions to violent events (Renda 1993; Mattoni 2013). Significantly, this is happening in a phase when mafias are more latent and have moved away from reminding people of their existence through acts of physical violence, and instead toward performing acts of structural and cultural violence (Galtung 1969). What strategies does a movement deploy to keep itself alive in the absence of such intense events?

Libera: The Foundation of an Umbrella Organization

One of the most important events in making the anti-mafia a national movement was the foundation of the Libera Association in 1995, which was born out of the necessity to coordinate all the anti-mafia efforts that were blossoming nationwide. Libera soon became an umbrella organization that today unites more than 1,600 associations. The full name of the organization, "Associations, names and numbers against the mafias," innovatively pluralizes the term *mafia* as well as the actors involved in fighting it (dalla Chiesa 2014a). As mentioned in the introduction, this is indicative not only of the expansion of the mafias' field of action but also of the multiplicities involved in its opposition.

Interestingly, Libera was founded by a Catholic priest, Don Luigi Ciotti, who had been particularly active doing social work with marginalized groups in Turin. His association, Gruppo Abele, emerged in 1965 and became increasingly concerned with drug abuse and AIDS, which gradually led it to concentrate on the problem of organized crime. The shift in focus became evident in 1993, when the group launched a journal specifically dedicated to analyses of the mafia, called *Narcomafie*.

In many activist groups within the anti-mafia movement, it is typical to observe this trajectory: their primary objectives frequently align with broader themes related to mafias, rather than focusing solely on combating mafias from the outset. Diversity is perhaps one of the essential characteristics of the contemporary panorama. My own fieldwork has led me to meet activist groups that self-identify as pacifist, environmentalist, anarchist, cooperativist, and Catholic, as well as some cases I would classify as conspiracy fantasists. Other important themes include social justice, refugee solidarity, drug and gambling dependence, austerity, corruption, and truth and reconciliation for mafia victims.

The movement has also expanded internationally. The German NGO Mafia? Nein, Danke! emerged shortly after the Duisburg killings in 2007, which saw the deaths of six 'Ndrangheta members in western Germany. The NGO collaborates closely with Italian associations, as well as the pan-European anticrime-network, FLARE (Freedom, Legality and Rights in Europe), which promotes legality through advocacy and lobbying in the EU. Ties with South America have also become stronger, particularly through solidarity movements involving the family members of victims of *desaparición*[19] and, in Mexico, of the wars between the drug cartels.[20] These different expressions of grief and grievance have managed to coalesce under the anti-mafia theme.

Despite the multiplicities involved, it is possible to point out at least three general themes that have become central in the past two decades of activism: education, memory, and enterprise.

Libera has played an important role in influencing all three trends, but as it is an umbrella organization, it has often merely coordinated the organizational and thematic trends in the movement.

Education

Ramella and Trigilia (1997) describe the anti-mafia mobilization of the 1990s as rotating around three main practices: crime prevention through social work in the areas with the highest levels of mafia infiltration; awareness-raising activities, particularly through educational institutions; and the organization of celebrations and demonstrations.

These are the central elements of what is often defined as the cultural anti-mafia, which focuses on transforming society through "knowledge" and "conscience formation" (*conoscenza e coscienza*; dalla Chiesa 2014a). Writing about and against the mafia has often been considered an important part of the anti-mafia struggle. Numerous forms of literature have been dedicated to understanding, describing, and analyzing the mafia phenomenon, including novels, such as *The Leopard* (Tomasi di Lampedusa 1958) and *The Day of the Owl* (Sciascia 1961), but also pamphlets, essays, and reports (Alongi 1886; Dolci [1955] 2024, 1960; Falcone and Padovani 1991; Falcone 1994; Franchetti [1877] 2024).[21] A large part of the contemporary movement against the mafia is in fact carried out within schools and universities through teaching and the production of texts. This is often referred to as the "cultural" stream of the movement, which has been particularly rich throughout the 1990s (Mazzeo 2014). The idea that producing investigative reports and analyses of the mafia is part of the struggle against it is not new. The novelty lies in the size of the effort and on the idea that it is by fostering a civic culture that the mafia will be prevented from taking root. The practice of spreading knowledge becomes more ambitious than the focus on accurate documentation, becoming an active project of fostering new "civic" subjects through educational development.

To begin with, the number of information sources has grown. There are, for instance, several websites dedicated to collecting and diffusing textual and audio information. Among examples of this are Radio Kreattiva, a streaming radio station financed by the Bari municipality since 2005 and run by the city's students, and Stampo Antimafioso, a website that emerged in 2011 with the aim of documenting and cataloguing news and research related to the mafia in northern Italy (Mattoni 2013, 346). Wikimafia, the first encyclopedia entirely dedicated to the mafia, also emerged in the north, in Milan, and recently developed a mobile phone app,[22] MafiaMaps, thanks to a successful crowdfunding campaign in 2015. Some of the more established mafia research centers, such as the Centro Siciliano di Documentazione Giuseppe Impastato, have also created websites that share information and articles. Transcrime and CROSS, two research centers that focus on international crime, are especially active in publishing reports, statistics, and papers on their website and social media platforms. Apart from academic content, other activists and associations, such as Sottoterra Movimento Antimafie, (R)esistenza Anticamorra, VALORIzziamoci and Casa Memoria Felicia e Peppino Impastato (to mention just a few) post events, thoughts, experiences, and news that are collected daily and shared by other members.

Most importantly, contemporary informative activities are aimed directly at schools and universities. Libera itself had four thousand collaborations with schools and sixty-seven universities in 2014, even signing a formal protocol of collaboration with the Ministry of Education and Research (dalla Chiesa 2014a). The content of this pedagogical exchange is often not specifically mafia oriented, but aimed more generically at building a context of legality and responsible citizenship.[23] It is therefore not surprising that these pedagogical projects are often carried out in collaboration with Catholic and scouting groups, both traditional engines of Italian civil society.

As we shall see in later chapters, the mafias have historically controlled information and even actively cultivated ignorance (Jerne 2024) to gain and maintain social consensus and power. Thus, the strategy of augmenting cultural capital via education and information counterimitates the mafias' very own power tactic in a preventive and also reactive logic.

Memory

Another important figure is that of the mafia victim family member. Parents, siblings, and partners, with their testimonies of mafia killings, play a central role in the contemporary project to forge anti-mafia subjectivities, and are directly invited to speak in workshops, seminars, and lectures.

Upholding and informing a collective memory has been a key strategy in the past thirty years. Libera itself was founded by two relatives of anti-mafia victims: one more famous, Rita Borsellino (sister of Judge Paolo Borsellino), and one less well known at the time, Saveria Antiochia, whose son was killed while escorting Inspector Cassará in 1985. One of their initial concerns was to act as a support group for the less prominent or indirect victims of the mafia,[24] burdened with both facing an uncomfortable and politically sensitive loss alone and the attempt to seek justice and discover the truth about the deaths of their relatives.[25]

One of the first actions of the association was to organize a mass commemoration of all the victims of mafia murders. Importantly, this means only "innocent" victims, those who were not members of these criminal groups themselves.[26] Since the first commemoration in Rome in 1996, the event has taken place in twenty different cities and has grown exponentially in magnitude. In 2016, the event took place simultaneously in different cities in an attempt to make it easier for everybody to participate.

Many activists I talked to during the 2015 commemoration referred to it as the most important day of the year (Jerne 2017). The event has a dual nature to it, as reflected in its title, the Day of Memory and Commitment: on the one hand it expresses solidarity with living family members who have suffered a loss, seeking justice and truth regarding the murders of their loved ones and insisting that their deaths are worth being publicly remembered. On the other hand, it is an annual occasion to reflect on what has been achieved by the movement so far and what the next steps should be. However, it is also an event the movement uses to engage its network in long-term activities that culminate on March 21, such as artistic projects that schools exhibit, theatrical performances, and thematic workshops.

Other than the event itself, numerous monuments, archives, and museums have been dedicated to documenting and increasing collective knowledge of and sensitivity to this difficult heritage. One example, which we will explore in chapter 4, is Addiopizzo Travel, a travel agency that connects tourists to hospitality enterprises that refuse to pay protection money, as well as to sites with high historical importance for the mafia/anti-mafia seesaw. Many of these are sites of atrocious murders and thus represent traumatic losses for the witnesses who intervene to mediate the tourists' experience. The tours are thus highly emotional and to some extent represent induced forms of collective mourning.

What characterizes these attempts at heritage preservation is that they are increasingly interconnected and aimed at communicating their political importance to inform a different future, not only for their own territories but also for other communities. The past has in this sense been a valuable asset for educating, communicating, and spreading the movement beyond regional and, more recently, national borders.

Enterprise

The idea that in order to fight the mafias, it is necessary compete with them has gained traction in the past two decades (Jerne 2015). The conception that mafias are thereby a strictly criminal phenomenon and that the most important form of action lies in investigating and denouncing their illegal activities and seeking justice is starting to lose ground. This rights-based, criminalizing approach is being complemented with ideas that relate to the welfare of the communities that are most affected by mafia criminal activities. Many activists refer to this as a passage from the *civic* anti-mafia to the *social* anti-mafia.

Underlying this shift is a realization that mafias are not merely criminal actors but also, importantly, entrepreneurs. Their power relies on a certain form of social consensus that grants them territorial control and wealth. Despite being violent, mafias often provide jobs and protection (Varese 2010); their entrepreneurial talent lies to a large extent precisely in their ability to create the necessity for these services. Extortion is the most obvious example: through the use of intimidation and blackmail, they create a market for protection money, or better, they capitalize on people's desire to live undisturbed lives, thereby creating a web of dependency. Moreover, they make it difficult for other business to compete with them in the market because of the incomparably higher costs of running a business legally. This allows them to grow in size and revenue, which in turn makes it possible for mafias to provide jobs. Drug dealing, counterfeiting, smuggling, prostitution, electoral clientelism, and corrupt tenders generate returns that allow many to earn their monthly bread, particularly in times when unemployment and poverty levels are high.

Anti-mafia activists have started to react to this business model by competing for social consensus through their own forms of enterprise (Jerne 2020). In other words, they try to convince people that it is "convenient" to be against the mafia. In the words of one Libera activist:

> When I go to the Zen[27] and talk to kids about the Mafia as something horrible, and I tell them the story of the heroes who have stood up to it and been murdered, they look at me and think: "Great. My father is in jail and my mother is a whore." What do they care about [Judge] Falcone? That's why we have to show them that the anti-mafia is a concrete alternative; that it works, that it employs people. (Libera activist, personal interview, July 10, 2014)

The underlying idea is that if you want to defeat your enemy, it is not only necessary to know him and understand him (through the practices we have examined so far); you also have to *imitate* his movements and spheres of action in order to outshine him on his own territory by taking over his assets and social influence.

A concrete example of this shift in attitude is a legislative innovation that occurred in 1996. Just one year after its establishment, Libera initiated a petition with one million signatures to push for law 109/96, providing for the social use of confiscated mafia assets. This law basically permits citizens to use goods that have been confiscated to actualize social projects. As the properties that are confiscated are often prosperous businesses, freezing them is not a total victory on the part of the state because in fact many jobs and capital assets are frozen with them. The law circumvents this problem and caters to these needs by reclassifying these properties: that is, by allowing them to be used collectively, the law aims at circumventing this problem. The 109/96 law thus expresses a double realization: that mafia *assets* are at the heart of the problem, and that the networks that depend on these assets need to be taken care of rather than abandoned. What begins as a penal measure of seizure thus develops into broader strategy of social *reutilization* (Jerne 2020, 84).

Confiscated mafia assets play a central role in contemporary activist projects, where education and commemorative practices coincide with questions of community welfare. The 109/96 law is in fact aimed at ensuring the community-oriented management of previously enclosed assets. One of the primary organizational forms that has proved to be best suited for this role is the anti-mafia cooperative, a key form of organization ensuring that the care, use, responsibility, access, and benefits regarding the asset are commoned (Gibson-Graham et al. 2013). Under Italian legislation, many of these cooperatives are aimed at employing "disadvantaged subjects" (*soggetto svantaggiato*),[28] such as people suffering from mental health issues, drug and alcohol addictions, or physical disabilities. A large share of the assigned assets is agricultural, being used to construct food chains that do not involve the use of industrial pesticides and trying to replace machines with human labor. The produce they grow varies greatly and includes legumes, fruit, vines, dairy products, wheat, and vegetables. In order to maintain their competitiveness in the market, because their production methods are more expensive, many cooperatives have formed networks to help them market their products. Libera Terra Mediterraneo is a professional union that emerged in 2008, collaborating with alternative banks, organic farmers, and market analysts to ensure the competitiveness of products made from confiscated assets.[29] RES (Rete di economia sociale, Social economy network) is a regional example of this that emerged in Campania in 2015, with the aim of contrasting the Camorra with an ambitious political economic project.[30]

Not all assets, however, are suitable for agricultural activities.

Assets include villas, supermarkets, pools, clinics, and industrial sites. Addiopizzo, for instance, manages a confiscated apartment that is situated in the center of Palermo. This activist group emerged in 2005 with the aim of economically and psychologically supporting entrepreneurs who refuse to pay extortion money and of empowering consumers by making visible their agency to support these "clean" businesses (Forno 2011; Gunnarson 2014). The group has now consolidated into an association, and uses the confiscated building as its main office, from which it coordinates and expands the network of enterprises that refuse to pay protection money. Their labor thus focuses on providing different kinds of services that support enterprises opposing extortion.

While confiscated assets have become central instruments to compete for social consensus, they are not the only ones. Gruppo Abele has also made statements concerning issues of unemployment in campaigns such as Miseria Ladra (2014), focusing on the recession and the consequent impoverishment of many citizens who are prone to collaborate with mafia. Other projects are aimed at supporting mafia victims, their relatives, and justice collaborators (e.g., SOS Giustizia and Interesse Uomo) in order to give those who have entered into close contact with criminal groups a support network. A last example are projects directed at juvenile detention centers (e.g., Nuove Opportunitá and Amuní), which are concerned with reintegrating minors into the workforce and take a restorative justice approach (dalla Chiesa 2014a). This is an important area of intervention, given that criminal groups play a traditional role in managing the lives of their affiliates both during and after incarceration to ensure their loyalty.

Overall, one could say that contemporary anti-mafia activism demonstrates a nuanced repertoire of action that in many ways mimics the growing sectorial and geographical extension of the mafia phenomenon. To tackle this increased complexity, activists have resorted to articulating forms of self-organized action that are increasingly moving away from pointing toward institutions as motors of change and rather enforce the change themselves. This entrepreneurial shift, which also involves the practices of commemoration and education discussed above, is increasingly articulated through economic activities. Unlike past forms of opposition, these actions are aimed not only at those who are directly prone to entering mafia-type relationships but at society at large.

This testifies an awareness that crime is not external to a given culture, but simply one of its extreme manifestations. Thereby, ordinary people take part in enforcing and/or changing the cultural humus upon which crime feeds, implying that preventing crime requires more than the prohibition of a given action performed by a group or an individual. It is a fundamentally *collective action* that operates precisely by diving into the culture that mafia reproduces, and fully recognizes itself as an active protagonist of the very same.

Becoming Anti-Mafia: A Methodological Digression

From the very beginning, my attitude toward this research has been a constructive one: I wanted to find nonexploitative ways of living in Italy that were already working and to understand how they worked. The anti-mafia movement fell upon me in a supermarket, where I was surprised to find such complex entanglements in a package of pasta. But perhaps it would not have touched me had I not had personal ties to a mafia heritage. The town I come from, Alcamo, is a stronghold of the Trapanese branches of the Cosa Nostra, and the consequences of these types of relations continue to torment my community, family, and friends. This struggle spoke to me because I was personally affected by it.

Only later did I encounter the work of feminist, poststructuralist thinkers who helped me understand and confirm my own positions. I learned that others too realized that "knowledge," "the knower," and "the known" are not neutral, objective facts and that their specificities and relationships are themselves generative of new realties (Gibson-Graham 2000). My own engagement with this case, the fact that I was affected by it, was suddenly not a problem, but rather represented an opportunity for me to build on (Sedgewick 2003). Indeed, in the eyes of Lisa Blackman (2015), research projects are always "haunted" by the researcher's ethos, by her way of being and having been. This is an issue that is commonly ignored, or worse, forcibly repressed in most scientific approaches.

Encouraged by these authors, I began to actively explore *how* this book was being shaped by what affected me, from when I began it to when I finished it. This led me to embrace the idea that the process of selecting cases, choosing theoretical approaches, and choosing what to leave out were in themselves normative acts. The result of this selection process, namely, this book, is therefore actively aimed at affecting the way we can think of and can do grassroots politics, as well as establish and maintain non-mafia relations. Therefore, throughout this exercise I have (consciously) become an anti-mafia activist.

I have chosen to focus on practices that are "working," meaning that they had a certain duration, were economically sustainable, and had attracted a growing number of coproducers or sympathizers. This means that the challenges, struggles, and contradictions implicit in shaping anti-mafia economies are only mentioned, not prioritized, in this book.[31] As an engaged part of the movement, I could equally have chosen to take this perspective in order to improve the maintenance of these economies.[32] I hope somebody else will take up the task of highlighting moments of anti-mafia failure not as an opportunity for criticism, but rather as a reconstructive strategy (Knudsen et al. 2015, 10).

Accordingly, between 2014 and 2019, I carried out ethnographic fieldwork (Wolcott 1995, 66) in several areas of Italy: Sicily, Emilia Romagna, Campania, and Apulia. I took part in workshops, demonstrations, work camps, anti-mafia tours, and commemorations. I took forty of my students on an anti-mafia tour in Palermo on two separate occasions, combining teaching and research. Through these activities, I contributed to the upholding of anti-mafia economies by paying to stay in specific hotels and purchasing food and other objects that were created in the anti-mafia ethos, thereby becoming part of the valuation circuit myself. I also volunteered my labor in the forms of farming, cooking, cleaning, and workshop organization in collaboration with several anti-mafia associations and enterprises. Contributing my labor and following the training and direction of the activist groups that I collaborated with gave me the inspiration to work autoethnographically, thereby using my own body as a site to be read for processes of anti-mafia "indoctrination." I also shadowed many of the groups I was interacting with in their publicly available material online. Finally, I took part in seminars and met mafia scholars and activists throughout Europe, which often led to formal interviews. In total, I recorded having learned from 147 anti-mafia activists, 47 of whom are professionals. However, many more have informed this study.

My initial impulse was to study Libera as an organization. However, my experience of volunteering made me realize that the practices, the use of confiscated assets, the attempts at communalizing, and the material and symbolic appropriation of territories were *in themselves* organizing movements. Libera was but one of these forces that brought people together. So instead of studying the representation of the organization (i.e., what people said the organization did, its formal structure, its logistics, etc.), I began to seek out the technologies (legislation, affects, objects) that in one way or another effectively led to the emergence of organizations that revolved around the anti-mafia issue. This meant that I began to interact more openly with different types of nonstate actors that engaged with the issue.

Indeed, what I discovered was that many of the more generative sociotechnical configurations were not really central to Libera per se. If I had kept my focus on the formal organization, it would not have been possible for me to trace what I see as the movement's more productive and interesting parts. Of course, many of these practices are also present in Libera and in some way intersect with the umbrella organization. But the knowledge I might have produced if I had stuck to the "organizational" and "geographical" boundaries I had neatly traced would have given me different answers to questions I had begun to disagree with. While this book is empirically grounded in multisited analyses, my aim is not to map out specific "regional" traits in a comparative manner. Rather, I use specific anti-mafia practices to reflect on broader questions such as the transformation of this movement and the possibilities offered by its contemporary expressions in order to rethink, among other things, the relationships between social movements, economy, and contention. The ethnographies that make up the rest of this book enrich the existing corpus of literature with my own experiences of these collective actions.

━━━

After a dense yet speedy summary of the past one and a half decades of mafia and anti-mafia history, my hope is that readers will not be overwhelmed with information, but rather will have solidified a few points in their minds.

The first point is a more nuanced understanding of what the mafia is and what it is not. What this historical chronicle tells us is that the mafia is a lot more than a group of gangsters who wear *coppole,* smoke cigars, and build secret bonds with one another through kissing hands and codes of honor. Through time, mafia have been synonymous with exploitative forms of land tenure, public procurement, the drug trade, and terrorism. Mafia has also suggested the international trade in human beings, weapons, and human organs, as well as electoral clientelism, political patronage, and corruption. Mafia hardly means family: the children, wives, and brothers of its members have been murdered without scruple. Mafia mostly means power exercised through violence, the enforcement of silence, social control, and market enclosures.

Similarly, we can now assert that Italians have been active and alert to these types of phenomena for years and that it is untrue, as some international journalists have noted, that Italy has only recently experienced some sort of "civic epiphany." The anti-mafia repertoire has been rich and unrelenting. Worker's strikes and union marches accompanied self-directed experiments in collective ownership as far back as the late nineteenth century. Contentious radio stations have been intertwined with poems, scientific documents, and, most recently, digital maps tracing the presence of mafia through space. Grassroots enterprises have developed into high-quality marketing agents, organic food producers, and even tour operators.

This chapter has laid the foundations for the reflections that follow, having established that anti-mafia is a social movement that has witnessed a transformation in the repertoires, actors, and media involved. This makes it a suitable case through which to reflect more broadly on the diversity and transformation of collective action and its conceptualizations.

Part I

Resignification

2 *È Cosa Nostra*

Reclaiming Mafia Assets

For a long time, the mafia was perceived as a distant, parallel, or even nonexistent phenomenon. Today you can walk into a supermarket and diminish mafia power by buying a packet of pasta that is produced following certain principles. You can also choose to spend your holiday in hotels that refuse to pay extortion money, or download an app that tells you where and how to support the anti-mafia movement through your daily acts of consumption. Not only does the existence of these commercial encounters make apparent that mafia is a very tangible entity; it also spells out that regular people have a reservoir of economic agency that can be deployed to oppose it.

As a consequence, the spectrum of sites and actors involved in anti-mafia actions has been immensely amplified. This important cultural transformation is the result of many instances of resignification: actions that disrupt dominant narratives and norms through the creation of new meanings that challenge the status quo.

Several beliefs and societal expectations are being challenged by these economic actions, but three are most relevant for our purposes. The first, most obvious one is that mafia is something external or parallel to society that does not touch the ordinary person going about her day. The second is the idea that political action belongs in parliament, voting booths, and demonstrations, and that, consequently, political power resides primarily within the state apparatus. The last is that the answer to defeating mafia lies in a more thorough enforcement of criminal law.

This chapter is about the norms that are constructed to replace these. More specifically, it illustrates some of the powerful processes of resignification that lie at the base of the growing number of political economies that oppose mafias. It describes different ways in which dominant normative frameworks that relate to mafias are collectively resisted, explored, questioned, replaced, and/or subverted via economic activism.

It is noteworthy that none of the three abovementioned beliefs are central to mafia praxis. Quite the opposite. As we shall see, mafias are highly skilled at navigating a variety of noncriminal social settings and capitalize on all kinds of people to enforce their power. They also manipulate legal institutions to their own advantage, testifying that they have historically played an important role in shaping institutional politics. Lastly, mafias have felt threatened by (and thus tried to subsume) trade-unionists, sexually liberated women, and neighborhood priests as well as judges and police officers (dalla Chiesa and Jerne 2024). These insights lie at the base of the mimetic opposition: rather than following the dominant societal conceptions of crime and crime prevention, anti-mafia activists tactically shadow the hybrid, multiple, and paralegal spheres of *mafia* power, and select these as sites for resignification.

We can call the actions involved in processes of making-meaning *acts of valuation.* The term *valuation* implies an abandonment of value as a substantive feature, and an acknowledgment that value comes to be through a series of empirical acts (Dewey 1939; Muniesa 2012, 2014). Value, then, is the signification that emerges from social interactions and is continually constructed and negotiated. Meanings, norms, and values are in fact works in progress that reiterate, negotiate, and rupture former versions of themselves. Indeed, situations of valuation are by their very nature sites of rupture and contention (Antal et al. 2015, 4).[1] Yet some entities are more difficult to change and break than others. Tracing the processes involved in resignifying them—challenging them, expressing them differently, and materializing them—makes it possible to locate sites of struggle and, consequently, nodes of power.

Following pragmatism and science and technology studies, language and meaning cannot be reduced to spoken words, signs, and interlocutors; different sociotechnical arrangements take part in materializing a discourse into the world (Callon 1998; Muniesa 2014). Therefore, I will also illustrate how various nonhuman actors are involved in the networks that resignify mafia power.

Because there are precedents of economic activism within the anti-mafia movement, I begin by reflecting on how this form of opposition has evolved in time. The empirical focus lies on various kinds of mafia assets, in particular agricultural lands, which are, in different ways, expropriated from mafia and used as sites to reconstruct relations and subjects that oppose mafia. I engage with the case of E!state Liberi!, a volunteering program coordinated by Libera that connects actors managing assets confiscated from mafia with tourists and activists who are willing to spend their summer investing their time and labor in generating anti-mafia value. I consider it a particularly effective mode of valuation because it attracts a growing number of activists every year[2] and is a form of political mobilization that is spreading across regions. The remainder of the chapter zooms in on my own experience as a volunteer in the E!state Liberi! program and reconstructs ways in which activists frame mafia and make anti-mafia real.

One Hundred Years Later: Capitalizing on Contested Property

In the previous chapter, I mentioned the example of the collective rentals that emerged at the dawn of the twentieth century.[3] At that time, farmers in fact opposed the mafia by collectively renting land to eliminate the intermediation of the *gabellotti*, who hoarded wealth and repressed the peasantry. Today's anti-mafia is similarly trying to circumvent mafias, but in far more intricate and heterogeneous ways. Both cases illustrate that activists imitate the mafias' own way of exerting power (here, by dominating relations of agricultural production) and oppose it by trying to outwit them at the very same activity. Comparing current practices with this historical precedent[4] allows me to bring forward the peculiarities of contemporary repertoires. In particular, I aim to highlight how economic signification is used today to mobilize *others*: individuals and groups that are not necessarily directly affected by mafia-type relations.

As l already discussed the phenomenon of collective rentals, l shall briefly introduce the E!state Liberi! program before comparing the two. After some years of experimentation, the program was officially set up by Libera in 2007 in order to capitalize on confiscated mafia assets. It is often believed that Libera directly manages these assets, though in fact it simply promotes and facilitates their reuse through its expertise and its vast associated networks. When the program began, the reallocation of confiscated mafia assets was still in its embryonic phase, and different associations were experimenting with different ways to manage and value buildings, land, and enterprises. These assets were often in a terrible condition, and it required a lot of work and money to restore them. Furthermore, despite being formally confiscated or frozen, many of these assets were still being "watched over" by the fearful and/or collaborative local population and were thus not fully detached from their previous owners or their networks of influence.

Bringing in volunteers to deal with this property became a fundamental strategy for gathering support, both material and emotional. Today the volunteering program is open to individuals, groups, and businesses (now both national and international) that can spend an average of one or two weeks restoring a confiscated asset for about €20 a day. The associations and social enterprises connected with the program are various in kind,[5] as are the confiscated assets on which they operate. These range from agricultural land, villas, and apartments to outhouses. During their stay, volunteers interact with local institutions, associations, enterprises, and testimonies of mafia-related activities of various kinds. The role of the family members of mafia victims is extremely central, which is why Libera calls the program "the most effective representation of memory that becomes commitment, the tangible sign of the necessary change that needs to oppose the 'material and cultural mafianess' that is so widespread in our territories" (Libera 2024).

Indeed, the E!state Liberi! program coalesces the three main themes l have identified as being central to the contemporary antimafia movement: education, memory, and enterprise. Now let us look more closely at some of the historical developments that forms of reappropriation have gone through, in terms of actors, issues, instruments, and activities.

	Collective Rentals (20th Century)	E!state Liberi! (21st Century)
Main Actors	• Private citizens • Labor unions • Political parties • Catholic credit unions	• Private citizens • Civil-society organizations • National and local institutions • Consumers • Volunteers/tourists • Relatives of mafia victims
Issues	• *Gabellotti* • Labor laws	• Local and international mafias • Environmental degradation • The welfare system
Instruments	• Proto-cooperatives • Legal instances • Microcredit agencies • Local markets • Agricultural land	• Social cooperatives and associations • Legal instances • Ethical banks • Local and international fair-trade markets • Agricultural land, buildings and enterprises • Difficult heritage sites
Activities	• Demonstrations • Petitioning for formal statutes/agreements/claims	• Demonstrations • Petitioning for formal statutes/agreements • Brand development • Tourism • On- and offline recruitment and promotion • Immersive forms of commemoration

Figure 2. Mafia expropriation compared. Adapted by Christina Jerne from (Jerne 2015, 201).

Main Actors

Although the two sorts of mafia "expropriation" occur in different periods in time, each with extremely different historical conditions, they both tackle a social issue by directly substituting the actor they are opposing over control of an asset. During the period of the collective rentals, these initiatives were taken up by groups of farmers who were politically linked to socialist or Catholic labor unions. At the same time, Catholic credit unions supported poor farmers in their financial struggles against usury.

Today's landscape is mainly made up of private citizens forming associations, organizations, and cooperatives, although an important number of them are still linked to Catholic voluntarism and workers' unions. E!state Liberi! acts as a broker, and connects these groups to tourists (individuals or groups) who want to visit them and support them.

An important novelty is that local and national institutions are directly involved in these practices: it is through the judicial and executive systems that these assets are confiscated, and it is a national administrative organ[6] that reallocates them to cooperatives, associations, and local administrations that compete for its use. The 109/96 law is in fact aimed at commoning public property (Gibson-Graham et al. 2013, 138); although the confiscated private assets become public in terms of property, effectively they often remain enclosed in terms of use. This is indeed what often happens to most confiscated goods today: although the amount confiscated is growing thanks to effective institutional efforts,[7] many of such assets remain frozen state property because they are difficult to reallocate to new owners.[8] Managing a confiscated asset requires a lot of capital investment, particularly when it comes to agricultural land that has been abandoned for years. Indeed, a frequent problem cooperatives face is access to credit, as these assets are only made public in use terms for definite periods of time but formally remain state property. Therefore, banks are not willing to lend out money without security for their investments.[9]

Nonetheless some forms of "ethical banking,"[10] coupled with state and EU subsidies, are helping cooperatives and associations access credit and alleviate the pressure of the mortgages which weigh on the asset from previous owners (Forno 2011, 106). There have been numerous discussions about the possibility of selling the confiscated real estate, and suggestions that the state should run them directly. However, Libera, which has become one of the main actors involved in promoting the reallocation of these assets, has taken a clear stand on avoiding these policies, as it believes there is a risk of these assets being acquired by corrupt private persons. In their use, attempts are therefore made to keep such assets as open as possible, even though it is clear that Libera dominates the scene,

making it difficult for cooperatives and enterprises that are not affiliated to the network to compete with its expertise and voice.

Another important difference in terms of actors is the massive
increase in the numbers of people involved. While collective rentals were aimed primarily at enforcing a shift in power relations on
the specific terrain in question, E!state Liberi! uses the assets to
catalyze different power relations *across* space. For instance, in the
summer of 2023, 3,007 people travelled to spend seven to fourteen
days on one of the assets that was hosting volunteers connected
to the E!state Liberi! Program, demonstrating national participation. In July 2014 I participated in Libera's first International Camp
in San Giuseppe Jato, which hosted a group of German volunteers
and further demonstrates a tendency to expand participation
across national borders. Many other similar volunteer experiences
have emerged outside Libera's own E!state Liberi! program. In this
sense, it is the *type* of engagement with confiscated assets, based
on a somewhat open-ended governance model aimed primarily at
spreading awareness and public participation, that travels to other
sites and thus other relations.

Lastly, and fundamentally, contemporary engagements are
strongly connected to the relatives of mafia victims. These are
present throughout the entire summer season, where they participate by communicating their experiences of loss and injustice and
use the occasion to demonstrate their commitment to opposing
mafia-like relations. Their role is pivotal for the direction these
enterprises take; their testimonies are drawn from and used to
educate the participants.

Issues

The issues that spur contestation today are obviously different
than they were in the nineteenth century. Protocooperatives
sought to oppose the agrarian mafia of the time, which were conceived of as a network of individuals (*gabellotti*) who unjustly
administered the aristocracy's land and repressed the poorest
members of the farming class. The protocooperatives attempted
to circumvent the problem by collectively renting their own land,

but they were also linked to labor unions and socialist parties, as they also aimed to improve their formal labor rights.

Despite the clear difference in today's (formal) employment conditions, many of the same themes are still relevant. One of the main objectives of today's cooperatives is in fact still to create fair and legal employment opportunities for young and disadvantaged members of society. As a result, the forms of production they initiate on these assets are also aimed at creating jobs. The difference lies in the fact that today's anti-mafia has further expanded its referent object from a concrete group of mafiosi to a much broader set of relations that undermine collective well-being.[11]

Importantly, the E!state Liberi! program collectivizes this issue by exposing tourists and volunteers to the difficulties that local populations are facing, as well as to the strategies they use to cope and live well. While the collective rentals also experimented with similar strategies, these were primarily aimed at the worker-members; the claims for broader changes to welfare were directed at labor laws through trade unions. Today it is the associations, cooperatives, and social movement organizations themselves that try to facilitate and realize these changes. This challenges the idea that the state is the main agent of welfare, and stresses that it is the community that takes part in the enactment of welfare. This is achieved through systematic research and collaborations aimed at understanding how to sustain these types of relations, but also by concretely linking vulnerable workers and volunteers, and facilitating exchanges of time, money, and labor.

Another expansion in terms of what is being contested is geographical in nature. The fact that the mafias have expanded nationally and internationally is apparent in both the fact that the confiscated assets, and consequently the E!state Liberi! camps, are physically located from the south to the north of Italy, but also in the types of activities that the associations are promoting in relation to these assets. These include supporting mafia victims, learning about social enterprises, farming, and mending parts of an asset, among many others.

What is also central to today's anti-mafia is the attention it pays to nonhuman others connected to the enterprise. The cooperatives in fact prioritize the use of organic farming methods, avoiding industrial pesticides other than copper and sulfur. This is in line with the shift in interest of the mafias themselves, which, as we shall see in the next chapter, are increasingly investing in renewable energy and the waste disposal sector, as an environmental disaster in Campania made particularly evident. In this sense, the two forms of enterprise mirror each other in terms of types of investment. Moreover, many of the activities of the summer camps are directly involved in clearing the local area of abandoned waste.

Instruments and Activities

The expansion of the mafias has necessarily required a broader spectrum of resources and activities by today's anti-mafia. Although formal demonstrations, petitions for legal amendments, and pamphlets remain important tools to realize anti-mafia enterprises, a series of other instruments are included in the contemporary repertoire.

For example, the very organizational form that engages with the land is far more nuanced today. While the protocooperatives that emerged in the nineteenth century were aimed at increasing access to land and empowering farmers, the claims of today's cooperatives are far more multifaceted and diverse, as is most obviously mirrored in the complexity of the cooperative form. Protocooperatives only shared use of the lands and initial investments between members (Santino 2009, 125–26): more than a century later, the cooperatives' and associations' objective is to *expand* the use, access, care, benefit, and responsibility regarding the assets to the community (human and nonhuman) at large.[12] The aim of these cooperatives and associations is in fact to mobilize and include as many living beings as possible in their activities, in Herbert Blumer's (1951) words transforming themselves from expressive into active social movements.

The confiscated assets are also used as platforms to resignify a difficult cultural heritage. In this optic, the assets have a much broader immaterial value ascribed to them: the narratives, the stories, and the information connected with them are much more extensive than those that are indexically connected to the sites. The educational[13] activities that take place on the sites are based on intense corporeal engagements with both the material assets and the more territorially abstracted histories of the mafias. As I shall explore further in chapter 4, the sites are used to communicate violent pasts and to negotiate other possible futures through the bodies of the volunteers.

Another important tool utilized in this respect are the brands with which the E!state Liberi! program is marketed. During the period of collective rentals, produce was primarily sold in local markets and was not framed within the same political issue. Instead, many of the goods that are produced by the social enterprises that collaborate with the program are branded under the same name (e.g., Libera Terra). In itself, E!state Liberi! is a brand that connects volunteers to this type of *experience,* as well as to enterprises that make material anti-mafia products. Brands thus act as material vectors of the anti-mafia issue, allowing it be transported, shelved, and selected by consumers in diverse spaces. Both the consumers and the volunteers contribute to the brand's value in material terms as well as symbolically. In fact, not only do the volunteers donate wealth in respect of their work, they also pay a fee[14] that contributes to the expenses of living there and to some extent also to the budget of the association as a whole. This is part of a broader evolution of brands as aggregative technologies, which have progressively been transformed from mere representations of identity to the concrete entrepreneurial productive force of that same identity (Arvidsson 2006).

One hundred years later, the modes through which anti-mafia forces create meaning are far more numerous and complex. In the case of collective rentals, we were dealing with rather simple forms of valuation: the land was utilized to establish relationships of labor and production that were independent of the control of the *gabellotti*. This reclamation strategy redefined farmers as masters of their own labor and destiny, demonstrating that their class status and identities were not fixed or innate, but shaped by the distribution and organization of resources in that specific time and place (Resnick and Wolff 1987). Thereby we are dealing with a subversive symbolic resignification: the term *peasant* no longer meant mafia victim, and the agrarian mafia no longer signified absolute master.

E!state Liberi! can instead be considered a far more extensive example of collective *capitalization*. If capitalization is to be considered the most intense form of valuation (Muniesa 2014)—that is, as a particular form of encoding that has an organizing and *generative* force (Guattari and Alliez 1983)—then this is the semiotic dynamic at play today.

To begin with, there is a realization that mafia power is not solely related to a specific network of criminals (like the *gabellotti*), but that it is by reshuffling the many relations that compose mafia power that the latter can be weakened. In other words, anti-mafia power is no longer built only on the idea that the presence or absence of certain individuals (*gabellotti*) will constrain or liberate others. This is exemplified not only in the case of confiscated mafia assets but also in the general institutional attitude toward organized crime that is gradually developing beyond merely punitive measures to open itself up to educational, welfare, and commemorative[15] approaches as well. Indeed, anti-mafia power has also developed, in a Foucauldian sense (1982), through different technologies of the government of the *self*, attracting and contaminating *others* to engage in the same forms of behavior.

This collective capitalization thereby involves two levels of abstraction. The first is characterized by the multiplication of the terms associated with mafias; the word *mafia*, now significantly pluralized in common tongue, is more than just a sign that symbolizes a network of criminals but refers more broadly to a way of relating to the world. The second level of abstraction pertains to the amplification of the kinds of actors involved in encoding these new meanings; anti-mafia is exercised by numerous and varied agents, far beyond those directly suffering from mafia violence. Both these forms of abstraction might be understood as semiotic shifts away from symbolic representation and toward presentational logics; as movements from the symbolic to the real. In the words of Scott Lash and Celia Lury (2007, 12): "In the real, meaning is no longer interpretative; it is doing, it is impact."

Indeed anti-mafia activists are making meaning by rearranging objects in ways that make them function as vehicles for collective investment (Muniesa 2014, 40): brands are utilized to generate networks of production and consumption; property is communalized (in a much more extensive way) to make possible alternative lifeways; legislation is amended beyond a strictly penal approach, allowing novel types of relations to form with confiscated assets; and heritage is brought to life to promote different kinds of knowledge of and relations with the past. Brands, property, legislation, and heritage are being used as vehicles of abstraction, as tools that are generative of diverse relationships in the future.

But how is this achieved in practice? How is it that these things are now considered valuable, true, and meaningful? So far, I have drawn a somewhat "finished" scheme of the results of many of these forms of valuation. Yet, in his seminal work on encoding and decoding[16] that gave semiotic paradigms true sociological significance, Stuart Hall reminds us of the complexity involved in the production and dissemination of messages. Hall illustrated, among others, that discourses are circulating entities that have various interactions throughout their trajectories that can either cause them to develop or bring them to an end: "If no 'meaning' is taken, there can be no 'consumption.' If the meaning is not articulated in practice, it has no effect" (Hall 1980, 129). At each stage of communication, messages are imbricated in structures of dominance, of relations of power. They also need to be recognized as appropriate or decipherable at given times and places. I will now go through some of the processes involved in making these meanings real, providing some ethnographic detail of some of the powers at play in these processes of resignification.

Here and Now: Orienting Bodies toward the Space and Time of the Law

The case of E!state Liberi! represents a political collective practice of valuing a norm: opposing and challenging mafia norms, and encouraging others to do the same. As the work of Michel Foucault has importantly shown, norms are expressed through a series of regulatory technologies that orient bodies to behave accordingly (Foucault 1977). The case of prisons is of course emblematic: cells function by spatially isolating bodies, as well as regulating what they do at certain times, on the basis of what is considered "normal" (Borch 2015, 10). Yet Foucault's most insightful contribution was to point out that these types of mechanisms occur in the everyday and are not bound to particular spaces, institutions, or subjects. Normative power is instead something that we do everywhere (e.g., by stopping at traffic lights, by choosing cruelty-free products in the supermarket, by going to the gym, by having children). "It is also something one creates oneself as" (Borch 2015, 16). Foucault's work has essentially countered the view of power as something merely repressive and negative, and instead promoted the idea that power is productive and generative of different forms of life.

Foucault's project can be seen as being broadly engaged in uncovering the diversity of ways in which people are subjected to and subjectified by power via normative standards. The fact that these regulatory mechanisms operate in implicit, even hidden ways, is perhaps why governmentality studies have so often been focused on critiquing some forms of power in a negative,[17] exposing sense, but less frequently on the shaping of other, desirable, types of subjectivities. I find this an interesting occasion to explore this, particularly as the bodies that are being disciplined here are not criminal bodies ("abnormal" or deviant), but bodies that are meant to be shaped in dissonance to crime (not unlike soldiers or judges). The question that shapes the rest of this chapter, then, is which technologies are at work to orient volunteers away from mafia. In other words, how is anti-mafia valued? And on the flip side: What, in these cases, is then revealed as constitutive of mafia power?

An important starting point is the schedule we were given throughout our stay,[18] which oriented our experience through space and time (Figure 3). As can be seen from the words in bold, every morning was dedicated to physical work. We would start tending to the vines at 6 a.m. and finished as soon as the sun was too high (between 12 and 1 p.m.). Alternatively, we would spend our time cooking, cleaning, and tending the garden of the house we slept in, which had been confiscated from the Brusca[19] family. The afternoons were spent primarily on workshops that had international themes, or on meeting local activists and witnesses to mafia-related murders.

Day	Activity	Location
Monday	<u>Morning</u>: Portella della Ginestra Visit (site of mafia massacre, meeting witnesses) *Afternoon:* Workshop on transnational mafia (information, research advocacy led by Libera educators)	San Giuseppe Jato (SGJ)
Tuesday	**Morning:** Work on fields with Placido Rizzotto cooperative <u>Afternoon:</u> Commemorative ceremony (Nino D'Agostino, mafia victim)	SGJ Palermo
Wednesday	**Morning:** Work on fields with Placido Rizzotto cooperative *Afternoon:* Workshop on Danilo Dolci and anti-mafia pedagogy (led by Libera educators)	SGJ
Thursday	**Morning:** Work on fields with Placido Rizzotto cooperative, *Visit* the canteen where grapes of three Libera terra cooperatives are transformed <u>Afternoon:</u> Trip to Giardino della memoria (site of murder of Giuseppe di Matteo, child mafia victim, led by liberessenze association)	SGJ
Friday	**Morning:** Work on fields with Pio La Torre cooperative <u>*Afternoon:*</u> Visit SGJ archive and library, meeting with archivists	SGJ
Weekend	Time off	

Figure 3. Anti-mafia camp sample schedule. Figure key: **bold** is volunteer work; *italics* is education; <u>*italics underline*</u> is networking; and <u>underline</u> is commemoration.

Day	Activity	Location
Monday	**Morning:** Work on fields with Pio La Torre cooperative *Afternoon:* Workshop on European organized crime and the EU directive on confiscation (held by myself) *Evening:* "100 passi" film screening	SGJ
Tuesday	**Morning:** Work on fields with Pio La Torre cooperative *Afternoon:* Workshop on international campaign "Peace for Mexico" (held by Libera educators)	SGJ
Wednesday	**Morning:** Work on fields with Pio La Torre cooperative *Afternoon:* Workshop on transnational mafias and judicial measures (held by magistrate Vittorio Teresi)	SGJ Marina di Cinisi
Thursday	**Morning:** Work on requalifying the mafia-confiscated house we were living in *Afternoon:* Workshop on narcomafias, from international drug trade to consumption (held by myself)	SGJ
Friday	*Morning:* Participation in court hearing on state-mafia treaty Afternoon: departure	Palermo

Clean Territories

Upon arriving, we were told that we were to sleep and eat in a house which "the mafia had lost" and the law had won. In general, the spaces we were directed to had clear boundaries, and our work was to be confined to them. One day, while working on the lands administered by one cooperative, a worker-member stepped aside toward me and beckoned me to follow him. He took me away from the Grillo vines and led me to the fence (Figure 4). He was going to tell me a story, he said, because he knew I could understand. "You see that land over there? That is mafia land, or at least, that's what the *pentiti*[20] say." According to him, the land had not been confiscated because of a lack of evidence. Laughing, he told me that now I knew where I was to go if I needed the toilet. "Just make sure you aim right, lady, because this is clean land. The fence is at the top of a slope: it could go both ways." In this sense, he directed my own bodily waste toward land that was not clean. Anti-mafia land was to be kept clean, while mafia could (and should) be pissed on.

At the same time, he pointed toward their land and remarked how neat it was compared to the land we were working. He explained that it was because they had access to wealth that they managed to keep it so well. "It's like the houses of the bosses," he continued. "You'll never see anything out of place because they have the money to pay for big fences, gardeners, and house-cleaners."[21] They, on the other hand, had to work really hard to make money because their cooperative farm was concerned with providing labor and sharing wealth among the workers. Indeed, their vines required a lot of attention, as the land area was extensive and the workforce small due to the necessity to having to share the profits so that everyone had enough money to survive.

The labor we were engaged in was primarily aimed at managing the canopy: weeding, removing stones from the soil, bundling up branches and leaves, and training vines on to a trellis to protect the grapes from growing downward and being burnt by the sun. At the end of the day, we could see the results of our work, as the rows we had taken care of appeared neater than the other vines. Our labor was heightening the value of the vineyards. "Now it al-

Figure 4. Fence between mafia and anti-mafia land. Photograph by Christina Jerne.

most looks like the land of a mafioso," the farmer joked, looking back at our progress. "Now it's really *cosa nostra!*"[22] In this sense, we were directed to tend the "clean" but messy anti-mafia land in opposition to the "dirty" but orderly mafia land. In other words, there was a strong connection between aesthetics and ethics in this process of valuation.

Our bodies were also used in other ways. We were not only directed toward valuing legal spaces; we were also used as vehicles to communicate these normative spaces. For example, every time we went into an open public space, where the line between the legal and the illegal was not as clear cut, we were asked to wear the official E!state Liberi! T-shirts. "Of course when you are farming, you might feel more comfortable in your own clothes. That is entirely up to you. But it is important to show the local population that people are doing these things here. It is a sign of change."

According to many of the farmers I talked to, when they first started working on the confiscated lands, they were fearful, and their friends asked them why on earth they would take such risks. Despite the lack of employment, very few people applied to work on the confiscated assets. Indeed, their activity was obstructed, as the land and the agricultural machinery were vandalized.[23] In the eyes of the Libera activists, this was a sign of victory because, when the mafia was annoyed, it meant that their stagnant rule was being disrupted. Now, after years of demonstrating that it was possible to work on this land and that many others thought it was possible too, they had achieved consensus that was "the most important weapon for the success of the movement." In this way, our bodies and our volunteer uniforms represented and spread this consensus regarding the norms they observed on this land. And importantly, this happened on assets that used to belong to the enemy.

Moreover, the consensus was also directed inward, toward our own bodies. Throughout our stay, we ate food and wine that was almost entirely produced by the cooperatives that were part of the Libera Terra Meditarraneo consortium. In this way we became attuned to the taste of the norm, as well as its visual manifestations. Many of our evenings were spent discussing the different types of grapes we tasted in the wines, the quality of the legumes, and the colors of the grains. In this sense we were also directly ingesting parts of these territories. Not only were we learning to appreciate their sensorial qualities, we were also valuing them by eating them, thus becoming a corporal component of the production cycle. We also entered the valuation cycle by paying for them, as well as, of course, working to transform them into a commodity. In this way, we were oriented toward revaluing the territories through our very movement, both outward and inward. Throughout our stay we therefore became anti-mafia subjects by encompassing "legal" objects in us and by contributing to shaping "legal" objects. We were thus turned at once into the receptacles and vehicles of anti-mafia.

Just Velocity

One of the challenges connected to producing food the "legal way" was maintaining a level of efficiency and competitiveness on the market. One farmer told me that when Brusca owned the land, everything worked really well. For example, there was an artificial lake that was constantly full because Brusca had pierced a hole in the public pipelines that bled water directly on to his farm,[24] ensuring easy and cheap access to water all year round. Getting access to water legally, by contrast, was a long process that failed on several occasions, making production and labor very inefficient and costly. Instead, the temporality of crime is fast and effective.

Indeed, one of the farmers told me he knew Brusca personally and that, when he found out that the lands were to be administered by the cooperative, he told him that he was happy because at least when he got them back (which at the time he thought he would), they would be in a better condition than when they were in the hands of the state. In general, the farmer explained, things worked really well during the golden years of the Cosa Nostra. Construction was booming, and everybody in the city was employed. But times were violent. "Sometimes you would just hear shooting and think to yourself, ah, there goes another one. I wonder who. We even had scores going between SGJ [San Giuseppe Jato] and Cipirello [a neighboring town]. We would compare the number of deaths. 1–4 for SGJ! We weren't even scared any more, it was simply natural." When the police arrested many of the SGJ district members, the city became deserted, and nobody had jobs. Building up alternative livelihoods was a difficult and slow process.

Indeed, when we were farming together, he confessed that volunteers were sometimes a burden to the work. Many of them had never been in a field before, were easily frightened by insects, fainted in the sun because of dehydration, were very sensitive to the stinging of sulfur in the eyes, or just did not do their job properly. He told me that many of the other farmers envied him when he worked with volunteers because that meant that he would be working less hard than the others. "They don't understand how tiring it is to communicate with all these people under the heat! It may be slow, but it's so important because only then can you city folks understand the fatigue of this work." He was right: we were exhausted. Not only were we not used to this type of labor, but our daily schedule was also packed with other activities that stimulated us and required a lot of attention and engagement. "Anti-mafia is hard work!" they repeated. In fact, we were told that, although everything worked well in the mafia period, it was never the mafiosi who did the physical labor. Brusca merely sat down, smoked his pipe, and asked passers-by which family they belonged to ("A cu apparteni?"). Mafia power was fast but lazy, or better, "energy efficient" (Jerne 2024).

Figure 5. Confiscated land. Courtesy of Gabriele Fantoni.

The cooperatives were also slowed down by their own members. According to Italian legislation, social cooperatives should be oriented toward "socially disadvantaged subjects,"[25] including people who operate at a speed that is different from most. One volunteer was a migrant who lived in Palermo and thus had to be picked up at a rather distant bus stop every morning so that he could take part in the work. Another member was deaf, so they had to find other ways of communicating, which took up time. Another one had heart problems, so had a different rhythm in his work. The least able bodies set the speed of the work.

On top of this, the types of products that were to be produced had to respect the temporality of nonhuman beings. The use of industrial pesticides was not allowed, which meant that the produce that came out of the land was far more prone to disease and more delicate. Meticulous and constant manual work was therefore required to ensure the productivity of the fields. Often, complained some of the farmers, they would be forced to leave half their vines to rot because they did not live up to the standard of excellence demanded by the organic certification standards. "It takes patience," they added.

One morning one of the farmers approached me and looked at me sternly: "Can I ask you a question?" I nodded. "Are you paying money to work for us?" "Yes, I am," I replied. "Why on earth are you doing this?" This question struck me. I reflected on why I, along with hundreds of others, was choosing to immerse myself in an experience where I would have to work hard, and on top of that pay for it. Contrary to conventional conceptions that theorize power in antithesis to the exercise of freedom, Foucault (1982) noted that power and freedom are in an agonistic relationship. In other terms, power and freedom are not mutually exclusive, but rather complementary. Thus, power operates precisely on individual freedom, and it does so by structuring the degree and type of agency of others. In our case, we were struggling to determine our own subjectivity by actively confronting dominant mafia norms, a manifestation of their power. In doing so, we testified that we had agency, that we were capable of exercising a collective and individual resistance, of investing our free time and surplus. It was our choice to farm and thus to limit our movements in time and space in a particular direction. By interacting with these sociotechnical arrangements set by other anti-mafia activists, we were practicing a form of habituation (Foucault 1977), where we disciplined ourselves to living at this speed and confining our movements in spaces of the law. In this sense, we resisted modes of being that empower mafia subjects, that is, operating fast with disregard for the needs of others (human and nonhuman) or appearing orderly but disregarding the legal order. We cultivated alternative subjectivities that disrupt mafia values and practices. By countering these ways of life, we were enforcing the anti-mafia norm, valuing it by making it real.

"It Would Have Been a Trip to the Zoo": Disorienting Bodies through Exposure

Meeting the Distant Others

A significant part of E!state Liberi!'s camp schedules is dedicated to explicitly educational activities. In what follows, I will describe some of the learning processes I took part in in Apulia, where the camp was connected to two social cooperatives, Piera di Scarto and Terra AUT, who were contrasting the mafias' international trade in food and labor. Among other things, they express their opposition by creating legal seasonal workplaces for migrants.

One afternoon we were taken on a field trip to the Rignano ghetto, a semipermanent settlement of illegal workers in the province of Foggia, southeast Italy. The trip was framed as a learning experience: we were to acquire knowledge of the kind of economies we were contrasting ourselves with through our experience of volunteering, which in this case was concerned with producing tomatoes. In particular, we were to be exposed to the harsh realities of gang-mastering (*caporalato*) in Apulia.

In a nutshell, gang-mastering is an organized form of labor recruitment, management, and trade that often relies on the trafficking and exploitation of workers and that follows wage levels, work hours, and conditions of work that do not meet legally recognized standards.

Work Conditions under Gang-Masters

- No protection or rights guaranteed from labor contracts and law
- Average salary 50 percent less than national minimum
- Average salary between €22–30 per day
- Average hours of work per day: 8–12
- Piecework: €3–4 for a 375 kg crate
- 60 percent of workers do not have access to water and sanitary services
- Payment for transportation according to distance (average €5)
- Payment for basic goods (average €1.5 for water, €3 for a sandwich etc.) (Federazione Lavoratori Agro Industria 2017)

Activists considered it one of the most problematic forms of contemporary mafia. Apulia is historically one of the largest agricultural regions of Italy. Due to its coastal position, it has attracted seasonal workers for centuries, particularly in the production of tomatoes, or "red gold." This specific context is characterized by a high number of seasonal workers trafficked and smuggled from eastern Europe and West Africa.

We drove deep into the countryside, until our bus approached numerous barracks and pedestrians carrying objects on their shoulders. The bus came to a halt in front of a large crowd surrounding a Caritas[26] worker who was engaged in a heated conversation with several women. When we got off the bus, thirty of us wearing bright yellow volunteers' T-shirts, the crowd turned toward us. A woman was yelling: "We don't want anything from anyone! Leave us alone! We just want to live in peace!"

Our guide asked us to stay put and ventured into the crowd to speak to the NGO worker. We waited and observed silently from a distance. A man selling live chickens approached us, inviting us into his restaurant. Many cars passed by, overloaded with passengers, car parts, and poultry. One of the volunteers took out his phone to take a photograph, only to be stopped by the glares of the group: photographs were not appropriate. Our guide returned hastily and told us that it was not a good time to be there. There had been some conflicts, and we could not visit Rignano as planned.

Instead, we were driven to the outskirts of the settlement, where we met a doctor who worked for the NGO Emergency. His role was to provide first aid for the workers of the area. Due to their illegal status, they had difficulties in accessing public health-care, as well as in circulating freely more generally, as their documents were withheld by the gang-master and their movements were monitored. The doctor told us that the workers were not even allowed to choose the means of transport to take them to the fields where they farmed, and would have to pay the gang-master an average of €5 to get there. In addition, the gang-master required the workers to pay for food and water that was provided under monopoly conditions by his organization. The restaurant we encountered upon arrival was indeed one of the main sources of food for the 800 inhabitants.[27]

Listening to this distressing testimony made me so uneasy with my own position in the field that I took a long walk, silently distancing myself from the group I was a part of. On the way I met several locals who showed me around the ghetto. One man told me that each zone was inhabited by a different group, primarily divided by language (Francophone and Anglophone[28]). He showed me one of the barracks and told me that he paid the rent for the bed. Only a small number resided permanently in the area, as the winter season made it difficult to live in aluminum shacks. The Roma community was in charge of providing infrastructure, such as spare building equipment "for when the wind came" and car parts for transport facilities. One area was reserved for women. Here, he explained, guests of the restaurant could entertain themselves after dinner, if they wanted. I asked him if there were many guests. He said that it was good business. Italian men liked African women.

Our conversation was interrupted. "I think they are here to get you," he said, pointing at the frantically waving woman at the horizon. I had to leave. Shamefully, I walked toward the guide and the bus that was waiting for me with the rest of the volunteers. They had been worried, she reproached me, asking me where I had gone. I apologized.

The bus was buzzing with such heated conversations that my absence was not questioned. Many of them were asking questions: Where were the police? How could this be happening? For how long had it been going on? Two volunteers started debating loudly, and attention turned toward them. One of them argued that she was really happy to have visited the ghetto because she could actually see how people lived:

It's really different on TV; sometimes you're even in disbelief: could they actually live in such conditions? Now I know that this is the real thing. This is it. And they live horribly. I was happy that I was able to experience the truth.

Her counterpart was upset:

OKAY. I also liked the fact that I was outside television. I could smell, see, feel. . . . This brought about strong emotions, and emotions make you feel engaged in what you're doing. At the same time, I started asking myself what my role is in all of this. What is my function? How can I help these people? When the *caporale* who welcomed us asked us: Who are you, what are you doing here? and we answered "Visiting," he said "Only visiting?" I felt awful. What are we doing here apart from observing their awful living conditions? This must mean that the other cooperatives are also just visiting and not doing anything. What's going on?!

Indeed, this woman took a far more critical stance on her own position. Her statement was a strong self-reflection on whether this was simply a form of voyeurism that anti-mafia associations were taking advantage of. At this point our group leader intervened:

Alright everyone, I know this trip didn't go as we planned. But it's not true that people are not doing anything. Now we are going to visit a place where things work differently, where these people are given different possibilities. We are not here to observe, but to learn.

Here the encoded message was made explicit: they wanted us to learn what should be done or what could be done, within the framework of the law. In other words, the experience was meant to orient us toward the desired norm and away from the gang-mastering we had been exposed to.

Dignity

We were taken to Eco-village, a regional project whose aim is to create alternative livelihoods, and particularly to replace the tattered tents covered in cardboard and bags with safer houses. Indeed, the village was primarily intended to provide alternative housing (*tendopoli*[29]), either through tents or "eco-friendly" homes made of wood. The project manager who took us for a tour repeatedly underlined that these housing units had been built by migrants themselves.

One of the most severe issues that were presented to us was the lack of dignity inherent in the ghetto houses: "[In Eco-village] it is much better. At least in terms of dignity, it is. I mean, what you see now is a good day etc. . . . But in the winter, there is mud, the wind blows. You die of cold here!" Throughout our tour, indignity was similarly treated as something that attaches to the way the migrant presents himself to others—particularly in the clothes he wears, his access to hygienic services, and whether he lives in types of housing that are homogeneous to the territorial context. Conversely, dignity was a norm of order, a certain level of presentability.

One of the difficulties in the way of realizing the project was to convince undocumented migrants to move into the village:

> But you'd think to come here and say: "From tomorrow, you have the possibility of staying in a tent, comfortable . . . even with air conditioning, shower etc." More dignified conditions. You'd think that people moved, right? En masse! In reality, we experienced a lot of ostracism from the guys. Why? It's simple. Because here in the ghetto, the people that have been here for more years have an interest. You see. Those that have cars: they take people to work. They put fifteen people in the car,

and get five euros per person, and don't work. Those who have a restaurant: they make them go to the restaurant, and they don't work.

Although illegal labor, such as transporting workers or providing food, was called "nonwork," it represents one of the essential ways in which undocumented migrants provide for themselves and have some level of independence. Moving away from this particular source of income represents a challenge. Indeed, the Eco-Village project was based on a realization of this, as it was intended as something more than just an alternative housing system. It was meant to foster alternative livelihoods too, ones that fit into legality, and thus could be considered "work":

> The idea is not to substitute a bad ghetto with a good ghetto. The idea of an eco-village is to make the most of the capacities, the potentials, the vocations of every single guy. Because the majority of them have an education, have work experience.... In the ghetto you find people who used to make pizza, who were carpenters, who were bakers, who were builders, who had a gym.

Therefore, the village hosts small agricultural fields, art projects, and constructions that aim to engage the migrant in "productive" activities that can sustain him and the community.

In contrast to bubbling Rignano, the village was quite desolate, due perhaps both to its novelty and the resistance of the undocumented migrants to the idea of moving there. Yet I was surprised to find quite a diverse group. I talked to some Pakistanis, from the Kashmir region. They had come to escape violence from the Taliban and the Indians who were also bombing the area. They took a boat to Libya because that is the easiest and cheapest route. "Libya is still a nightmare in my mind," one of them told me. Another family I met were Kurds from Iraq who had just arrived in the village, thirty days before.

Many migrants do not remain in Italy by choice. The Dublin Regulation[30] requires countries where illegal migrants first enter the EU to handle their paperwork and possible asylum claims.

Italy and other Mediterranean countries therefore often become countries of destination, even though they are intended as countries of passage. Furthermore, the status of illegal migrants, which is that of most victims of human trafficking, is even more precarious. Eco-Village testifies to this: if migrants are to live within the law, all they can do is to live on the outskirts of the local community, at best making artwork and providing food for themselves for an indefinite period. In order to be become "legal" subjects, capable of circulating and working in the normal way, migrants need to go through a long bureaucratic process that often involves them being shipped to different countries and/or being arrested. They are excluded by the law, but subjectively produced by it at the same time. They are dependent subjects.

Indeed, throughout the tour, migrants were framed as *ragazzi* (the kids). They were infantilized, involuntarily derided as weak beings that needed to be made into dignified subjects by the responsible local population. The language with which they were referred to expresses the asymmetry of the relationship. Who would trade clean drinking water, food, and a warm bed for a situation of slavery, poor hygiene, and vulnerability? The fact that the migrants preferred living in Rignano to inhabiting a "dignified" detention center exposed some of the paradoxes of legality. If dignity is a matter of well-being, then the law in both its actual and potential manifestations did not equate to dignity. In all legality, illegal migrants are excluded from most types of transactions, and thus unable to freely enter relationships of exchange. On the contrary, in Rignano there is the potential to earn some money both in the fields and by entering other forms of exchange within the community and sending remittances back home. In some "fortunate" cases, there is even a chance of making a career by ascending the gang-mastering ladder. This is why some consider illegality, even when it borders on slavery, to be a more empowering alternative.

Distortions as Critical Openings

Our tour of the empty village of legality came to an end after an "ethno-ethical" dinner. Many of the volunteers were cheerfully chatting to the residents about the exotic dishes they were preparing. Unlike Rignano, where illegality was the norm, here the volunteers felt comfortable taking pictures of themselves playing with the children. One volunteer sat next to me. We discussed some concerns we had with the EU's migration laws. His reading of the trip was dramatic. "Today I saw the region [of Apulia] and the financial associations playing on the mafia and on the shoulders of the weakest."

Our group leader drew the day to a close by justifying the form of the trip in relation to its intended outcome: "See why we took you to Rignano? You wouldn't have seen the severity of the problem if we just came here, where things are working. Otherwise it [going to Rignano] would have just been a trip to the zoo."

Once more, the encoded message was that the law was right. E!state Liberi! directed its volunteers to a legal environment, one that is encoded as good, and then opposes it to the illegal Rignano setting, encoded as bad. From the most obvious point of view, the valuing strategy being deployed here is one that disorients the participants by exposing them to a failure of the norm (Rignano), which was uncomfortable to be in, in order to reorient them toward a space where the norm (legality) was succeeding.

Yet, there is also an *unintended* type of disorientation at play. Many of us were not convinced by this dichotomy, and the legal situation was not so easily accepted as good. Asymmetries between what is encoded and what is decoded are common features of communicative practices. Stuart Hall calls this a "distortion" or "lack of equivalence" (1980, 166) between the emitter and the receiver. These types of openings are the home of performativity, where meaning is reiterated, and thus also where critical instances are accommodated.

On the one hand, this case might be taken as an example of performative failure, that is, of the subject of the speech act (Libera) failing to bring a new reality into the world (*increased faith in legality*). The semantic domain labelled "legal" did not overlap with the "well-being" of the migrants in the reception center, and thus the decoding volunteers were not fully attuned to the regime of truth that was being emitted. In Butlerian terms (2010), however, we can consider this a successful example of a performative operation. Despite and precisely *because of* the lack of alignment, something else was brought to life by making visible an opening, a distortion: by "slipping," the norm of "legality" was challenged as the "natural" order of things, thus making critique possible. Critique, and, linked to it, the cultivation of virtue and the moral self, occur when subjects interrogate the very limits and terms of a certain category (Foucault 1978, 1982; Butler 2002). In this case, this lack of alignment deautomatized the "goodness" of the norm of "legality" and made *visible* the very fact that it is a naturalized order, in doing so exposing its cracks.[31] Here, the sociotechnical arrangements connected to the tomato value chain led the volunteers to encounter a far more complex axiology than that of the norm. Even the volunteers who were aligned with the absolute righteousness of the law were exposed to ways in which it was being challenged and had been suspended in such a visible manner for over two decades. State power was either too timid or inappropriately categorical in its treatment of the weaker links of the criminal trade. The experience made evident the ways in which legal power performs, enforces, or at least complements organized crime. The value of legality was suddenly made fragile, imperfect, and liable to being subverted.

What is more, in reaching this epistemic limit, we witness a possibility for interrogation *and* the imagination of different paths of action:[32] is the law the only option in dealing with undocumented migrants, or are other structural fallacies at stake? In fact, it does not matter whether the volunteers and the group leader agreed on the degree to which legality is the way to break mafia. What is more important is to note that this experience made these types of confrontations happen: the trip made the gang-mastering issue matter, and it made it matter with force. E!state Liberi! directed us into a neglected territory, a configuration of paradoxes and information that we could learn from, act upon, and tell others about. In this context, anti-mafia action was about exposure, awareness, and also facilitating an unforeseen type of critique: a critique of the law. Here it was by disorienting rather than successfully aligning bodies that anti-mafia is effectuated. It was a gesture that broke the idea that the legal/illegal binary has a *natural* parallel in an anti-mafia/mafia binary. It triggered discussions on where that boundary could and should lie.

Importantly, being presented with these failures made visible the fact that here was a site that *could be* and needed to be filled by someone, or something more organized. And indeed, this disorientation was materially channeled into the work we were called to carry out. During the day we contributed to the production of tomatoes and the requalification of buildings that were in the hands of two cooperatives that were actively working toward providing seasonal legal labor for the local population, particularly for migrants who were faced with the types of choices I have described. While these cooperatives complied with the legal requirements of only admitting documented migrants into their formal membership, thereby conforming with the hegemonic discourse that equates anti-mafia to legality, they also carried out much work in the grey areas of this legal/illegal binary. They collaborated with trade unions and lawyers involved in aiding victims of gang-mastering, they supported some of these victims to establish their livelihoods by providing temporary shelter or food, they lobbied and networked for legal and local institutional change, and as described thus far, they invited other activists into their enterprise. In this sense, this experience not only valued anti-mafia discursively; it also valued it in practice by directing our labor and money toward constructing a more dignified space of employability. Thus our bodies actually took part in filling the opening. It is in these kinds of critical openings that we find a politics of possibility, the basis for the construction of a community ethics founded on the disposition to negotiate the conditions of interdependence, rather than the affirmation of a preestablished way of *being* "we" (Gibson-Graham 2006a, 82; Nancy 2000; Young 1989).

At a time when economic meaning is increasingly expressed in the form of experiences rather than goods and services (Pine and Gilmore 2011; Knudsen et al. 2015; Knudsen and Jerne 2019), these forms of corporal, immersive communication have been fundamental to spreading anti-mafia norms and attracting supporters who are not necessarily immediately affected by mafia-type relations.

As we have seen, the incorporation of volunteers who contribute their resources and time on confiscated assets allows circuits of production that value slow paces of input, hard work, and legal rules to be affirmed. Importantly, these are enforced and extended beyond the in situ mafia relations. For instance, these collective enterprises critique and interrupt ideas and correlated networks of mafia power that operate rapidly, exploit others, and circumvent physical and bureaucratic fatigue. In addressing such a range of norms and praxes, anti-mafia activists demonstrate their awareness of the manifold spheres of mafia power. And they imitate these modes of exerting power and influence by strategically selecting the very same sites for their own acts of social resignification.

However, the values that are contested are various in kind and are by no means "finished": they are cocreated and collectively negotiated. Indeed, these collective actions do more than just resignify what the terms *mafia* and *anti-mafia* represent and how activists understand their content. There is also an interesting shift in the *forms* through which these ideas are articulated and practiced. In other words, in this movement, the economic turn represents a shift in semantic content *and* register. The very fact that volunteers are invited into these circuits, for instance, highlights that these assets are recurrent sites of collective valuation and action. As a mode of collective action, E!state Liberi! presents and thus spreads anti-mafia as a particular way of being in common.

More broadly, this allows us to think of economy as more than something that social movements fight *against,* and thus as something external to politics. Similarly, these cases challenge the idea that economy is simply a matter of resource optimization, of allocating things in a manner that mobilizes the rational interests of activists and ensures their engagement with a political issue. Rather, economic acts represent specific forms of signification that can be highly political *in themselves.* Economy is a mode of existence (Latour 2013), a particular manner through which life is organized and livelihoods are negotiated (Miller 2019). The next chapter will look more closely at some of the *structures* that permit the affirmation of livelihoods that resist and interrupt the reproduction of mafia ecologies.

Part II

Rearrangement

3 Disrupting Structures of Mafia Dependency

A farmer drags the corpses of his dioxin-filled sheep into a black plastic bag and tosses it onto pile of rubble. His wife explains that they had been feeding their children and their customers poisonous milk for months before they found that they were eating and reproducing death. "They will put them all down" she says looking at her lambs, wondering how her family will survive in the toxic ecology without their main source of income.

This is just one of the scenes from the macabre documentary *Biùtiful Cauntri* (Calabria et al. 2007), which tells the story of how criminal economies are polluting the region of Campania beyond repair (Figure 6). Eco-mafias, as they call them, span across numerous sectors and types of material, demonstrating a violence that is particularly eco-diverse.

Struck by the gloom of these thanatotic images, I set out to explore what strategies activists were using to stop, circumvent, and navigate the pollution of their territory. I soon found that this particular struggle is difficult to represent because it transcends categories, forms of expression, and types of protagonists. Here the struggle against mafias is very literally about life and death. This sense of urgency gave rise to an incredibly creative set of entrepreneurial activities, a bricolage of economic activism that works by restructuring and/or interrupting the proliferation of harmful livelihoods.

Inevitably, these livelihoods depend as much on nonhumans as they do on people. And the forms of activism that I will shortly

Figure 6. Toxic grazing in Terra dei Fuochi. Photograph by Mauro Pagnano. Courtesy of Mauro Pagnano, Etiket.

address demonstrate that nonhumans can also play a fundamental role in *creating* political opportunities and shaping repertoires of action. That is, nonhuman objects are not only sites for political action, but their very materiality structures and shapes collective relations (Knorr-Cetina 1997; Lash and Lury 2007; Bennett 2010; Marres 2012).

This is of course also the case for mafia relations. Mafias aggressively shape landscapes and ecosystems, but their own entrepreneurial models in turn also depend on the composition and state of the territories they operate on. This is by now crystal clear to many anti-mafia activists. It is here that we once again find the mimetic element of their opposition; activists work by rearranging the composition and state of their territories that are opportune for mafia investment and *make them inopportune.*

This chapter illustrates several of these instances of rearrangement, highlighting how the new configurations of things, spaces, institutions, and people interrupt or hinder networks of mafia dependency. The previous chapter also partly addressed the role of nonhumans in shaping these political economies, but it did so to illustrate that they partake in meaning-making processes and the construction of norms. I will now move beyond from the strictly semantic aspects of collective action and more broadly toward its syntactical dimension. This means that I will address the way objects (human and nonhuman) and their configurations[1] take part in structuring and ordering these political economies.

In doing so, I choose to tell you how some of these realities are associated through an object. The thing at hand, a jar of peach jam, has an analytical function: it opens up different associations within the movement, rather than being a determinant explanatory factor. Yet, not only does the jar of peach jam allow for the methodological tracing of an organization, but it actively allows for the making of that political organization. This is not to say that it is the jar that plays a singular political role in itself; rather, taking the perspective of the jar can help us see that together with *other objects,*[2] its assemblage can be disruptive.

The choice of the jar was dictated by the fact that I kept bumping into it. This could, however, have happened with a word, a logo, a chant, or a heroic figure for the movement. In theory, one could choose to take any object as a point of entry. What makes the jar relevant for this case is that it is plugged into different arrangements in ways that increase the affordance, the potentia,[3] or the ability to act, of the movement in relation to its object of contestation: the Camorra.

The real power of the mafias has been theorized as lying outside of the concrete mafia organizations (dalla Chiesa 2014b, 21). As terms such as *inside* and *outside* can be misguiding, as they are often used to describe spatial relations or worse, monolithic totalities, here I need to be more precise. Mafias, such as the Camorra, can be understood as heterogeneous organizations that have historically manifested certain ways of relating, not just internally (i.e., between affiliates), but with the world around them. Indeed, following assemblage thinking (DeLanda 2006), the identity of an assemblage, such as the Camorra, is not defined by the parts that constitute it, but rather by a series of repeated *types of interactions* between parts. This implies that the Camorra has emergent properties and thus exceeds its singular parts and what they actualize (Harman 2010, 184). These parts are connected by relations of exteriority: relations in which the whole (Camorra) does not constitute the identity of the single parts (affiliates, drugs, cement, trash, etc.), and in which it is not the single parts' properties, but rather the particular exercise of their *capacities* that constitutes the whole. Thus, the parts can express themselves in different manners: they are capable of taking up different material and immaterial arrangements, which implies that the identity of mafias are contingent on these configurations. It is thereby possible to think of mafia power in Latourian terms, not so much as *a strength,* but rather, as *an array of weaknesses* (Latour 1988, 201). This means that mafias thrive because certain objects (i.e., corrupt public officials, waste legislation, and abandoned land) are *configured and expressed* in a manner that increases the mafia organizations' movement and influence. The task then lies in identifying and reconfiguring these objects.

This idea has become central to the movement itself, as it informs its contentious practices (Ciotti 2011). For obvious reasons, the movement rarely tackles criminal organizations up front, in their actualized form; this task is relegated to executive and judicial forces. Instead, their activities aim to shift the "weak" links that strengthen mafia organizations into ones that enable anti-mafia relationships.

One could say that anti-mafia practices are thus working to rearrange mafia relations in virtual terms, and not solely in their actualized form (DeLanda 2006, 35). That means that activists work with the sets of conditions and constraints, risks and opportunities, that shape the development of mafias (virtual), and not only the ways in which mafia has *already* manifested itself (actual). Herein lies the distinction between crime prevention and crime reaction: while crime prevention operates by reducing the likelihood of criminal acts occurring in the first place by addressing root factors, vulnerabilities, and opportunities (virtual aspects), crime reaction works by responding to offenses after they have occurred (or actualized), via instances such as criminal investigations, arrests, trials, and incarceration.

Italian law defines mafia-type associations as exploiting "the force of intimidation of the *associative bond* and of the conditions of subjection and omertà[4] that it yields"[5] in order to carry out their activities. Ian Hodder (2012) reminds us that dependencies, such as these associative bonds, are not inherent in things, but are contingent to the relationship between things. In a context where mafia-type relationships have been repeated over time, and are thereby difficult to uproot, dependencies go beyond actualized relations (i.e., arresting a boss is not sufficient). Because of this reservoir of cultural heritage, it has become necessary, even inevitable, to also operate in virtual terms, and thereby imitate the *potential* configurations that mafia has shown itself capable of actualizing throughout time.

This is a truly creative exercise, as it entails both "knowing thy enemy" and its affordances, and imagining how it might operate in a new context. Let us look more closely at how this reconfiguration works. But first, some Camorra talk.

Aggregative Shape-Shifters: Contracts, Debris, Poison, and Fire

Representations of the Camorra are in many ways a lot more relatable than that of its insular cousin, the Cosa Nostra. The time of the charismatic godfather—protector of a traditional family, international diplomat, and defender of an "integral" ethos—is long-gone. The readers of the Anthropocene can better relate to environmental apocalypses and tradesmen that make little distinction between living bodies, organs, toxic asbestos, and guns. This fluid, amorphous organizational form, whose volatile ethos is driven by nothing more than thirst for wealth and power, speaks better to contemporary imaginaries, as testified by the success of Saviano's bestseller, *Gomorra* (2006). Indeed, while the symbol of the Cosa Nostra has traditionally been the octopus, made of a central body with arms that worked under its direction, the symbol of the Camorra is the hydra: a Greek mythological creature whose heads reproduce themselves uncontrollably the more you cut them off.

These symbols in many ways actually correspond to the contemporary criminal reality. While the Sicilian Cosa Nostra has witnessed severe power losses due to the successful incarceration of many of its key leaders in the early 1990s, the Campanian Camorra has proven its resilience in recent years.[6] Incarcerating a Camorrista has in fact often led to the proliferation of new, anarchic organizations that are far more difficult to control, given their horizontal structure, where clans are highly independent from one another.

One of the developments of their power escalated to the infamous "waste emergency." For readers not familiar with this conflict, I shall dedicate some space to explain it, and begin by rewinding to the Irpinia earthquake of 1980.[7] The 6.9 magnitude tremors shook central Italy, destroying entire cities and killing almost 3,000 people. The amplitude of the disaster required public finances to cover the costs of reconstruction, which were supplemented with foreign aid from, among others, the United States and Germany. The earthquake radically transformed the landscape and the speculative interactions with its components. This is why I do not begin my reading with the official proclamation of the "waste emergency," a loud but less irreversible event. The earthquake instead, in Graham Harman's terms (2016, 49), initiated a new phase in the life cycle of the Camorra. It became *symbiotic* with land.

Land became increasingly deployed to construct public infrastructure, schools, hospitals, and private enterprises. The "economy of the catastrophe" (Becchi 1988) was made of cement, sand, and other aggregates. At that point in time, these materials had far more potential in generating wealth than agricultural products. Land thus often became a source of aggregates, but also a site of transformation, transport, or construction.

Given the scope of the disaster, the state had a large role to play in the reconstruction, thus making contracts the main point of access to these activities. Thereby, public contracts became increasingly attractive for entrepreneurs (Barbagallo, Sales, and Becchi 1989). Monopolizing these was a way to control the most flourishing labor market in the territory. Controlling labor relationships has been a strategy historically employed by Camorra and other mafia organizations to control a territory (Catanzaro 1988; della Porta and Vannucci 1999; Lupo 2004). Thus, the earthquake sparked a series of dependencies between land, public contracts, workers, sand, roads, politicians, and Camorristi that later made waste cycles particularly appropriate or "fitting" (Hodder 2012, 113).

As the reconstruction expanded throughout the 1980s, other national and international partners joined the enterprise. The role of transport companies thus grew in importance. An apt development for such mobile enterprises is to move across space and connect to more markets. This proved crucial for the expansion of the cement cycle, which in various ways proved to be foundational to the establishment of the waste cycle.[8]

In fact, in the same period, many European governments started to be more rigid in terms of urban and industrial waste disposal regulations, causing heightened costs in waste management (Saveria Antiochia Omicron n.d.). This led to the proliferation of a national north-south trade in waste that often circumvented the law. Some have connected the growth of the internal market to the concurrent increase in the patrolling of the seas, sparked by a series of shipwrecks in the 1980s that exposed the illicit waste trade between Northern Italian firms and extra-European countries (Saviano [2006] 2016; Cantoni 2016). These factors provided a fertile ground for the collaboration between northern industrial enterprises, public officials, and organized crime groups.

Other than the aforementioned convergences linked to the mobile nature of the two enterprises (waste and cement), it was the roads themselves that proved beneficial. For one thing, roads facilitated transportation, but they also allowed these shape-shifting mafia entrepreneurs to blend waste into the asphalt that the roads were made of. This also occurred with bricks that were employed in the construction of public and private buildings. The malleable nature of asphalt and concrete allowed for multiple composites.

The highly convertible properties of land lent themselves well to this type of industry. The sites of excavations and the pits that were employed to produce concrete and construct new buildings were, for instance, well-equipped burial spots for masses of hazardous waste.[9] Their size and extension were apt for storing and dumping dangerous and expensive materials. Furthermore, the monopolization of the real estate market allowed entrepreneurs to purchase land at low cost, which expanded the territorial area that could be employed for burial.

Given the level of infiltration in institutional settings, the chain of dependencies linked to this toxic cycle grew to paradoxical levels. By the early 1990s the Camorra was not only managing the transport and transformation of industrial and urban waste but was also being hired by the state (in many cases, embodied by itself) to treat it, as it had the power to purchase and manage the large waste plants and the labor connected to their operation. The resulting levels of pollution led to a state of emergency in 1994, where public waste plants were declared saturated.

The official emergency lasted for fifteen years, under which the governments' primary policies were preoccupied with constructing and reclaiming waste treatment facilities. One of the largest policy failures was the concession of a public tender to a conglomerate of enterprises (FIBE) that were entrusted with the management of the regional waste cycle in 1998. FIBE did not build the promised incinerators, but only managed to present waste in a new, compact form, eco-bales,[10] that were physically unsuitable for incineration. By 2008 these eco-bales amounted to 12 million tons (Cantoni 2016, 105) and were scattered in highly exposed areas without prior negotiation with the local communities (Caggiano and De Rosa 2015, 535). The overall mismanagement of the cycle resulted in periods where domestic waste filled the streets, causing substantial urban unrest and violence.

Different governments tackled the problem either by sending waste to unfit treatment plants, shipping it abroad, or opening new incinerators. This infuriated the local communities who had severe clashes with the police on various occasions, culminating with the militarization of treatment facilities. The "emergency" officially ended in 2009, when the Berlusconi government removed 170,000 tons of trash from the streets (Cantoni 2016), coherently crowning a season marked by "sweeping under the rug" policies.

The damages to the Campanian ecology are great. Not only are flora and fauna contaminated to levels beyond repair, but child mortality, cancer, and congenital malformation in various organisms have been found to be linked to the levels of pollution (Senior and Mazza 2004; Comba et al. 2006). These factors have had harsh consequences for the reputation of Campania (now internationally known as the Terra dei Fuochi, Land of Fires[11]), and particularly for the local agriculture, the most toxic of all the human-nonhuman entanglements.

Grassroots reactions to these intoxicating conditions have been both numerous and varied in kind since the beginning of the crisis: national and international petitions, legal accusations, violent and nonviolent resistance to the construction of incinerators, and street demonstrations. Here I focus on political actions that do not speak to powers that represent them, but rather that present their own power. In other words, I focus on nonrepresentational types of collective action (McDonald 2006; Tormey 2006, 2015). Monica Caggiano and Salvatore De Rosa (2015) too have pointed out that in the past years anti-Camorra activism has shifted toward collective forms of territorial reappropriation, through for instance, commoning practices (Gibson-Graham et al. 2013). In particular, I aim to show how these diverse forms of economic action are reshuffling the arrangement of things, the syntax, around three nodes of Camorra power: land, labor, and reputation.

Production: Reclaiming Land and Labor

"You are lucky enough to be standing on the only occupied Camorra estate in Italy," were S.'s words, when I asked him where I was. In the 1990s the terrain was the building site of a luxurious apartment complex named Vomero 2. During the construction phase, there was a methane explosion that raised the authorities' attention to the nature of the building site. At the time, it was managed by the Simeoli family, which was affiliated to some of the leading building speculators in Italy during the 1970s, the Nuvoletta and Polverino clans. After the incident in 1997, the state seized the asset, and confiscated it effectively in 2001. Until 2008, the 14 hectares of land remained abandoned and unsurveilled, allowing illicit economies to keep proliferating on it. In that period, the Simeoli family was working on the construction of an illegal landfill, digging a 270-meter-deep hole using European funds.

Interrupting Unfavorable Chronologies

S., the president of an anti-Camorra association that has been active in the area since 2008, decided to take matters into his own hands, and occupied the land in 2012. This was a crime in itself, because once the state confiscates an asset, it remains under its administration until it is formally allocated to a cooperative/association that has competed for and has been granted the tenure of the property. This democratic procedure can require years, and in this case, the local administration had not even launched the public tender. So S. and his association irrupted on the asset and started materially claiming the public nature of its ownership, effectively challenging the Camorra's influence through direct usage.

As this particular asset is an agricultural estate, leaving it barren augments the costs of retrieval, as living beings such as fruit trees and vines need uninterrupted care to generate produce. In November 2014, S. harvested the first illegal yields of his occupation—illegal because it interrupted the time of legality, which in itself allowed for illegality to flourish. In practice, his illegal act was considered illegal to a lesser extent, because in fact, it sped up the formal allocation of the good (in all legality), which was unsurprisingly granted to his association. His act challenged, and hastened, the temporality of the state.

The occupation thus dictated novel arrangements of power and control over the land.[12] In this case, S. wanted to empower one of the actors that is most entangled in Camorra power: their workforce. As I have discussed, one of the main ways that mafias gain power over a territory, is by trying to manage and monopolize labor relationships. In this specific territory, much of the labor is concerned with drug dealing.

S. was born and raised in a Neapolitan neighborhood named Scampia, home to one of the most disastrous ghettoized public housing projects in the world. Uncoincidentally, it was built to provide new homes for many of those who had lost theirs due to the earthquake I described at the beginning of this story. Today it is primarily known for setting the backdrop to many of *Gomorra*'s scenes. The area houses around 100,000 people but has nearly no services or facilities. This has resulted in the creation of one of the largest drug hubs in Europe (Pollichieni et al. 2016).

S's association grew out of the necessity to keep the children of the neighborhood in school. The squalor of the living conditions, coupled with infrastructural failures, has left many of the inhabitants without jobs. Many of the resident children therefore drop out of school at an early age, often due to the night shifts they take dealing, packaging, or guarding drugs. S.'s project was aimed at these kids. According to him, his association had some instances of success when it showed up at their door and took them to school forcefully. What they realized, though, was that the problem was only an effect of a generalized necessity to survive. Going to school was not the solution to this problem.

Fruitful Awakenings

S. began to experiment with ways of creating alternative livelihoods to drug-related ones, to contrast Camorra power. His social project, now organized as a cooperative, employs six young detainees with the aim of reintegrating them into the labor market. Two of them became worker-members and continue to work there for the duration of their prison sentence. Moreover, the confiscated asset is being used as a training ground for two juvenile justice centers, whose detainees are taken to the property to learn how to farm. The estate has become both a training center and a terrain for the cultivation of a mafia-alternative market.

Here they produce grapes, lemons, and peaches. Peaches are the fruits that they then turn into jam and juice, and that are connected to the larger network, which I shall delineate shortly. Though peaches are not the central determinants to this new reconfiguration, they allow for the tracing of broader reconfigurations. Indeed, while these peaches have been living on this land for a long time, they have not played a mobilizing role in the lives of those interacting with them until recently. Reconfiguring things' capacities, connecting them to others, has the power to transform relationships from those that cause constraints to ones that instead open up potentials. Power, as noted by Hodder (2012), is tightly connected to questions of dependency. The web of relationships in which an object is immersed, the so-called entanglement of which it is a part, can in other words either constrain or potentiate the object's ability to act. The irruption of the association on this land initiated a chain reaction that reconfigured the role of things on this land. As the target of the association is the "disadvantaged subject" (*soggetto svantaggiato*) the weakest actor of this social arrangement, here I focus on how this reconfiguration of property and usage of land potentiates them in the production site.

Initially, the criminal (now serving time in prison by working on the estate) had no direct relationship to the land. The land was a site for recycling the money that his employer, the Camorrista, would spend. In other words, the drug profit generated by the criminal was reinvested on the land and was transformed into a construction site. In this sense, he was entirely alienated from the final product, as any faithful Marxist might note.

Indeed, the Camorra worker was detached from the revaluation process that occurred on the terrain. The relation between the land and the worker was loose: the revenue derived from drug trade, on which he was highly dependent for his livelihood, would be transformed into construction sites that he could not access. Unlike Marx ([1844] 1959), I do not ascribe the negative effects of this estrangement to a loss of a "real," "organic" self, or what he calls species-being (*Gattungswesen*). The drug dealer is not oppressed because the product of his work, the money generated by the trade of drugs, veils the relationship to its final usage (alienation from the use value), but rather because the relationship detaches him from the plurality of values that *could* be exchanged for his labor. So this is less a question of authenticity than of potentiality. In other words, there is no "original" foundation to the subjectivity of the worker that is somehow contaminated in the process of estrangement. The worker is simply rendered immobile. He is constrained from *becoming other* than what he currently is in that configuration of relations.[13]

Indeed, the stability of an identity is not merely given by the conscious associations we make between ourselves and specific goals/ideas/tastes, but rather by the *repetition* of these associations (DeLanda 2006, 12–14; Tarde 1895). In the case of the Camorra worker, his identity is in fact highly stable in the Camorra relationship, as he is entangled in a web of relations that confirm that his only way forward is to deal drugs. Drugs closed the worker in a very specific network that repeated itself: worker-drugs-buyer-money-boss. He had no access to networks in which that value was transformed into another (real estate/public funding) as he was dependent on a smaller network of relations, to work. Drugs confined the worker in a condition in which he had little mobility. Drugs were thereby, in that configuration, valued by him as the most important object because in that equation they are the objects that carried the highest level of potential: money. S. and his association interrupted this formula with their action. The occupation of the terrain reconfigured the possible land-labor relationships. In the new configuration, the worker's identity is *destabilized* as he acquires new skills and is in contact with different networks (DeLanda 2006, 50).

Shaking Up Syntactical Capacities

Importantly, it is the specific syntax (the order in which things are arranged) that plays a central role in enabling this new political enterprise. This space of production is in fact linked to a series of material and expressive elements that augment the potential for the inmates to reconfigure their action.

Technically speaking, there is a particular status granted to confiscated assets granted by law 109/96. They are given in custody to associations (or institutional actors) that have "social aims," which then might receive particular benefits from holding such a responsibility. For instance, S.'s association managed to stipulate a contract with the Department of Juvenile Justice, which entails that the workforce deployed in transforming the peaches is serving time in prison. This makes it then possible for inmates to exit the walls of the prison and encounter alternatives that they were previously even unaware of: different people, different forms of labor, and importantly, different skills that they are trained in.

Thus, this new configuration confronts the prisoner (who has been employed by, or is prone to work for, Camorra) with an opportunity for transformation. Importantly, it does so by using the same nouns in the formula (the Camorra's connection to the land, its use of it, and the criminal as part of the entanglement) but extends it to include different actors (the state/activists and their connection to the land, their use of it, and the prisoner/potential laborer as part of the valuation process). If the inmates had been employed in say, a shoe factory, which could potentially employ more people, the association between labor and Camorra would not have been disrupted. It is the mimetic citation of parts of the previous labor configuration (the former syntax) that allows for the subversion, that is, via the act of oppositional repetition.

Indeed, as Deleuze reminds us, difference does not consist in negation, but is connected to an affirmative movement. When we negate, we are dealing merely in actualized terms and are cut off from the potential of objects: "The negative is always derived and represented, never original or present" (Deleuze [1968] 2014, 270). In our terms, if the Camorra workers had been employed in a shoe factory, they would not have been *present* in the opposition, because that configuration would not produce novel associations between preexisting terms of which they were generative. Becoming other, actualizing a true difference, requires a repetitive reiteration,[14] in this context, a movement of *re*subjectivation. Indeed, according to Deleuze's reading of Gabriel Tarde's seminal work *The Laws of Imitation* ([1890] 1903), difference emerges between two types of repetition (Deleuze [1968] 2014, 164). By repeating the association between labor and Camorra, on a territory that belonged to the Camorra but that is replaced by new actors, difference is enforced. The syntax of this assemblage thus plays a fundamental role in generating different subjects.

The material properties of the land also determine what kind of difference can be enforced. The fact that fruit trees and vines are already present determines the enterprise that can take place on the land. It would be a lot more expensive to start a different form of enterprise there, as it is the cooperative that manages it that is responsible for the investments on the terrain. True to the law, the property formally continues to be in the hands of the state, so these become private investments in the public. Therefore, most banks are less willing to lend out money to this type of enterprise, as the possibility of seizing and reselling property in case of insolvency is unlikely. Nonetheless, the costs of renovating agrarian land are high, especially when the land has been abandoned for many years.

Indeed, fruit requires constant attention due to its physical properties, and thus determines the type of labor needed to requalify the asset. Furthermore, competing with the mass production of fruit from big corporations would be impossible, so the better alternative for this market is to concentrate on a niche that values quality and the labor relations implied in its production—in other words, fair-trade markets. This entails, among other things, utilizing traditional farming methods and no "artificial" fertilizers. This type of production requires a major human workforce per hectare, which in turn allows for the asset to be a resource for more detainees. The properties of this asset thus afford (or are most capable of enacting) the cooperative form (Hodder 2012).

Distribution: Reputational Battles

Many activists that work with confiscated assets address them as bearing the potential for "territorial redemption" (*riscatto territoriale*). Due to the extent of eco-loss, territorial redemption has particularly vitalist connotations in this context. Food in particular, a source of life, income, and identity, plays a central role in these struggles. Here I shall zoom up a scale and discuss some strategies that are used to make these food chains appetizing, in turn, allowing the networks connected to products such as our peaches to sustain their struggle for life in larger fora.

While the first part of the peach network analysis focused primarily (but not solely) on the *material* properties that interrupted certain chains of dependencies, at this scale it is the *expressive* properties of the assemblage that matter more to the development of the conflict.[15] Therefore I shift the direction of the focus to how particular anti-mafia expressions (linguistic and otherwise) influence the material components of the networks, bearing in mind that these are, however, not independent of one another.

Activists have for decades been demonstrating against the poisoning of the Land of Fires. Although they have achieved important legislative reforms and prosecutions, the ecological disaster effectively remains unresolved. Consequently, the reputation of the territory has been devastated, severely impacting the livelihoods of small- and large-scale farmers: nobody wants to eat toxic food.

Inhabitants of the affected areas have, since 2012, increasingly responded to this problem with collaborative forms of material and symbolic territorial reappropriation (Caggiano and De Rosa 2015). Hybrid coalitions between environmental organizations, cooperatives, scientific communities, municipal committees, and farmers are ever more common. These are providing support of the most vulnerable groups, but also effectively monitoring the area, preventing its further expropriation and contamination.

One of the largest networks is RES (Rete di Economia Sociale; Social Economy Network), which was formed in 2015 and unites twenty-nine different private and public subjects. The network has an ambitious political agenda to enforce infrastructures that can serve as "antidotes to a criminal economy" (Caggiano and De Rosa 2015; DeRosa and Baldascino 2016).

One of its key strategies is to work with confiscated assets, which are often termed as powerful communicative tools. Indeed, an entire part of the network is solely dedicated to communication. Etiket,[16] a branch of a social enterprise, diffuses the network's activities through a web radio station, a recording studio, a data archive, photographs, text, and brand design.

> The first thing they [a business in crisis] cut is communication. . . . The population doesn't see that there is Camorra, underdevelopment, the destruction of the agriculture: this is the problem. So we are aiming at . . . our objective is fulfilled when we manage to give a contribution toward this thing [communicating the presence of the Camorra]. (F., Etiket employee, personal interview, June 16, 2016)

F., one of the key communicators in Etiket, explains that their enterprise is not about giving people a voice (by speaking on their behalf), but rather a platform to express it themselves. Indeed,

Figure 7. Wall surrounding Etiket studio. Courtesy of Pasquale Corvino.

Etiket's studio, located in Casal di Principe,[17] is an open space where potentially anybody can enter. Its interface is communicative of this openness (Figure 7). As I walked through the city, I documented a particular taste for high, thick walls that marked a strong separation between the private and the public space. Here, the walls were literally punched through and broken. Interestingly, the choice was not to tear them down, but to alter them in a way that made the closure visible.

Mockery

Keeping the wall and interrupting it can be seen as a form of mockery. Mockery is a distinct form of mimicry, which purposely opposes and ridicules the imitated subject by slightly altering something in its form. As we have seen earlier, mimicking always implies reproducing an object, with a slight difference. Indeed, a copy always differs from the original as it is not-that. But most importantly, when mimicry takes the form of mockery, it does something else. It reveals that the *process* of imitation is occurring, thus implying a meta-communication of some sort.[18] What becomes central in mockery is thus the nature of the relationship between the imitated and the imitator: in this case, the power hierarchy between the Camorra and anti-Camorra.

On the one hand, it reveals that there is dominant praxis; a fear of others or a wary enclosure of one's private domain. On the other, it reveals a subordinate, minor object (the hole in the wall, the activists), that, in order to make themselves heard *have to* refer to, mimic something else.

Yet, in visualizing asymmetrical relations, mimicry carries a critical transformative potential too (Bhabha 1994). In other terms, not only does it *represent* the presence of asymmetries of power, but it can directly be employed in challenging it via mockery. Here the hole mocks the very purpose of a wall (normally used to keep others out; here it is designed to invite people in). Through this ridiculing critique, it belittles the "protective" function of the mafia. "We don't need your protection to survive; we are not afraid of fighting for ourselves," read the belligerent postures of the bodies portrayed on the wall.

Mimetic Sign Entrepreneurs

Indeed, this type of mimicry is not merely a communicative strategy used to represent a conflictual issue, but also a strategy used to organize in opposition to the Camorra that I encountered on several occasions.

For instance, the overall idea of communicating anti-Camorra experiences is imitated from the Camorra's own practices. The Camorra increases its power by communicating its territorial control through murders, but also by directly libeling anybody who opposes their activities through printed media and rumors.

> Until a couple of years ago [when the Camorra's power was stronger], a lot of gadgets circulated during the Christmas season, which gave them money. . . . Like a sort of masked protection fee [*pizzo mascherato*], let's call it that. And they ordered a lot of pens, for instance, or calendars or things of this sort . . . because they like . . . veiled the racketeering

activity through these things. (Personal interview, F. Etiket
employee, personal interview, June 16, 2016)

Gadgets and publicity were thus also used to create relations
of dependency. Sometimes they would force print shop owners to
produce items for free. This meant that not only would the shop
owner's own business be deferred, causing a loss of money, but
also that his business would be associated to the Camorra, as the
printed items carried their logo. Other times, they would force
businesses that wanted to market themselves to use specific channels that were controlled by them. In this sense, they would ob-
struct the possibility of choosing the most convenient and fitting
business relations for the enterprises. In other cases, Camorristi
would simply communicate their presence by forcing business
owners to exhibit products they controlled, such as calendars and
pens, in their shops, not unlike dictators that impose the display
of their self-portrait or statue. These market relations would thus
depend on, in the sense of being constrained by, the Camorra.

In a sense, Etiket is mimicking their enemies by communicating their presence on the territory, but once more, with a difference. The difference lies in the ethics of their praxes: they are
sharing, rather than imposing, their vision of social organization,
and thereby making it possible to freely take part in theirs. The
difference also lies in their aesthetics: they do it with a very refined
and well-researched sense of humor that demystifies and undoes
the machismo, the fear, and the other sad passions that resonate
most commonly with Camorra environments.

One important aspect that emerged from my interviews was,
accordingly, the importance of being highly professional and
tech-savvy:

These are excellent entrepreneurs. They've got high-skilled
workers operating for them. . . . If we want to have a chance
to compete, we need to be even more professional. Today's
battle is not the one of Camorra stories [killings] anymore,
but to take apart that grey zone made up of great professionals, REALLY good, of the best, that respond to the Camorra;

those are the ones we should be afraid of. (T. RES founder, personal interview, June 11, 2016)

And if you close yourself, let's say, only to the "nonprofit third sector world" [*l'ambito del sociale*] without also expanding yourself to the profit sector, it means that you . . . are already losing. Because the real world is out there, I mean it is outside our networks; so, we need to slowly open up. (F. Etiket employee, personal interview, June 16, 2016)

What these activists point to is that in order to compete with Camorra influence on the territory, it is not sufficient to oppose their ethics by representing a different position. It is necessary to mimic their skills, work within the sectors they invest in, and become capable sign entrepreneurs. As the last quote suggests, this requires expanding beyond a fair-trade niche, and mastering a language that resonates with different types of communities, so as to move them. As Franco Berardi designates with the idea of semio-capitalism, the exchange of information and signs increasingly characterizes current economies (Berardi 2014, 92). In this sense, communication is not merely functional to a different order, but is *in itself* an enterprise in which the activists (and mafias) are investing.

Wit

One of the first, smaller networks of social enterprises is called NCO (Nuova Cooperazione Organizzata; New Organized Cooperation). Being sign entrepreneurs, their name is not accidental. NCO is an acronym that copies that of the Camorra structure that emerged in the 1970s: Nuova Camorra Organizzata (New Organized Camorra). T., one of the founders, shared the evolution of his communicative strategy. His story highlights the fundamental role that expressive components such as signs can play in stabilizing and enforcing the identity of an assemblage. In particular, it allows me to further explain how the peach jam's networks have been transformed and empowered by language.

Initially NCO (the legal one) created a common box, where they placed the various goods that are produced by businesses that work with an anti-mafia ethic (among which, our peach jam; see Figure 8). They called it, "pacco letterario," or literary package, due to the inclusion of books in the box. The first year, they sold 1600 boxes. The second year, they aimed at 2000, but then something unexpected happened, which T. defined: "an unsolicited stroke of luck" (*botta di culo non richesta*). During the public launch of the box, one of the speakers accidentally made a pun:

> Il *pacco* letterario è in realtà un grandissimo *pacco* alla Camorra. Facciamoglielo sto pacco!

> The literary package is, in reality, an enormous blow to the Camorra. Let's blow them off!

While the word play does not have much force in translation,[19] it had a strong effect on the crowd at the launch. They all cheered and laughed, and stood up to clap. T. was called up and told to interrupt the production immediately.

The punned rebranding increased sales by the hundreds. This discursive shift tapped into something that allowed for their market to expand. What was at work? T. described this event as something that triggered a new phase in the life of his networks. He explains how, initially, his team was characterized by good intentions, but lacked "know-how" and "street credibility." Through repetitive failures (and unsolicited strokes of luck) they learned that they needed to shift strategy, both in the internal organization of their networks, but also in the way they presented themselves to the public:

> I mean, you buy the products, regardless of all the value aspect that lies behind it, because they are quality products, because they are products of quality that should be prized. Not because they are products made by the "good guys" but because they are good products. (T. and F., personal interview, RES, June 16, 2015)

What T. underlines is that the market for solidary, ethically driven buyers, is far smaller than the market that recognizes a

Figure 8. *Un Pacco alla Camorra,* Etiket box containing jam and several other anti-Camorra products. Photograph by Christina Jerne.

clever wordplay. This new image was indeed far more successful: by 2012 they managed to make €300,000 in revenue, selling over 24,000 packages.

While the content of the box remained essentially unaltered, this new syntax gave it a new force. It was thus inherently not the meaning (the anti-mafia ethics of the products) that made this box seductive, but its form (the disposition of the words). Indeed, as Christoffer Kølvraa (2015) points out, affective discourses work on bodily dispositions and have little relation to "truth," that is, deeper cognitive interpretations of coherence. In order for these types of effects to be reached, however, the signs that circulate need to be shared and familiar: only then can a meta-communicative relation be achieved between emitter and receiver. Gabriel Tarde called these "syllogisms of action" (1902b, 132). Indeed, these syllogisms, which are essentially rhetorical tools that allow us to communicate, have to be intelligible:

> Either through authoritarian suggestion or through demonstration, we can only communicate our thoughts to others (which is equivalent to a *gift* of assets, the unilateral beginning of an *exchange* of goods) on condition that we present them through their measurable and quantitative aspects. If it is a question of forcing our judgement into someone else's head, through demonstration, we will need a more or less explicit syllogism, that is, a relationship between species and genus or between genus and species, established between two ideas, which means that one is included in the other, is of a *number [type]* (undetermined or determined but real) of things which are *similar,* and perceived as similar, that the other, the *general* proposition, encompasses and contains. (Tarde 1902b, 199, my translation, emphasis in original)

We must not confuse Tarde's reference to the quantitative with numerical language. Indeed what he is referring to is the broader ability to assess, the abstractive capacity that allows us to *value* something similarly to others.

Markets are made up of relations that are established at points of juncture (i.e., shared currencies, converging tastes, physical points of contact)—in this case, shared linguistic and humoristic frames of reference (i.e., understanding the double meaning of the word *pacco*). Indeed, we are dealing with two markets: a market for puns, humor, and wit, as well as a market that is specifically disposed against the Camorra. By linking up to the collective value of wit, which is higher than that of fair trade at this point in time, the box obtains a greater capacity to sell. It is therefore possible to intensify and extend a network by "latching up" or merging with another market that is already thriving.[20] This can be considered a case of "cross-appropriation" (Spinosa et al. 1997, 27), where the "world" of political activism appropriates techniques from the "world" of marketing, thereby enabling different mechanisms of diffusion.

Inside-Out

The new concatenation of words in fact enables the box and its content different opportunities: now the peaches and the other food chains in it afford a larger market. Importantly, this novel disposition has retroactive effects on the activist organizations that relate to the box assemblage. Indeed NCO was formalized as a consortium only in 2012, after the reputational success and the expansion of the market, as it required stronger ties between the cooperatives. In fact, this resulted in the establishment of common logistical frames that facilitated information exchange and coordination, and has allowed them to employ about sixty people, with an approximate turnover of €2,500,000 (Caggiano and De Rosa 2015, 543).

The year 2012 was also a terrible year for the Terra dei Fuochi stigma: the media increasingly represented deaths, tumors, intrigues, and mutated organisms, making sales drop drastically. As the intensity of the toxic discourse grew, so did the need for different expressive and material strategies that could support the farmers and the surrounding grassroots networks.

These external shocks to the network thereby also played a part in the way the box and its parts were disposed. The expressive elements of the assemblage became a lot more central, so Etiket's communicative strategies grew in complexity and attention. The box itself witnessed several internal and external transformations. The cardboard used for the container is now entirely made of recycled materials, resonating with the broader ecological crisis and concern. At the same time, the books that were included in the box were replaced with images taken by the network's skilled pho-

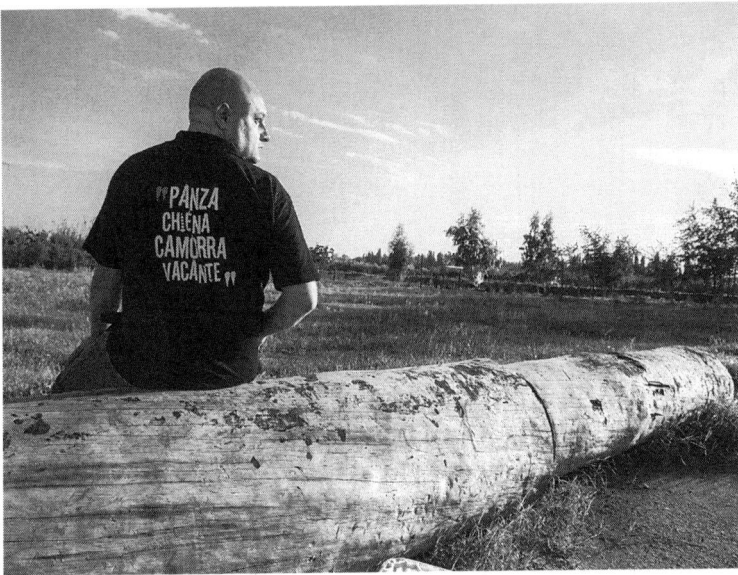

Figure 9. Farmer wearing an NCO T-shirt that reads "Panza chiena, Camorra vacante." Photograph by Mauro Pagnano. Courtesy of Mauro Pagnano, Etiket.

tographer, Mauro Pagnano. Once more, these often use irony and dialect in a playful manner. One example is this image of a farmer wearing an NCO T-shirt (Figure 9).

The text reads "Panza chiena, Camorra vacante" (Full stomach, empty Camorra). This is a mash-up of an old Neapolitan saying: "Panza chiena, tasca vacante" (Full stomach, empty pocket). The proverb taps into the idea of poverty; in order to be fulfilled in life, you need to have money. The NCO twist adds another layer: that you can be fulfilled in life *while* blowing off a specific type of money: Camorra money. More so, it refers to the fact that their market is connected to food, as it is quite literally the stomach that is filled, because the currencies of these economies are gastronomic. Importantly, the text uses dialect and not Italian to express the wordplay, which points to the local, territorial grounding of this maxim, but also, of the anti-Camorra struggle.

Not only did the toxic media discourse shape the aesthetics of the box, but it also changed the way the anti-Camorra associations *interacted* with the territory. For example, the role of the farmer is revisited: no longer is the farmer a mere producer, but he becomes a guardian of the territory. Monitoring the area, reporting on the status of the lands, becomes part of daily activity. Indeed, as the region gained media prominence, it also became the playground of scientific researchers who officially declared that only 5 percent of the soil is not safe for agricultural purpose. So the technical attention to these soils becomes a possibility, as there is no land that was more monitored in the entire nation. In turn, lands that *are* found to be unfit for farming are not left to die but rather, are reformulated. The network has in fact begun to foster the experimentation of different types of crops in risky areas: hemp, flowers, poplar, and soil-cleansing/nutrient-creating plants. Crops that are not ingestible but nonetheless valuable.

A shift in the types of products grown on the safer lands becomes necessary too. The box's own aesthetic refinement complements a substantial transformation in the way that certain parts of the network began to interact with the *territory*. NCO began to dig into the depths of their niche market, realizing that it is attuned to a taste of "excellence." The use of recycled cardboard was for example accompanied by a deeper attention toward nonhumans living on the territory. Indeed, activists search for healthier human–nonhuman relations in their cultural heritage, seeking to revive ecological practices from their past. Therefore, they start incorporating ancient recipes in their production, such as making sauces without water. They recuperate traditional fruits, such as the Asprigno grape, which is harvested horizontally, as the vines that grow in height and not in width. They start drawing on their cultural heritage, adding novel touches to it, for instance by reframing buffalo mozzarella as a dessert, rather than a savory dish.

Thus the reactive communicative strategy, the ensemble of signs and materials, actually had effects on the *practices that the activists* engaged in and their relationship to the territory. Indeed, as mentioned earlier, the associated actors grew from being four cooperatives to the much more complex organizational form (RES) that includes twenty-nine public and private subjects, ranging from banks to universities. This indicates that the development of this conflict has led to an expansion of the skills and capacities required to tackle this criminal ecology. Furthermore, the hybridization of these alliances and their articulations demonstrates a need for investigations that take into consideration how objects and people interact, and that move beyond the study of how humans define these interactions. These can generate knowledge about how collectives form and are transformed by their very relationships.

———

The peach jam entanglements illustrate a rich diversity of collective actions deployed to hack the structures on which Camorra power relies. I have identified both material and expressive components of these modes of association. The first, represented by the reconfiguration of peach trees and the legal framework, is providing the possibility of novel labor relationships that are not dependent on the Camorra. Using the dispositions of these objects (trees, laws, and land) in novel ways has resulted in the establishment of labor and income that are independent of the Camorra, at a speed that the state interventions, entangled in bureaucratic loops and ambiguous affairs, could not afford. The direct usage of the land also represents a battle over the mafias' territorial influence; a tactic that exemplifies an imitation of the hybridity of its material components and sources of dominance. In these new configurations, land is in fact less prone to becoming entangled in waste and cement cycles, as its new relations of property and usage diminish the risk of Camorra control.

The second scale of action has been the creation of a vector that expresses and sustains these types of relation on a larger plane. By mimicking (and mocking) the Camorra's own expressive modes of territorial control, based on enhancing their reputation through the spread of fear and subjection, the anti-Camorra is promoting opposing sentiments and connected livelihoods. Indeed Camorra power is enhanced if nobody realizes that different, nontoxic configurations are not only possible but also actual. By drawing attention to other kinds of collective orders that already exist, activists promote the idea that the anti-mafia is possible (virtual), but also promote their own position on the market, thus actually strengthening those that already operate on it (actual). The use of wit has here been effective in captivating the attention, and money, of the public that is so attuned to the horrid. Jointly, these movements are *rearranging* Camorra entanglements with land, and shifting virtual and actual relations of dependency into relations that afford more livable worlds.

Overall, these cases illustrate how nonhuman elements play a part in both shaping mafia relationships and in rearranging them. My engagement with anti-Camorra activists has taught me to open up to the complexity of this struggle and recognize how different elements play their part in shaping the identities, networks, and conflicts involved in this field.

Understanding how organized contention operates across preestablished actors (e.g., human/nonhuman, activists/nonactivists), sectors (e.g., economy, environment, the social) or categories (e.g., meaning, structure, and emotion) is not only a necessary epistemological advancement for studies on collective action. It is of fundamental importance to grasp ways to interrupt relations of dependency. By softening categories and recognizing their effective interactions, it is possible to sharpen our knowledge of how small alternations can have large-scale results and vice-versa. This way it is possible to recognize and perform different topographies and chronologies of power.

Part III

Affective Reframing

.

4 Mobilizing Mafia Heritage

Techniques in Critical Tourism

> "What happens in Vegas, Stays in Vegas." Well what
> happened here all started with the Mob. Join us as we
> return to the 1940s and travel in time to the 1980s when
> the mob's influence reached its pinnacle. You will visit
> sites where mob murders, burglaries, a car bombing, and
> underworld activities occurred. Learn about the ruthless
> mob enforcers and hear how they operated in the shadows
> while dodging law enforcement officials.
>
> —Vegas Mob Tour 2023

Vegas Mob Tour is one of many enterprises that offer tourist experiences that give you a glimpse of the "mob," a preview of true
"thug life," a taste of "omertà." Drugs, gambling, and public tenders
are no longer the main commodities and services associated with
mafia economies. Today, organized crime has also become a mediatized universe that can be experienced through books, films, and,
increasingly, immersive spaces such as walking tours, hotels, and
restaurant chains. In an era where consumers increasingly seek experiences rather than merely goods or services (Pine and Gilmore
1999; Boswijk et al. 2007; Knudsen et al. 2015), there is a large market capitalizes on the desire to witness criminal worlds. And mafias
capitalize on this allure to build consensus and exert power.

While many businesses and tourists are profiting from these
types of experiential enterprises, some have contested the specu-
lation on what may be considered a difficult heritage (Macdonald

Figure 10. Vegas Mob Tour. Screenshot from https://vegasmobtour.com.

2006). In 2015, the General Court of the EU even backed this indignation, stating that the Spanish trademark "La Mafia Se Sienta a la Mesa" (The mafia sits at the table) was contrary to public policy and to accepted European principles of morality. This statement underlined that eating at a mafia-themed restaurant is no innocent endeavor, as its criminal activities are a serious threat to security throughout the EU.

The commercialization of difficult heritage presents many ethical challenges for tourists and tour operators (Knudsen 2011). And whether explicitly dealing with sensitive heritage or not, tourism in general, as a form of experiential commerce, is far from unproblematic. Its recent massification has in fact led to aggressive transformations of urban landscapes and economies, to the increased pollution of ecosystems and to the enforcement of cultural stereotypes that have belittling effects for local populations. On the other hand, certain forms of tourism are being deployed to bring different cultures to meet, to requalify natural resources and cities, and to redistribute wealth in ways that nation-states could not. In 2007, the World Tourism Organization officially became a United Nations special agency, leading the UN General Assembly to formally recognize sustainable tourism as a resource for the eradication of poverty, community development, and the protection of biodiversity in 2014 (World Tourism Organization 2015). This is an important shift in discourse, because for a long time tourism was considered a mere side effect of an increase in wealth, and thus not a consequential phenomenon in its own right. Moreover, this acknowledges the political nature of tourism (i.e., Krippendorf 1982; Laarman and Durst 1987; Weaver 2013; Fennel 2015).

In this chapter, I reflect on the potentials that tourism offers to mobilize people to join in a critical political movement. Just as mafia-themed hotels and tours begin to pop up worldwide (some even owned and hosted by mafia affiliates or relatives), so are anti-mafia forces capitalizing on the desire for "real" criminal experiences and sensations. In fact, in the past decade, tourism has become a prominent mode of contention in this movement. So far, we have seen how activists enforce anti-mafia through different forms of discursive resignification. We have also addressed the importance of reassembling objects and networks in a way that opposes mafia relationships and affords different relations. Here, we will look more explicitly at the affective trajectories that activists engage others through, and the challenges and opportunities these techniques carry in making non-mafia relations possible.

These activities can be read as acts of affective reframing. That is, activities that "insert and stage a legacy into new narratives and create experiential material, environments or curatorial spaces around them to offer public leisure activities that *can* sensitize larger audiences . . . [to] a difficult past." (Knudsen 2018). In this understanding, reframing thus includes both semantic and material aspects, and is in this way tightly related to resignification and rearrangement.

What makes this mode of opposition distinct from the others is that it works by attuning publics through the tactical use of *affective* methods. In this context, this implies capitalizing on emotions and affects[1] to enhance the public's attunement to the anti-mafia cause.

It is in this tactical use of emotions that we once again find the imitative node of the opposition; for mafias have proven to be outstanding at manipulating emotions (Jerne 2024). The most common emotion they seek to trigger is, of course, fear. But there are also other types of emotions that are central to enforcing mafia power, such as pride, contempt, and a particular kind of vanity that is tied to the act of silence. We can call this omertà. We have already encountered some examples of this in the previous pages. This chapter will look more closely at the way anti-mafia activists work to interrupt and reframe this legacy with new affects: their own.

I begin by introducing the case of Addiopizzo Travel, a tour operator that allows travelers to support entrepreneurs who have refused to pay *pizzo* (protection money) to organized crime while engaging with the local cultural heritage. It represents the largest anti-mafia tourist enterprise in Italy but is far from the only one.[2] My reading is based on several years of collaboration with various anti-mafia tour operators. I also designed and participated in two different weeklong Addiopizzo Travel tours with two groups of Danish travelers in 2016 and 2019.

First, I will take you through the semiotic history of this struggle against protection money, which allows us to place the isolated tourist experiences in a broader discussion on the shifts in modality of these collective actions. I trace Addiopizzo's nuanced changes in communicative structure, which have been highly successful in mobilizing a city like Palermo and beyond.

Second, I focus more directly on the genre of commemoration. I bring forward certain affective uses of narrative and content that work well (and less so) in the context of making a subjunctive use of a difficult past (Jerne 2017).

My overall aim is to bring forward different techniques and media configurations that use desire to orient bodies away from mafia and seduce them to become anti-mafia, in what Luc Boltanski might call a politics of pity ([1993] 1999). In broader terms, these cases suggest that capitalizing on immersive affective experiences can be a strategy incorporated in existing social movement repertories, as the staging of political experiences through travel design has here become a novel mode of contention. Thus, it is beneficial to think of tourism as a type of *practice* rather than an isolated social realm (the tourist "sector"), which can be a valuable tool for the diffusion, financing, and enforcement of collective action and community economies.

From Sticker to Brand to Experience: The Semiotic Life of Addiopizzo

In terms of diffusion and outcomes, Addiopizzo ("Farewell protection money") represents a particularly successful grassroots
mobilization. In the past decades, it has undergone rapid transformations, providing valuable examples of how experiential
design can be functional for contentious forms of economic organization. The social movement organization (SMO) started
up in 2004 when a group of friends, upon deciding to start up a
business in Palermo, Sicily, realized that they faced a very high
chance of paying *pizzo* (protection fees). These fees can come in
various forms: cash, goods, favors, forced supply of products/labor,
or even partnerships (Gambetta 1996; Partridge 2012). Similar to
what I traced in chapter 3 with the jam assemblage, extortion operates by coercing relationships of dependency that grant mafias
control over a territory. The Palermitan neo-entrepreneurs recognized the malaise of automatically considering *pizzo* as a cost in
their budget: they realized that these relationships of dependency
had become naturalized. They decided to act upon it and materi-
alized their indignation into a sticker[3] that they spread throughout the city (Figure 11a). It read: "An entire people who pays *pizzo*
is a people without dignity." The media coverage of this message
was broad, particularly because previous antiextortion activism
in Palermo ended tragically, as described in chapter 1 with the case
of Libero Grassi. The group of friends decided to ride this wave of
attention and started (wisely) acting upon consumers rather than
entrepreneurs:

> We said to ourselves: "Going to shopkeepers is already diffi-
> cult. If we do this with a list of names [of consumers], maybe
> it is less difficult." This is not to say that it turns the situation
> around, but "Hey! There are people who follow this situation,
> who are interested in change, etc." We took this initiative, and
> then we started the "hunt" for business owners. And then we
> did a door-to-door. Beginning with the friend, the relative,
> the shop downstairs that you know. (Addiopizzo activist,
> personal interview, May 30, 2014)

According to the activist, it was necessary to start with consumers who were opposed to protection money because they had a much smaller stake than entrepreneurs in voicing their opposition to mafia. A regional newspaper supported their campaign by publishing the entire list of names of consumers: after only one year, 3,500 people were willing to make public their critical stance (Forno 2011; Gunnarson 2014). Only when they had collected enough signatures did the association turn to entrepreneurs.

By making this choice, Addiopizzo created a market for *pizzo*-free products that might have not existed otherwise: they made visible the potential gain this choice could bring entrepreneurs, thus making it possible to imagine. Indeed, entrepreneurs did not only imagine the gains, but they actually joined the network. The encounter with the list of names instilled the belief that it was possible to do, thus forming the basis for action. What started as a list of 100 adhering enterprises in 2006 is today a network of 1,049 businesses, formally supported by over 13,285 consumers (Addiopizzo 2023). The maintenance of the underlying organizational structure of Addiopizzo is further supported by other SMOs such as Libera, but also by actors that are not traditionally tied to the anti-mafia movement, such as consumer unions (Forno 2015, 539).

An important choice that strengthened the movement was the creation of a brand in 2010 (Figure 11b). The brand certifies that the underlying product is 100 percent *pizzo*-free. Gaining this type of certification implies a greater level of collaboration between enterprise and SMO: a willingness of the enterprise to be monitored and a joint effort of rendering the supply chain transparent. According to the official website, it is aimed at

> further promoting the products that are characterized by excellent quality level but also by the fact they are made respecting lawfulness, principles of sustainability, and respect for the environment. The agricultural products are strictly organic, while the crafted products are aimed at recycling, reutilizing and promoting small artisans or cooperatives that work with the social inclusion of subjects that are particularly at risk of being marginalized. (Addiopizzo 2017a, my translation)

Many of the activists I collaborated with noted that the visibility and credibility gained through the brand was of great importance. For example, it made it easier to denounce violent acts because it represented a broad consensus around the shift in norm. It also facilitated the connection to entrepreneurs who had experienced standing up to *pizzo* and therefore could provide knowledge, resources, and emotional support.[4] Furthermore, it made extorters afraid of coming into the branded shops because "the network is too loud now."[5] Indeed, one of the methods employed by the movement is to place an Addiopizzo sticker in the window of the shops that are part of the network. Essentially, this is a strategy that allowed the reputation of the movement to grow solid. In turn, it also connects more consumers to the enterprises and, consequentially, directs money and networks into the movement. These resources are redistributed following crime-preventive logics,[6] thereby strengthening the anti-mafia movement's status and force on the territory.

This transition from the sticker as a symbol of expression to the brand as aggregative technology resonates with what market theorists see as a constitutive property of brands: their capacity to form affective publics (Arvidsson 2006; Arvidsson and Peitersen 2013). This means that brands are not merely the outcome or symbolic evidence of existing publics, but that they actually play a part in their formation (Lury 2004). In other terms, the passage from sticker to brand in this movement is a semiotic move from the representational to the presentational.

Adam Arvidsson and Nicolai Peitersen (2013, 51–55) note that originally brands were primarily symbols for products, which gave these some sort of specific identity that consumers could identify with and thus purchase. Already at this initial stage, brands were a "new kind of connecting device" to others who manifested similar choices in their purchases. In the 1960s, with the spread of television and more differentiated media, companies began understanding that consumers had fluid lifestyles rather than fixed tastes for particular things, so brands began constructing communicative contexts within which particular tastes for things could be hybridized and matched (a good example is Marlboro's forging of new types of masculinity). As media became further diversified throughout the 1980s, the products and the consumers they appealed to became increasingly global, so the "mixes and matches" between different normative fields and objects became even more diversified, making the connection between a brand and a specific product—Marlboro and a cigarette—more difficult. On top of this loss of referentiality, there is a parallel abstraction of agency and direction: the increased availability of communication technologies has additionally shifted the boundaries between production and consumption, making it easier for people to make their own music and fashion or, in this case, political products. This means that brands themselves come to rely more and more on consumers (or prosumers) to evolve their products and that brands become less and less symbolic and more and more social. Brands (and their underlying communities) have transformed from being a mere symbolic expression of identity to the concrete entrepreneurial productive force of that same identity. Brands assemble things and people (Lury 2004, 2009), and they do so symbolically, performatively, and affectively:[7] by moving bodies to engage with them, wear them, eat them, join them, buy them, do them.

A simple and common affective strategy has been the association's choice of linking celebrities to the brand. Popular Sicilian comedians—such as Ficarra and Picone and Pif—have supported the campaign with their image, contributing to popularizing the brand by making it speak to a broader public. It is no secret that celebrities and charismatic figures have mobilizing potentials for publics, both for social movements (Meyer 1995) but also for other formations such as fans (Dilling-Hansen 2015) or consumer tribes (Cova et al. 2007; Hamilton and Hewer 2010).

A more substantial transformation came in 2009. Like many other enterprises that seek to further intensify a brand's affective resonance in the experience economy (Knudsen and Jerne 2019), Addiopizzo has developed immersive experiential activities connected to the brand. This project started with the initiation of a travel component, Addiopizzo Travel (Figure 11c). The tour operator offers packages of various type and duration that connect tourists to Addiopizzo-affiliated enterprises. It also provides guided tours that are aimed at not only raising awareness and spreading

a

UN INTERO POPOLO CHE NON PAGA IL PIZZO
È UN POPOLO LIBERO

www.addiopizzo.org

b

CONSUMO CRITICO
ADDIOPIZZO

Figure 11. (a) Addiopizzo
sticker. Photograph
by Christina Jerne.
(b) Addiopizzo brand.
Screenshot from
https://addiopizzo.org.
(c) Addiopizzo travel
experience. Screenshot from
https://addiopizzotravel.it.

c

ADDIOPIZZO
travel
COMPAGNI DI VIAGGIO

knowledge on mafias and the anti-mafia movement, but also at promoting a positive image of Sicily through more generic cultural and natural excursions.

Some of the surplus generated by these tours is reinvested in associations that have "social aims" connected to the anti-mafia struggle. Examples include urban regeneration projects and social activities aimed at improving the lives of marginalized youths and migrants who are prone to take a path of crime. From 2009 to 2019, Addiopizzo Travel donated more than €104,000 to the network of associations and has hosted 35,730 tourists.[8] In other words, the brand's experiential development mobilized resources that are used to finance the anti-mafia movement's overall activities.

While the previous phases that led to the formation of the affective public—the sticker and the brand—can be seen as speaking to rather momentary actions, such as the choices of goods and services (purchasing an ice cream from one enterprise rather than another) this phase invades the individual's engagement with the world in a much more encompassing sense. The tourist is moved through spaces and speeds that have much longer duration. In the words of Jakob Linaa Jensen and Anne Marit Waade (2009, 31), this can be seen as a form of *hypermediation,* where the media object takes a spatial turn, in that it actually interacts with and affects the movement and behaviors of bodies on a given site.

As marketing (Pine and Gilmore 2011; Boswijk et al. 2007), cultural studies (Knudsen et al. 2015; Knudsen and Jerne 2019) and social movement theories (Melucci 2000; McDonald 2006; Roelvink 2010) have made evident, embodied affective experiences such as these are central to the production of individual and collective subjects. In an era of where intensity has become the very ethos of humanity (Garcia 2018), the "experience of difference" plays a central role in collective action; that is, becoming *other* than what one is (or of what oppressors want one to be) (McDonald 2006). This is also evident in the rise of political tourism, where travelers seek to transform themselves and the contexts they visit via their movement in space.

The semio-affective operations that structure these experiences are, however, only one organizational level. In this case, the content is just as paramount, as we are dealing with the very specific political experience of traveling into a mafia universe.

Authentic Activist Trajectories

Addiopizzo Travel offers three standard types of travel packages. The first is specifically aimed at schools and universities and has the duration of about one week. The second is day trips and excursions to the city of Palermo, but also other anti-mafia strongholds as well as broader Sicilian heritage themes that are both "cultural" and environmental in type. The last type simply refers to accommodation and food, and thus directs tourists to Addiopizzo-affiliated enterprises. This means that you do not have to be interested in the mafia "filter" to take this type of tour, allowing for a more accidental donation of funds to this struggle.

I asked the tour operator to visit four localities that they promoted (Palermo, Corleone, Portella della Ginestra, and Cinisi) because I had previously visited the areas and found them rich and different from one another. I also asked them to make a bid for a four-night stay in one of the networks and asked the students I was traveling with whether they were willing to pay the extra price of staying in the affiliated hotels/restaurants. After some days of researching other options, they agreed that the price of accommodation and food was competitive with other solutions, so we decided to stay in the network of suppliers.[9] This meant, as the tour guide kept repeating, that our experience was 100 percent anti-mafia.[10]

The majority of tourists that choose this type of holiday are, similarly to our group, students that are accompanied by their teachers (70 percent) or highly educated adults in the age range of 50–70 (Forno and Garibaldi 2016). The price is comparable to similar types of packages that have explicitly ethical dimensions to them. Since the network must guarantee the absence of mafia links in the supply, the area that is made available is prevalently in Palermo and in other mafia strongholds. The few excursions that are available in other provinces are made because of tight collaborations with well-known groups such as Libera or other small antiracket associations (Forno and Garibaldi 2016), confirming the importance of preexisting organizational ties in movement development (Krinsky and Crossley 2014, 4).

As mentioned, our schedule directed our activities entirely toward anti-mafia enterprises. We lodged at Hotel Torreata, which adheres to the movement but curiously does not choose to market itself as an Addiopizzo hotel on their website. Therefore, in order to have an anti-mafia experience at the hotel, you need prior information of its status, which you might only receive if you are already aware of the movement. This means that the network has an "opening" function in terms of the political experience you might have in the structure.

While I found the bright blue skyscraper in which we were staying dissonant with that part of the urban landscape, the students commented on how happy they were to be staying in the "authentic part of Palermo." Although we were in a rather residential area, they termed the neighborhood as a "slum," which opened my own perspective on the city. In contrast to the context we were coming from, Denmark, the area looked messy: building facades were not renovated, and there was little attention to urban planning. This was interpreted as a symptom of poverty (slum) but, importantly, it was met with excitement: it was closer to what the majority of the city's inhabitants experienced on an everyday basis and thus validated the tourist's desire for being in touch with the real.

"How do we ensure that we are not feeding mafia-type economies when we are out in the city?" they kept asking. Indeed, while our stay was designed entirely around anti-mafia sites, there were also moments that were left to wander freely in the city. As phenomenological approaches to tourism have shown, the media that establish the relation between place and body dictate ways in which the body itself appropriates place and senses it (Knudsen and Waade 2010). This entails that when place is explicitly mediated, such as in these kinds of tourist designs, the traveler's experience of it is rendered more "authentic" because it heightens the status of place through a specific filter. Compared to other quotidian encounters with place, such as when we walk to work or take the bus to the supermarket, as tourists we put place at the center of attention rather than at the periphery (Knudsen and Waade

2010, 6). Thus, the criminal theme immediately filtered the tourist's experience of place.

Other than the design of the tour itself, Addiopizzo provided us with another medium: a map of places that were affiliated to the network. The association has also developed an app that digitalizes the map. These instruments allowed us to be certain that we only fed into the Addiopizzo network, thus answering the tourists' concerns. Another medium that facilitated our use of these cartographies was the sticker that I discussed earlier, which is placed in the shop windows so that the ethos of the enterprise was immediately visible. One group accordingly reported having gone out drinking the night before and spotted a sticker on the pub window: theirs was a "clean hangover." This medium was actively sought out by the tourists because they were fully immersed in a travel experience that directed their gaze toward anti-mafia filters (Urry 1990). In other terms, the anti-mafia cartographic indexes intensified and augmented their sense of place (Jensen and Waade 2009).

The opposite also occurred. The anti-mafia filter was also appropriated in terms of the negative consequences connected to subjects we had become. On many occasions, this group of tourists asked whether we were in danger: Was there a particular type of insurance that covered such types of high-risk tourism? Was it daring to eat right in front of the Addiopizzo shops? Was it wise to be wearing their T-shirts in public? In other terms, the mediated experience allowed us to embody the larger struggle: we had become activists and, like others who had stood up to crime, we might be in danger.

On other occasions, some read apparently unrelated events through the filter by which we were traveling. For instance, upon arriving at one of our sites, we encountered many police cars and, ironically, signs of blood on the road. The entire street watched the dramatic episode of a migrant being taken out of a reception center and being forced into a police car as well as an ambulance taking away a severely injured body. Here, several tourists asked me what was happening, as they could not understand the language. They asked me whether it had been a mafia-related murder, or whether the migrants had been trafficked by criminal groups. There was a hint of excitement and fear in their questions, which I see as linked to the sensation of authenticity linked to the narrative filter provided by the tour. We were experiencing a real place of mafia.

Tourism studies have long emphasized the centrality of authenticity (Boorstin [1961] 1992; MacCannell 1973) in the practice of tourism. Perhaps above all, the tourist is hungry for the real (Knudsen and Waade 2010, 7): the more she approaches the sensation of authenticity, the more she values her experience. A central discussion has rotated around the question of *what* renders authenticity: is it the objective quality of a place (given by the level of factual coherence inherent in an artifact/site of an event) or the subjective, existential experience of authenticity (rendered by a touching experience, such as the contact with an alien place, that forges one's own mode of being in the world) (Wang 1999)? Similar to what I have discussed in chapter 2, this is a question of valuation. Performative understandings of authenticity instead highlight the process, the relationships, and the sensations involved in satisfying the *desire* for authenticity (Knudsen and Waade 2010). Authenticity is not an inherent attribute of a given object, but a type of drive.

Furthermore, these studies challenge the idea that tourists are mere spectators, that authenticity is only triggered by external factors. Tourists themselves coproduce the experience of authenticity; they are not passive subjects (Crouch et al. 2001). The discussions that the tourists had on the dangerous nature of the trip are emblematic of this: Addiopizzo did not address our position of vulnerability at any moment. Nor was it merely the inherent nature of the sites that made them "mafiosi," as many of these conversations occurred while we were in between sites that had an actual criminal heritage. It was the tourist's imagination, her re-mediation of the events, the sites, and the broader cultural associations that revolve around mafias that forged the sensation of authentic peril. They became anxious as they approached their object cause of desire. They also performed the activists: identifying with the cause as their own, even if only momentarily, they connected to the movement's affects and values.

Guiding the Tourist Gaze

According to many of the tourists' feedback, the guide was what made the tour the most effective. Much like the map, the app, and the tour design that intervened in our movement through space, the guide is also an important medium. Our guide, Stefano, was a particularly skilled communicator. The first day, he took us through his home city, Palermo. The tour was explicitly aimed at showing us important mafia and anti-mafia sites in the city, which is also where we could interact with our map.

He told us his own story, his activism, and the relation it had to the broader movement and the historical events that triggered his lifestyle choice. He was not just a tour guide: to him, improving his communication skills from day to day was a political struggle. He wanted the city to be *"pizzo* free" one day, and (as he kept repeating) "It is also because of you that this change can happen." His function is to mobilize others by raising awareness and by educating them. In particular, he emphasized how our presence strengthened and spread their narrative throughout the city. Many of the tourists in fact commented on how great it felt to be part of the same struggle, which they had only been a part of for a few days.

His specific knowledge of the antiextortion struggle, of mafia massacres, and of the overall cultural context made him an authentic witness and testimony of the movement. According to Paul Ricoeur (2004), testimonies are the link between memory and history. Testimonies actually shape past and future narratives—they make history—because they are true artifacts.

Stefano fully took on his testimonial role: he often spoke of his first-hand experience and did so with a high level of emotional engagement. For example, on one occasion he took us to an activist radio station in Cinisi where Giuseppe Impastato, a famous mafia victim, had been active in his youth. What was supposed to be a historical visit (guided by another witness, one of Impastato's close friends) became a heated discussion of a contemporary media event. The night before, the son of one of the most violent Cosa Nostra bosses, Totó Riina, was invited on a national television show (*Porta a Porta*) to discuss his autobiography, *Riina Family Life*. This spurred heated debates regarding the ethics of transmitting such testimonies on national media. Stefano simply could not hold back. He exploded in a passionate monologue that took up most of our time at the museum: he was red in the face and raised his voice. We stood quiet and watched him. I was touched, as were we all, because he was truly angry. His body expressed his commitment and disgust, which effectively communicated the sensitive nature of mafia heritage. Afterward we discussed the gravity of the situation among us for a long time, reflecting on the importance of public commemoration and its ethics. His rage was not merely cathartic, but catalytic: we were moved by him and with him.

Witnesses can play a political role; their ability to make testimonial utterances allows them to make visible the collective importance of certain events in a space of struggle (Knudsen and Stage 2015, 133–35; Ricoeur 1972). They have a structural capacity to move the social because "they were there." Indeed, every site we visited was mediated by a witness, either in the broader sense of the term—somebody who was personally involved in the anti-mafia struggle—or in the strict sense—somebody who was an eyewitness to a mafia massacre. Witnesses afford the tourist form; their role makes them apt candidates for the production of heritage. This also means that tourism is a potentially fertile activity for the diffusion of a political cause because tourism *is* a quest for authenticity. Thereby, tourism's very premises provide tools for history making: as tourists want to be in touch with the "real" nature of a place, so they are, in a sense, particularly predisposed toward being moved.

Other than connecting us to his own testimonies and to Addiopizzo's battles, Stefano's narratives were extremely effective because he took his point of departure from common frames of knowledge. The number of common reference points is of course more meager than if it had been a local group. In fact, several of the tourists noted that on many occasions it was difficult to follow the complex history and the Italian names of the protagonists that sounded alien—and thus homogenously incomprehensible—to their Danish ears. Unless these histories were mediated by images, objects, or witnesses, which added another sensory layer to the communication, the narrations that worked best were either Stefano's personal stories or his referral to stereotypes.

For example, Stefano started our tour of Palermo in front of the

Massimo Theater (Figure 12a). He explicitly addressed the scene
of the third *Godfather* film, which ended with the tragic murder of
Maria Corleone, on the stairs of that same building (Figure 12b).
He told us that he wanted to challenge mafia stereotypes, such
as the one promoted by the Francis Ford Coppola films, which in

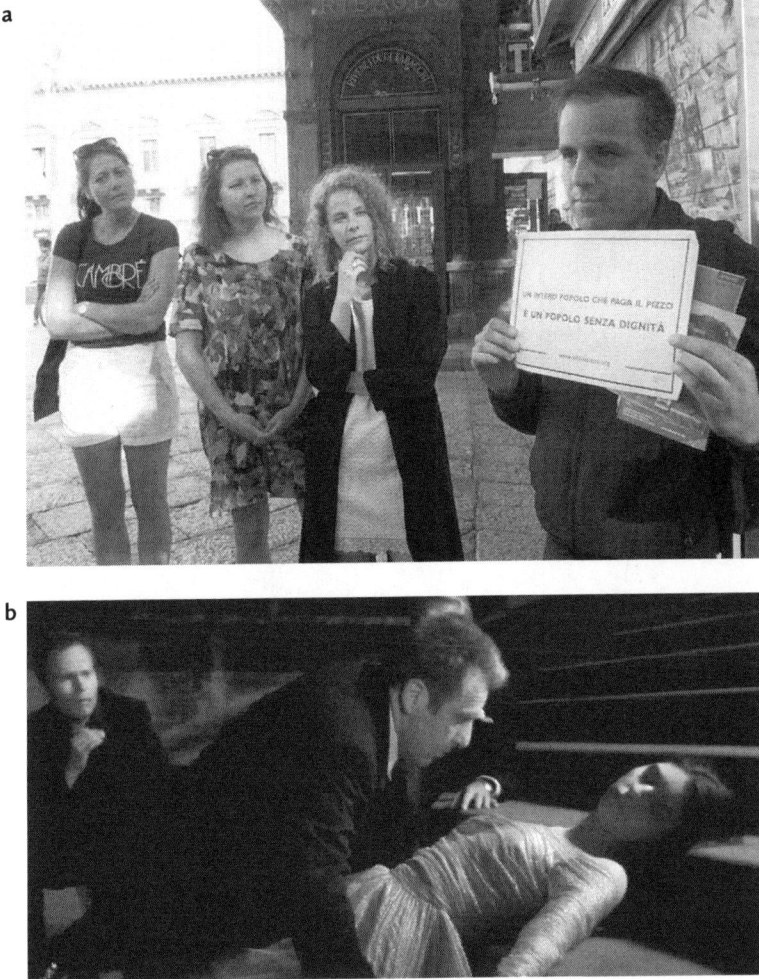

a

b

Figure 12. (a) Beginning of anti-mafia tour in front of the Massimo Theater,
Palermo. Photograph by Christina Jerne. (b) Murder of Maria Corleone on
the stairs of the Massimo Theater, Palermo. Screen capture of scene from
The Godfather Part III.

his view portray mafiosi as elegant, strong, patriarchal role models that are family centered and traditionalist. Instead, he conveyed a different reading, one based on how mafia did not care for family ties, giving us historical details of cases of fratricide, matricide, uxoricide, and even filicide.

Overall, in his narratives he often made other cultural references that were familiar (such as *The Sopranos* or Berlusconi) to us and started from them. These were appreciated among the students who did not have much prior knowledge of the Italian mafias, let alone the complex political history that surrounds it. It was through these narratives that they could start making critical reflections, thus connecting to the movement. This confirms the idea developed by David Snow and colleagues (1986) that the effective use of common interpretative frameworks is a determinant factor to the formation, duration, and even the success of social movements.

Hats That Keep Your Head on Your Shoulders

An enterprise that we visited founded its entire business model on reframing cultural stereotypes. Coppola Storta ("Kinked coppola") is an entirely Made in Sicily fashion enterprise that aims to give the *coppola* hat and its heritage a new life. Upon entering the production site in Piana degli Albanesi (Palermo), we were welcomed by stylish Guido, who was part of a cultural association that aimed at promoting Sicilian handcraft in the 1990s. Later, he developed his own cooperative enterprise, Coppola Storta. He told us his story and his desire to transform the status of his land. To do this, he took part in the organization of a design competition, inviting big names in the fashion industry (e.g., Crizia, Missoni, Ferré, Armani) to reinterpret the *coppola*. He told us that he was astonished to find that they all answered similarly; they kept the structure of object unaltered. The *coppola* is versatile, easy to carry, aerodynamic, and casual, but not rogue. From a purely structural perspective, it is one of the best hat models. What they all suggested was that, at most, one could rework the fabric.

Redesigning the interface of the *coppola* is an act of cultural reappropriation. Throughout time, the *coppola* has gathered a strong association to mafia culture particularly due to the film industry. It has also become synonymous to Sicily, which then by synecdoche has come to signify mafia. Coppola Storta aimed at changing this association by reworking a new communicative stratum into the object: a textile layer.

The textiles used by the enterprise are extremely diverse. There are both classic tweeds and silks, but also wilder retakes on the theme, such as hand-embroidered political slogans or the incorporation of protruding prickly pears, a characteristic Sicilian fruit. What spoke to me was actually the diversity and abundance in choice itself: hundreds of stacks of *coppole* were waiting to be worn and shone at me with their unique colorful interfaces. As Nigel Thrift remarks in relation to contemporary material culture, as consumers we deal with an unprecedented amount of affective stimuli: from sight, to taste, to sound, to touch. Thus, we have an incredibly (mostly unconscious) rich and intense cognitive heritage (2008, 15). To captivate an audience, to forge a field of attention—even if it is with the intention of disrupting or disturbing that very same material culture—it is necessary to modulate these affective fields using a comparable level of intensity. Color and ample choice were effective ways of exciting our bodies.

Another strategy was to construct an authentic setting by building a narrative around it (Nünning 2010). The factory tour staged the entire production as if we were not altering the manufacturing process with our presence. Men were ironing the textiles, and one woman explained the different parts of the assembling process by demonstrating them. She explained that, however, the cooperative's women perform the sewing at home and the factory simply sends out the different custom-made components based on the orders.[11] The final assembling of the hat takes place outside the factory walls. The reasoning behind this was framed politically. First of all, she explained, this allowed women to perform labor in the household and thus facilitate their traditional role as mothers or wives. The productive set-up was thus framed as a tool to ensure the employability of women and the preservation of their rich technical knowledge. Second, the enterprise meant to promote labor in the territory to provide an alternative for the increasingly dispersed local population. Like many other contexts, urbanization and industrialization have emptied Piana degli Albanesi of remunerated labor and people. In this way Sicily is reframed twice. Its cultural heritage is reinterpreted as a source of value rather than stigma, and the territory is reformulated as a place for employment rather than underdevelopment.

Whether or not we agreed with this type of gendered labor division, this form of community economy certainly made an impression on us all. Here, adhering to Addiopizzo does not just mean refusing to pay protection money but also refusing to accept broader cultural mafia references. It is a form of cultural resistance aimed at developing the local community. As Duncombe poignantly notes, cultural resistance can easily become an isolated utopian practice, a mere expression of resistance rather than an actualized pragmatic reorganization. "Cultural resistance, unless translated into political action, can become 'imaginary' solutions to real world problems and create 'magical' communities in the place of real ones" (Duncombe 2007, 498). In this case, the cultural resistance linked us to the economies that were underlying the resistance. We were, in other words, seduced not just into buying narrative reformulations but into investing our money into these organizational reformulations as well.

Indeed, at the end of the tour, we spent some time in the factory shop, and almost all of us bought (at least) one *coppola*. Everyone tried them on, took a look in the mirror, and took out their wallets. We desired the hats. My colleague noted while paying at the counter: "I don't even wear hats." The guided tour, the live marketing, the overall architecture of the community economy, and the beautiful *coppole* sparked a desire in us to take part in supporting the project by taking a part of it with us. The tour mobilized our resources, which go directly into valuing a project whose aim is to reconfigure mafia meaning and influence. Indeed, the fact that tourists bring money makes it more attractive for enterprises to join the movement. In this sense, experiential designs can bring together and mobilize different types of actors.

As McCarthy and Zald's work (1977) importantly highlighted in the late 1970s, social movements depend on skillful entrepreneurs that mobilize resources. Social movement success or failure is linked to the way funds, networks, and infrastructures are allocated. Their work, most commonly referred to as resource mobilization theory (RMT), was an attempt to bring forward the more pragmatic elements of mobilization that, in their view, were lacking from the prevalently psychological and irrational approaches to collective behavior of the time. Because of this historical opposition, RMT operates on an understanding of social action as driven by rational cost-benefit analyses. What this leaves out, and in a sense opposes, is the inherently sensual and affective part of what drives personal choice. Indeed, this SMO did entrepreneurially set up a network that connects tourists and activists, thus channeling their resources into the movement. But it did so using affective aesthetic strategies that activate desires away from mafia and toward the anti-mafia.[12] People's resources are mobilized through conviction, but it is not just the mind—an isolated, floating calculator—that is to be convinced. It is the entire body. Beliefs, and the choices that come out of them, work with desire.

Clearly, tourists that choose these kinds of experiences are already sensitive to certain political beliefs; there is a structural element of affinity in the type of people that might become involved. This is the general case in social movements, that preexisting ties and interests play an important part in determining the type of engagement and outcome that can be achieved (McAdam and Poulsen 1993). However, political tourism, as a genre of experience, in my opinion carries a different mobilizing potential than other practices that have been classically conceived as central to social movement repertoires (rallies, sit-ins, protest events, strikes, etc.).

First, there is something connected to the inherently pleasurable nature of the tourist experience. Sit-ins and protest events are intensely time consuming, energy demanding, and committing in terms of effort, which is why, for instance, McCarthy and Zald addressed the question of social movement entrepreneurs. It takes a lot to convince somebody to invest their energies and resources in causes that they only might feel a slight sympathy toward. Holidays, for which there is an increasing global demand, in this sense represent a valuable tool to engage individuals who might have a loose affinity to the cause. They also provide an opportunity for wealth redistribution, as only those who have enough economic and cultural capital might afford spending their free time this way.

Of course, tourists may simply be looking to be entertained and to distinguish themselves among their peers for having taken part in such laudable activities. Indeed, the tourist can just drop by, spend his money, and leave—and probably expects to do this. Sustaining engagement is a classic problem for any type of movement activity. Strikes, boycotts, and contentious digital networks also have a level of precarity: it is not unusual that only a core of dedicated activists takes care of keeping the movement alive while most join the demonstration just momentarily. Likewise, similar observations around social distinction and hedonism are also valid for other types of activism. The difference lies here: in many forms of political dissensus, resources are not necessarily mobilized (although they might be). In a tour, resources are a precondition. Tourism can therefore be considered a form of crowdfunding and, as such, can be a valuable tool for the sustainment of a cause.

The Difficult Spectacle of Noir

Although tourism bears much potential for resource mobilization, here it also has less pecuniary aspirations. Both material and expressive components partake in forming and stabilizing the identity of social unit (DeLanda 2006), that is, both material and immaterial elements partake in the territorialization of anti-mafia economies. So how do activists work to move tourist *sentiments* away from mafia? How do they design experiences that forge and fortify anti-mafia identities? The last techniques I want to address relate more directly to the genre of heritage making this tour engages with, and what it seeks to move in its participants.

Mafia heritage is particularly grotesque, secretive, and violent. If tourists choose to be exposed to this type of heritage, they are also choosing to be disturbed. As a tourist, one voluntarily exposes oneself to some form of disturbance of the everyday platitude: one wants to be affected. Even hiking a mountain, visiting a museum, or traveling at different speeds than normal are practices that in one way or another interrupt our ways of normally being in the world. Some tourists have a taste for more extreme interruptions. Thanatourism, dark-spot tourism, and slum tourism are all examples of this. And there is a growing market for this type of commotion (Seaton 1996; Knudsen 2011).

Dark forms of tourism can be highly problematic because they capitalize on sensitive material, usually death or some form of catastrophe. The manner in which this type of practice is expressed thus necessarily faces ethical dilemmas.[13] Several critical authors dismiss this type of practice altogether and classify it as a voyeuristic, distanced, mass consumption of the pain of others (Urry 1990; Sontag 2003). Others who have a more constructive perspective on tourism instead read this type of practice as urged by a sense of ethical responsibility toward others and a desire to connect to their suffering (Chouliaraki 2006; Knudsen 2011). In the words of Luc Boltanski:

> Now nothing promotes the formation of a cause more than the spectacle of suffering. It is first of all around the suffering of unfortunates that the *precipitate* is brought about which launches people who were previously unaware into a cause. It is through the cause that the public sphere and a politics of pity are connected to each other. ([1993] 1999, 30)

Following this second line of reading, I want to suggest that the fascination for the horrid can also be (and is being) used for the shaping of communities of care. Here I use two different experiences I have had that led me to reflect on the curatorial challenges of this genre of tourism. Both try to communicate the collective importance of death and both do so with the explicit intention of shaping a different future. Even so, there was a difference to the type of engagement they achieved on the tour, suggesting that death does not speak for itself and that heritage transmission is not merely a question of truth.

Telling the Facts of Loss

In a typically Italian manner, mafia heritage was often communicated to us through rigorously documented historiographies. What was important to the guides was to get the whole picture so that no detail was left unattended. This was framed as a form of moral commitment: *all* the names of the victims should be remembered in order to render them justice. The criterion of truthful *comprehensiveness* was, however, the one that, in my experience, seemed to work less because it made things less *comprehensible.*

An example: We were taken on a museum visit in Corleone, perhaps one of the cities in Sicily with the most burdensome heritage. Corleone had both suffered the fate of being used as a surname of the *Godfather* family, but also later became the hometown of one of the most gruesome mafia clans, known as the Corleonesi or *peri 'ncritati.*[14] At the same time, anti-mafia activism has been particularly strong in the territory, meaning that the town has many mafia victims. The museum was in many ways a tribute to them.

The building itself was confiscated from the Provenzano family. The part of the family that did not end up in jail lives next door to this day. We were taken inside, where the guide showed us what she termed as the "legality lab": a space for discussion, meetings, educational activities, and the selling of products from the local cooperatives. Upstairs, an exhibition hall hosted the bright paintings of a local artist, Gaetano Porcasi. The paintings represent innocent mafia victims and are dated 1943 to 1997.

The art pieces themselves were extremely violent in their representations. They reproduced famous photographs of murders, explosions, and kidnappings. They also represented mourning widows, blood, and Christian iconography—such as crosses and doves—that mafia bosses all looked away from. There was a clear distinction between good and evil in the choice of colors as well.

The guide in this museum followed the chronology of the paintings with utmost fidelity. She stood in front of each painting and told the exact details of their death, the political status of the time, the precise reactions of the press, and so forth. Despite having spent a long time researching mafia history, even I was enriched with a lot of new information. It was in this sense highly educational because it reported matters of fact.

Other guests were working hard to keep up. Their body language signaled something between politeness and impatience. Many were distracted. They looked out of the window, checked their phones. Yawns were also frequent. The questions asked after the hour-long tour of the room expressed that they had missed much of the information. They repeated much of what had already been said.

Once we went outside, the situation changed. Everyone seemed excited about peeking into the window of the neighbor, the "authentic" mafia house. This irritated me. I felt that it was disrespectful toward the tragic nature of the stories we had been told, and toward the tour guide and the managers of the building who had to deal with this uncomfortable neighbor on a daily basis. "But of course, I am invested in this struggle to a different degree. I have been attuned to those stimuli. My relation to those people and places is much more layered in time than theirs," I thought to myself. After all, they were being exposed to this information for the first time. And they were on a field trip.

One tourist, an eleven-year-old boy, had a different reaction. During the tour, he left the room. His mother hugged him and joined him. Later she asked me to talk to him. On the bus I asked him if he was all right. He told me that he was upset by the tour and how casual (*henkastet*) the narrative was:

> It's odd that she tells us all these names and deaths and then in some way makes is sound superficial, "normal." Why did she not tell us about the stories of the people? They are victims. Why are they just run through so quickly? (Addiopizzo tourist, field note extract, July 4, 2016)

He was particularly affected by the story of a boy his own age who was kidnapped and dissolved in acid. He found it unfair that the main part of the narrative was dedicated to commemorating Falcone and Borsellino:

> He [the child] is more innocent than them [the judges] because he had nothing at all to do with them. That is worse than being killed for acting against something. (Addiopizzo tourist, field note extract, July 4, 2016)

What this boy pointed at is paramount. In effect, the narratives that were passed onto us as tourists were structured around a collective trauma that is contextual to Italy. The killing of Falcone and Borsellino, the two judges who fought a solitary judicial battle against the Cosa Nostra, was a tragic event because of what it symbolized politically. But it was also a media event. The witnesses of this event are still hurt by it: many refer to those assassinations as "our own 9/11." In general, these deaths are naturalized in the Italian imaginary. This can be difficult to relate to. What the boy was upset about was a question of habituation. As I discussed in an earlier chapter, identity is a matter of repetition: he (and the others) did not share the same cultural heritage as myself and the tour guides. There was an asymmetry in the relation of equivalence between the encoder and the decoder, that is, between the tour guide and the tourists (Hall 1999, 501). This resulted in an overload of information. He wanted the guide to "tell the story of the people, not just treat them like numbers" (Addiopizzo tourist, field note extract, July 4, 2016).

I believe that this was also one of the reasons for the apparent disengagement of the rest of the tourists. Aside from confirming the allure carried by material relics compared to discursive interpretations (the next-door neighbor, the "real stuff," was much more interesting), the drop in attention is also tied to the difficulty in articulating, of becoming attuned to the information. Indeed, it is much easier to become affected by something if one has been trained to those stimuli. This confirms Latour's view that, while one can learn to be affected, it makes a difference to the learning process "if one uses propositions (which are articulate and inarticulate) instead of statements (which are true or false)" (2004b, 206). Here, the criterion was truth rather than proposition. It was a depersonalized fact race that, with the exception of the sensitive eleven-year-old boy,[15] failed to *nourish the imagination* of the spectators faced with the distant suffering (Boltanski 1999, 48–51).

Cocreating the Mourning

I want to conclude by sharing a different experience that attempted at the same effect, to sensitize others to a collective loss. In my view, this form of mediation can be learned from to build affective connections between different cultures. In this site, the transmission of heritage was framed as a form of remembrance that actively invites others to take part in the *mourning* rather than just in the learning. In other words, the decoding phase of the communication process was made explicit (Hall 1999).

The child that so struck the eleven-year-old boy at the museum was killed in 1996. His name was Giuseppe di Matteo. When his father Santino di Matteo decided to stop working for the Cosa Nostra and start working with law enforcement, the Brusca clan captured Giuseppe. They sent the family two photographs of the child holding a newspaper that read the date of the kidnapping. A message was enclosed: "Shut his mouth." Despite the menace, Santino continued to collaborate with institutions. Giuseppe was held captive for 779 days, in different homes of criminals affiliated with the group. His last period of imprisonment took place in a homestead that was used as a weapons deposit. After twenty-six months, he was strangled, and his body was disposed of in a tub of nitric acid. Then, the murderers smoked a cigarette and spent the night there, in the same building.

This is more or less all that we were told when we entered the site of the murder.[16] It is now a confiscated asset, managed by a cultural association in San Giuseppe Jato. Upon arriving at the site, the associates complained about how difficult it was to manage it with the municipality, which was not only disorganized but also (at best) did not seem to prioritize the heritage site. It was almost abandoned, and we had to wait for an old man to drive out into the countryside to give us the only key to the gate. Visits were not so frequent. "This is why it's important that we were there," they told us. "Giardino della Memoria (the garden of memory) is a powerful place. People prefer not to talk about it because it's easier." According to them, this was exactly the problem, and it became their mission to work with it.

We were taken around the building and into the small room of the homicide. In there, they told us the story of the child's kidnapping, the surrounding historical mafia events, and the exact details of the murder. They centered the story on Giuseppe, and how he might have felt. Not much more. I was really disturbed by the site. Looking back on my video recordings, I can see that they are interrupted several times. The photographs are shaky and blurry. In my field notes, which I wrote up hours later, I mention that it was difficult for me to breathe, that I needed to get fresh air. I felt disgust and anger. I felt compassion. The mediators were prepared for this: it was their intention to share the disgust.

After the short tour they invited us to sit outside in the sun. They told us that they wanted to give this space a different meaning. They termed it as a sad, white room. Therefore, they had brought colorful paint. We were all given little canvases and an hour of time. They told us that they would hang up our works afterward, and that, because we were the first group they welcomed, our paintings would be the first of a long series. It did not matter whether we were good at painting, they said. What was important was that we gave back our impressions to the place we had visited (Figure 13).

Painting felt initially awkward, but then deeply soothing. We were mostly silent. At the end we each presented our work and shared what we had thought of in creating it. We named the emotions; we interpreted the place and what we wanted it to mean. Many painted peace signs. Some drew different cultures uniting and explained that everyone had their own losses and that all cul-

Figure 13. Visitors' paintings for the Giardino della Memoria, commemorating Giuseppe di Matteo. Photograph by Christina Jerne.

tures should unite around them. Others worked more in abstract and expressed themselves through color. This led to a rich discussion on the general meaning of commemoration and the importance it has for the present.

Compared to the museum visit, this was a different use of heritage because we were actively invited into making it. The nature of the site itself (a murder scene) too played an important role in shaping the intensity of the experience, but in my view, it was the way the guides framed our visit that did something different. In this case, we were given the time and media to become part of the commemorative process.

As the experience economy literature suggests (Boswijk et al. 2007), participatory practices increase the value of an enterprise. The reason behind this is that taking part in creating value is a *generative* activity; loosening the grasp that the "producer" has on the practice, inviting others to cocreate meaning and feeling, makes it possible for subjects to cultivate *themselves*. In an affective economy, "value is sought in the expansion or contraction of affective capacity" (Clough and Halley 2007, 25). The value of an experience is thus a question of intensity, to which "the affected body responds immediately, and the physical response is the expression of the quality of the experience." (Knudsen and Waade 2010, 15). Here, it is the very abstraction of agency—the fact that the guides gave us the *means* to take part rather than entirely setting the *content* of the experience—that invited us toward the corporal connection with the pain of the other.

Furthermore, the material reelaboration of an affective encounter can set a direction for the future. "Once an affect is labeled, recognized, and made a common point of comparison, it functions as an ordering principle for future affects. Affects become the raw material for a socially recognized system of emotions" (Read 2016, 121). If affects are categorized, understood, and internalized, they can be used to transform the self and one's way of relating to the world. This way the past, and its painful remembrance, can be indexical.

These theoretical insights suggest that if sad passions are effectively triggered through a shared process of mourning, they become written in the body of the tourist. Your past becomes mine, and I will remember that which causes sadness because I experienced parts of it. By stimulating the conscious reelaboration of the sad passion as being caused by mafia, the tour aims at directing the body away from mafia in the future.[17]

In the eyes of Judith Butler, passionate encounters constitute us—do us and undo us—as subjects. "Passion and grief and rage (we feel), all of which tear us from ourselves, bind us to others, transport us, undo us, and implicate us in lives that are not our own, sometimes fatally, irreversibly" (Butler 2004, 20). Thus, these encounters not only shape us as subjects but also work to orient our mode of relating to other subjects and broader normative frameworks. This is why desire offers a possibility for political and ethical interventions. Desire wants to last (Deleuze 1988, 99): it is a disposition to maximize and stabilize the ability to be affected. Desire is appetite that has become *self-conscious* of that which causes joy and sadness, of which relations make us persist and live well. Therefore, encounters such as these that explicitly seek to enforce our emotive dependence upon others—that interpellate us as witnesses to the pain of others—are constitutional to the way we develop as subjects and subjectify ourselves to certain norms. In this sense desire is political; it orients how we are with others in the now and in the future.

Clearly, here it is only possible to speculate on the fact that anti-mafia uses desire to break mafia and on the most visible effects achieved by this strategy on the tour. I cannot know whether one or the other tour was more or less determining to the participant's overall orientation. Perhaps the immediate responses of compassion were not followed by anything but a sad Snapchat for a friend. Likewise, maybe the Danish tourists who were yawning at the museum are now adamantly committed to buying anti-mafia products. Processes of subject formation are irregular, nonlinear, and unpredictable. Studying the long-term impact that this type of heritage usage has had on the development and sustainment of these communities[18] would require different methodologies.

Furthermore, as Jean-Luc Nancy notes (1991), while communities are "revealed in the death of others," this does not occur because we align ourselves with other subjects (a specular, shared subjectivity would require a subject made of a durable substance; a phenomenon that I have yet to encounter), but because we experience their difference, their limit, their finitude. It is in fact because "death itself is the true community of I's and that are not *egos*" that community is revealed. Nancy thus reads community in a Bataillean sense: it is through the limit experience, in the borders between ourselves and the world that we find community. Community is thus neither a fully realized vision of something that must be achieved nor something that once was, but rather it is *the very experience of being outside ourselves* that is constitutive of community.

The details of these two different thanatotic community-making efforts, in my view, uncover some of the challenges involved in creating an empathic connection between different worlds. What emerged in the first case was that death does not speak for itself. The level of asymmetry between the frames of reference at play, and the curatorial choice of reporting "matters of fact" resulted in a sensory overload that quite literally moved the tourists' bodies away. It either resulted in indifference (most of the tourists) or agitation (the child). The second case instead suggests that working with smaller doses of information and inviting others into the process of articulating it might facilitate attunement to the new information because it is reelaborated by the very participants. Indeed, they might suggest that painful memories require time to be formed and communicated. Overall, both cases point toward the need to further refine communicative strategies in tourism, to avoid the much-feared "commodified spectacle" (Urry 1990). The key to this could lie in emphasizing the reciprocal nature of the process of learning to be affected: both the activist and the tourist can benefit from attentively reading one another. This way, it may be possible to move away from a vision (and practice) of tourism as an act of *consumption*. Both sides *produce* effects, both in terms of the immaterial components that are exchanged and in the material resources that are traded on the tour.

═══

How does one convince others to join a cause? This chapter has highlighted numerous affective strategies deployed by anti-mafia activists. Media such as stickers and brands have been functional in establishing connections between diverse actors that previously had no link to the anti-mafia. The further inclusion of immersive experiences that bring one closer to "the other" has provided means to live out a critique of mafia heritage. Here, the use of witnesses and common frames of reference were valuable to authenticating tourist experiences as "truly political" and thus connecting them to the movement. The incorporation of pleasurable objects, such as garments and textiles, but also gastronomic delicacies and beautiful landscapes all attuned the tourists to the cause in different ways. Importantly, these seductive strategies were carefully designed to feed into community economies, thus raising the money and the reputation necessary to counter practices of violent intimidation and extortion.

Seduction becomes trickier when we enter the realm of sad passions. The fascination with the horrid and the romanticized version of godfathers is something that has overall led mafia films, books, gadgets, and restaurant chains to sell. These uses of the past have had deleterious effects on Italy's image and its economies, enforcing negative stereotypes and attitudes. Mafias thrive on this allure and capitalize on these affects to subject affiliates and to promote their territorial control. The question this raises is a realist one: If this type of market exists and will probably continue to grow, then how can these affects be modulated in ways that are constructive? This is an important conversation to have in an affective economy. It is here that we find the space for ethical intervention.

Indeed, what these cases have suggested is that to diffuse a political movement, it is beneficial to tap into, rather than work against, the semiotic dynamic of the time. The desire for "real" mafia should not be ignored or repressed, it should be ridden, even (and I would say *especially*) if it is to be critiqued. The force of opposition thus also relies on the capacity to mimic the *intensity* of a given phenomenon.

In affective economies, meaning is not given hermeneutically, but rather depends on the emotional impact of an activity, the amount of energy invested. This is an insight that is often missing or, worse, considered toxic, particularly from progressive political economy. Consider this: Why is it so easy to speak self-ironically about how desire works on us in the everyday, in supermarkets, on billboards, and porn ads, but so difficult to accept that the same logic applies to the political? Why is it merely appropriate to criticize populist leaders for using market analysts and their insights into our use of social media and what we *like* to hear, but not alright to think of using the same logics to build political projects that are progressive? While ideas of postrepresentational/postfactual politics are currently in vogue, it seems that many are not yet ready to embrace the idea that the hyperreal (Baudrillard [1976] 1993), that is, the increasing diffusion of simulation and loss of referentiality, is not only a strategy of domination but also can be a strategy of critique and rupture.

I am not suggesting a simple acceleration of intensity for the sake of intensity. Rather, I am suggesting that critical movements (and their scholarships) might benefit from exploring the possibilities offered by plastic affective environments, such as the ones that characterize tourism design and their simulations. But this can happen only if the resulting desires and resources are carefully invested in concrete activities that work toward disrupting, in our case, mafia relations. More specifically, these experiences need to be designed in a way that fosters reciprocity, both in terms of resource flows and, importantly, in terms of setting aside spaces that are entirely dedicated to letting intensity "sink in": that invite toward a critical reflection of one's relationship to the experience. In other words, perhaps desire should not be seen as something that opposes deliberation, but rather as something that triggers and ensures its very occurrence.

5 Queering Social Movements

That there will be changes as a result of the crisis is certain. There is no going back to the world before the crisis. But the questions are, how deep and fundamental will the changes be? Will they even be in the right direction? We have lost the sense of urgency, and what has happened so far does not portend well for the future.

—Joseph Stiglitz, *Freefall*

A Crisis of Imagination

This is the dreary quote with which Alain Touraine opens his book *After the Crisis* (2014, 1). In it, the pioneering social movement scholar warns us about the severe consequences of the 2007–2008 financial crisis on the social body. He argues that through the deregulation of finance and the maximization of profits, the neoliberal regime has brought about the triumph of individualism. Coupled with the increase in unemployment, the uncertainty of being reintegrated into the formal labor market, and a weak and silenced political system, we are now facing an overall breakdown of society as we conceived it in industrial and even "postindustrial" times. The "postsocial" situation Touraine describes is one characterized by a complete separation of the economic system and the social system.

Several crises later, it seems that these worries continue to be reflected in different forms of activism worldwide. The Occupy protests were directed at the workings of the financial system and questioned its effects on wealth distribution. The anti-austerity protests around Europe questioned the power of public and private bodies in relation to national debt. More recently, people voiced their desperation at losing their means of sustaining themselves due to harsh lockdowns, inflations, and the increasing costs of living all over the world. The message these protests carry is that "the economy" is devastated, and someone should do something about it.

Yet, while these classical examples of social movements have been directed at national and international institutions and corporations, crying out for changes in the distribution of power, other forms of protest have directly changed power distributions through their actions (Bosi and Zamponi 2015). In the previous chapters, we have seen how activists are contesting mafias by rearranging the oppressive relationships of property, labor provision, marketing, and wealth distribution that these economies enforce. This exemplifies the different forms of agency involved in economic action and highlights the scope of cultural and political transformation that economic activism can in fact bring about.

The anti-mafia movement is indeed but one of many examples of contentious economic action. If an "economy" refers to a set of collective practices and technologies that sustain life according to a certain order, then "contentious economies" refers to interruptions or transformations of orders that are perceived as harmful or unjust. Examples include critical forms of valuation (reformulating waste as nutrition), rearrangements of property relations (commoning or piracy), interruptions of certain networks of exchange (boycotts), or organizational designs that counter the alienating effects of some modes of production (social enterprises). Do these forms of contention represent a new mode of collective action, a global shift in repertoire? Or has economic life always been a space where collective action, negotiation, and protest are possible? In other terms, does the Touraineian split between the "economic system" and the "social system" instead reflect a division in the way we *conceptualize* these two spheres of life?

I have already traced different empirical manifestations of collective action that can hardly be separated in these terms. The overall aim of this final chapter is to problematize this conceptual cleft and to suggest some tools that might bridge it. Since language and theory are forces that actively take part in shaping reality, these conceptual rearrangements are just as important as empirical reconstructions in developing an approach to economy that recognizes the agency inherent in economic action, and appreciates its potential for political transformation (Roelvink et al. 2015). Thus, this is also part of the specific political project of countering the mafias, as a tuned vocabulary makes it more feasible to recognize and support what already works in this sense.

I have already traced some of the origins of this conceptual tension in the introduction. Here I shall begin by digging deeper into the specifics of the sociology of collective action and tracing some of the theoretical tendencies that contribute to enforcing the separation between the "social system" and the "economic system"; a separation that contributes to a crisis of imagination and thus hinders the kind of collective experimentation we urgently need more of, but already have.[1]

The final part of this chapter suggests some conceptual tools that may be used to queer several binaries that accompany dominant conceptions of social movements. This move is inspired by feminist political economists J. K. Gibson-Graham who used the term "queering," which traditionally refers to the act unsettling dominant gender norms, to instead undo dominant conceptions of economy. The resulting method of "reading for economic difference" (Gibson-Graham 2020, 475–85) operates by bringing forth the radical heterogeneity of economic identities, relationships, and trajectories that exist in the world. My ethnographic accounts of anti-mafia activism have already implicitly unsettled several dominant conceptions of both economy (capitalocentrism) and politics (state-centrism). Here I will make explicit the theoretical tools that assisted me in the task of reading for difference, and thereby fully recognize the political force and status of these forms of economic action.

I am referring to the work that has emerged out of nonlinear thinking initiated[2] by Gilles Deleuze and Félix Guattari ([1980] 1987), and out of the more empirically friendly approaches of Bruno Latour (1988), Michel Callon (1986), and John Law (1986) (actor–network theory/ANT), and more recently, the speculative realists Manuel DeLanda[3] (2006) and Graham Harman (2016). I shall take the liberty of referring to this stream of thought as *assemblage thinking*. Despite the numerous divergences[4] and incongruences between them, I will pick and choose ideas that have been useful to reconstructing these collective actions. Collective actions that already resist what Max Haiven has called enclosures of imagination (2014, 23).

Events versus the Quotidian

> The everyday is platitude (what lags and falls back, the residual life with which our trash cans and cemeteries are filled: scrap and refuse). . . . Whatever its other aspects, the everyday has this essential trait: it allows no hold. It escapes. It belongs to insignificance, and the insignificant is without truth, without reality, without secret, but perhaps also the site of all possible signification. . . . Accordingly, it will be a question of opening the everyday onto history, or even, of reducing its privileged sector: private life. This is what happens in moments of effervescence—those we call revolution—when existence is public through and through. (Blanchot [1959] 1987, 12–14)[5]

Many contemporary conceptions of grassroots politics struggle to live up to Maurice Blanchot's poetic summoning, namely, to take the everyday, a difficult and slippery terrain of analysis, seriously. Although Alberto Melucci's work vitally set this agenda for social movement scholarship four decades ago (1985), the dominant approach to studying collective action remains focused on episodic, highly organized, contentious *events* that see claims makers and their opponents (most often governments) as the most important elements (McAdam et al. 2001).

Although still a minoritarian trend, important work has featured the identity-building, mobilizing force of everyday practices within social movements (i.e., Staggenborg 1998; Haenfler et al. 2012; Portwood-Stacer 2012; Yates 2015a, 2015b; Rodríguez-Giralt et al. 2018; Schlosberg and Craven 2019). Several scholars, for instance, have suggested looking beyond the category of social movement organizations (SMOs) (Snow 2004; Staggenborg and Taylor

2005) and instead exploring less manifest instances of "ideologically structured action" (Zald 2000). In many ways these are, as geographer Lise Nelson put it (2003, 564), attempts at decentering a unified understanding of "movement," "state," or "civil society" by following actors and tracing discursive practices through a variety of social and political arenas.

A relevant example of this shift of attention is the study of consumption. In recent years, authors from various disciplines have moved away from seeing consumption and production as individual, sovereign acts to treating them as collective practices (Jacobsen and Dulsrud 2007; Barnett et al. 2010; Forno and Graziano 2014). Some have pointed to the increasingly blurred line between producers and consumers (Boswijk et al. 2012; Bruns 2008; Arvidsson and Peitersen 2013), others to the increased politicization and governmentality of the everyday (Lewis and Potter 2011), or to a nascent realm for "individualized collective action" resulting from increasingly complex and global issues (e.g., climate-induced harms) that nation-states are failing to address (Micheletti 2003).

Recently, the study of consumption has entered into systematic dialogue with social movement studies. This has highlighted the need to broaden our understanding of both consumption and mobilization and opened up a much-needed space of dialogue between these fields (Wahlen and Laamanen 2015; Colli 2020). These thoughts point, among other things, to the need to move beyond neoclassical economics and its objectifying understandings of value and utility. Instead, they highlight how the act of consumption is part of a wider process of political valuation (Muniesa 2012). Overall, these moves have helped to challenge "loud" visions of collective action, those tied to the idea of the street and the visible mass as the focal point of contention. They have granted quotidian political action the attention that it deserves, recognizing its potential to have socially transformative effects.

Realities versus Repertories

Even though economic practices, such as selective purchasing or political marketing, are now regarded as worthy of the attention of social movement scholars, the need for this type of conversation testifies to an underlying separation between contemporary conceptions of the economic and the political. Indeed, the need for studies of consumption and everyday politics to "speak up" for their object of enquiry as being fit to be classified as a form of mobilization in my view reveals two things: first, that the "economy" is usually not conceived as a site for political action, and, when it is, the effort goes into proving that it is "contentious enough"; and second, and relatedly, that the term *social movement,* despite being widely theorized as promoting or opposing change at different scales and modes (Diani 1992; Melucci 1996; McAdam et al. 2001), resonates most strongly with the scale of action where power is represented by the state and resistance by the organized masses on the streets. As a result, commons, lifestyle, and consumer movements are often taken to be different from social movements in nature, rather than in degree. That is, they are considered ontologically different "social facts" (Toews 2003).

Yet, even one of the most government-centered social movement scholars, Charles Tilly, was wary of being essentialist. Famously, he described a shift in social movement actions between the eighteenth and nineteenth century in Britain (1981). He showed that through institutional development, the idea of citizenship began to form. This called for a shift from direct violent actions to "legitimate" actions such as petitioning, marching, and distributing pamphlets. He called this a shift in movement repertoire. In his words:

> Collective action usually takes on well-defined forms already
> familiar to the participants, in the same sense that most of
> an era's art takes on a small number of established forms.
> Because of that, neither the search for universal forms (. . .)
> nor the assumption of an infinity of means to group ends will
> take us very far. Because of that, the study of the concrete
> forms of collective action immediately draws us into thinking
> about the *cultural settings* in which more forms appear. (Tilly
> 1977, 5-1, my emphasis)

In this vein, one might think that the French Revolution was revolutionary not because of the specific action of cutting off the king's head (the essence of the act), but because *at that time and place,* it was unthinkable that the masses would do so (the social context within which the act is inscribed). As we have seen throughout the book, social change is made possible by collective actions that cite or differentially imitate an *existing* culture. Otherwise, the change would be irrelevant, undecipherable; simply unthinkable.

We might thus think of shifts in movement repertoires as Tardean inventions (Tarde 2000, 86), that is, as eventful interruptions of dominant norms that bring about a new kind of imitative series. Thinking of changes in forms of opposition as being embedded in a social context allows us to move away from defining things *in the absence* of actual constellations of historically and spatially grounded actors. This perspective allows us to take diverse forms of contention seriously, and to openly assess their socially transformative capacity.

Contemporary politics now makes it clear that in spite (and perhaps even because) of the recent resurge of authoritarian nation-states, the legitimacy of political institutions is increasingly draining away in many contexts. The emergence of concepts such as "postrepresentational" or "postfactual" politics (Tormey 2006, 2015; Manjoo 2008) are a testimony to this. It is not surprising, therefore, that activists find power in other arrangements and organize to confront these configurations in other ways that are more "fit."

Most likely, this very observation is informed by my own Eurocentric, Enlightenment-informed understanding of politics, meaning that collective action in other parts of the world has perhaps always also, and even primarily, expressed itself outside these representations of politics. This is a topic that I know little about and would be keen to explore with other scholars. What I can say with regard to this movement and many other Western forms of collective action is that organized forms of economic contention can be seen as shifts in movement repertoire.[6] This, as Tilly noted above, attests to a gradual shift in the cultural settings that surround grassroots politics, that is, in the way politics is *imagined* and can be practiced in contexts where the most legitimate form of contestation has hitherto been the kind that speaks to the state as the custodian of the "social contract."

Yet, dominant scholarly understandings of social movements tend to "conceptualize movements as externally focused, collective 'political' action, while often viewing other forms of collective action, such as lifestyle movements, as self-centered, largely individualistic projects of personal expression and affirmation, thus *marking movements as serious contenders for social change and lifestyles as trivial in comparison*" (Haenfler et al. 2012, 1, my emphasis).

In my view, this inherent hierarchy in the judgment of political validity can be traced back to a predominance of essentialist understandings of politics (and relatedly, economy) in studies of social movements, as I shall briefly illustrate below. These views are an obstacle for the analysis of a phenomenon as hybrid and dynamic as collective action, particularly at a time when international political bodies regulate toothpaste formulas and in which it is possible for individuals to crowdfund healthcare for poor families from the comfort of their sofas. In other words, at a time when it is becoming increasingly apparent that the sites and actors of political and economic action cannot be neatly confined to formal, institutionalized sociality, or separated into preestablished sectors, it is ever more necessary to recognize and analyze the existing diversity of collective action.

Social Movements versus Collective Behavior

Sociological studies of grassroots politics can be dated back to late nineteenth-century thinkers who were concerned with collective behavior (Le Bon [1895] 1960; Tarde [1901] 1989). Although studies of collective behavior gave birth to rationalist understandings of the social,[7] the term is most often associated with more psychological, suggestive approaches. Gustave Le Bon, for instance, focused on the contaminating force of crowds. He believed that individuals lost their ability to think rationally when gathered in a crowd and regained it only after leaving it. He used the French Revolution as one of his examples to describe the mechanisms of reversion to animal emotion within the group setting. Freud later echoed this in his book *Group Psychology and the Analysis of the Ego*

(1922). Robert Park and Ernest Burgess (1921), followed by Herbert Blumer (1951), also used the term *collective behavior* but pointed out that collective emotion can also be positive and not only express anger and fear. Blumer divided collective behavior into four categories that differ in intention and form: the crowd, the public, the mass, and the social movement. To him, social movements differ from the other three forms of collective behavior because of the degree of intentionality of their members.

As the sociologist Christian Borch shows (2012), the passage from collective behavior to social movement studies was connected with a desire to rid social theory of the irrational associations that the term *collective behavior* entailed. This coincided with the success of Durkheimian sociology, which was more inclined to rationalist and linear thinking, leading studies away from amorphous and disorganized notions of collective behavior. As a result, social movements became a separate field of enquiry, dedicated to collective enterprises that were deliberately trying to change or propose new social orders.

Furthermore, like other phenomena of interest to sociologists, social movements acquired the status of "social facts" (Toews 2003), that is, of collective wholes made up of the sum of individual acts. These types of organic whole are characterized by what Manuel DeLanda (2006) calls "relations of interiority," whereby the relations between the parts define their very *nature*. If a part of a movement is detached from it, it ceases to be what it was when it was in a relationship with the other parts, because being part of the movement is one of its *constitutive* properties (DeLanda 2006, 9–10). An example would be if a political ideology (part) such as "Greenlandic people have the right to speak Kalaallisut" were expressed through lobbying activities (part) and public demonstrations (part) against the imposition of Danish language in Greenland. Together, these would make up a whole: "decolonial Inuit movement." If instead at some point the ideology (part) were to be propagated through the joint practice of refusing to speak Danish, the ideology would lose its nature as a constituent of a social movement. It would be treated as something else of another, ontologically different type. Different schools have proposed different principles and mechanisms to order these organic wholes. Let us look at some of them.

Democracy, Utility, or Culture?

Some schools within this tradition are structuralist in type, such as the political process (or opportunity) model (Tilly 1981; Tarrow 1989; McAdam 1982). These study collective action in relation to macro-structures, seeing them as the extensions of traditional mechanisms of political participation. The focus lies on tracing the (perceived) resources and opportunities that are available to social movements at a given time, such as different forms of capital (cultural, symbolic, economic, political). Together this set of resources compose what have been called the "structural factors of mobilization" (Caruso and Cini 2020). Although these authors mostly use the term *structure* to describe processes that occur at the grassroots scale, rather than to analyze the relationship between these and the systems that operate on a "macro" scale (the State or "the capitalist cycle," as Caruso and Cini suggest [2020]), this tradition nonetheless grounds politics in collective actions that are ordered in a dialectic relationship with formal institutions. Social movements thus express conflicting social interests and are at once the results of and influential on institutional politics (Tilly and Tarrow 2006).

Unsurprisingly, the economy is also discussed in relation to institutional politics, particularly democratic distribution. Donatella della Porta's more recent work is exemplary of this line of thought (2015). She rightly notes how capitalism has been ignored by contemporary social movement studies, putting forward instead an analysis of the relationship between public demonstrations and the neoliberal structures from which they stem. This understanding of the economy is therefore primarily concerned with capitalist macro-structures; it is the structural nature of capitalism (neoliberal policies) that gives rise to its opposition (protest events). Social movements are thus on the receiving end of a unified economic system and represent their grievances by publicly expressing them. The agency of the movement is relegated to its ability to demonstrate, to mobilize, in order to publicly present its claims, which should then be taken into account by institutions. That is, a movement is essentially an engaged victim of an economic structure: it is because the structure produces problematic social consequences that the economic becomes a political issue.

A related paradigm is resource mobilization theory, which sprang directly out of neo-institutional economics. Mancur Olson (1965) drew attention to the fact that people mobilize to maximize their personal utility and not necessarily to forward other people's interests. This led the neoclassical paradigm of marginal utility being applied to the study of all collective action. As this made it difficult to explain why people actually often mobilize for interests that went beyond their own "utility," studies began to focus on the organizational aspects of mobilization and how SMOs could in some way guarantee mobilization (McCarthy and Zald 1977). While their interpretation of resources is relatively broad, their primary interest is organizational, concerned with how efficiently one could allocate resources to motivate and allow individuals to mobilize. Politics is essentially the process of acquiring access to and control over resources, which is facilitated by the entrepreneurial skills of a SMO. It is a political economy of rational maximization of utility.

This approach received numerous criticisms for its business-like tones, particularly because it emerged at a time when both utilitarianism and structuralism were declining in popularity. The 1980s were in fact also the breeding ground for cultural and constructivist approaches for studies of collective action.

In Europe, as a reaction to the weakening of labor unions and the overall transformation of labor and production, there was a need for a new narrative that could replace class politics. This led to the establishment of the new social movement (NSM) paradigm, which turned away from economic matters and drew instead on culture to explain what animates social protest. This approach underlined the emergence of new, non-class-based *values* to represent social and political conflicts that could no longer be voiced by labor unions (gender, the environment, human rights, etc.). Exponents of this school of thought, such as Alain Touraine (1981), Claus Offe (1985), and Alberto Melucci (1989), highlighted how social struggle is increasingly animated by identity and cultural and emotional needs, rather than class conflicts. In fact, this paradigm is often referred to as being postmaterialistic (Inglehart 1977). Yet it takes the economy, and particularly the fulfillment of a certain level of economic security, as a prerequisite for the transformation of the nature of protest, thereby reflecting its Marxist heritage: politics and culture are superstructures. That is, it is because Western societies have reached a certain level of wealth that people have turned to other "nonmaterialistic" matters.

The cultural turn in European[8] social movement studies can be seen as having replaced the idea of class consciousness with that of collective identity (Maheu 1996), since its very foundational category (culture) is a product of an analysis steeped in historical materialism. Of course, this is a genealogical observation, and does not by any means describe all NSM thinking. Nonetheless, the fact that this split occurred around materialistic issues has led to a great deal of work based on categories such as culture and identity to ignore resource-based politics and economic questions (Hetland and Goodwin 2013), as if economy were not a cultural matter.

As I have briefly sketched, the affirmation of the social movement paradigm around the 1960s as a reaction to irrational streams of thought[9] is accompanied by a tendency to rationalize and theoretically separate the political, the economic, and the cultural.[10] The political process model has, in a sense, "institutionalized" the economy by prioritizing analyses of protest events that are aimed at structural reforms, thereby making institutions the holders of economic agency. By applying neoclassical conceptions of value to the social movement "industry," resource mobilization scholars have instead "economized" the social by rendering it a sum of individual cost-benefit assessments. NSM studies and cultural constructivists have moved away from materialistic concerns as well as institutional ones because of these tendencies. Yet, as Francesca Polletta notes (2004, 97–110), meaning and culture are not merely in the actor's head, they are forces that shape, change, and uphold organizational structures in all sorts of ways. Her work challenged and made visible another predefined order, namely, that meaning and language are often used in binary opposition to "structures,"[11] which are often intended as "objective" external factors that determine mobilization (e.g., the economy).[12] In other words, Polletta emphasized that "meaning" is often framed as ontologically different from "structure" and debated as either more or less important than "structure."

In sum, for many years, social movement studies have been preoccupied with debating which order orders most. Yet all sides in this debate have tended to "soften" this division by acknowledging, for instance, the roles of "culture" or "political opportunities" in their analyses (Kurzman 2004). Exponents of all these approaches (Zald 2000; Goodwin and Jasper 2004; della Porta 2015) have, in their different ways, pointed out the need to challenge many of these separations and to construct a more fluid view of the political. Dichotomous and binary conceptualizations cannot fully grasp the complexities of certain current forms of activism, as "what we need precisely are a new set of transversal categories and forms of thought that elude both dualism and determinism" (Butler and Athanasiou 2013, 43). I therefore suggest turning to a theoretical tradition that is driven by a different style of questioning. If all sides acknowledge the influence of different factors, then the question should not be, "Which order is most important?" but rather, "How do these orders come together in ways that interrupt power arrangements that are harmful to the collective?"

The Syntax of Social Movements

The overall design of this book has been inspired by this question. Because of the divisions and conceptual hierarchies addressed above, I have intentionally chosen to collate my own analyses along the three most contended paradigms within this tradition: meaning, structure, and feeling. I have exemplified how these three modes of organization are all powerful, distinct, and yet mutually constitutive aspects of collective action. This implies that the corresponding mimetic political tactics of resignification, rearrangement, and affective reframing are symmetrical in potential capacity, but contextually asymmetrical in actual force. My argument, in sum, is that none of these modes has an ontological prevalence over the other.

In more practical terms this has meant that I have attempted to immerse myself in the contexts in which the anti-mafia issue circulates and traced the ways in which things assemble around them to generate more livable worlds. This has in turn allowed me to locate a variety of arrangements of mafia power (e.g., exploitative labor relations, cement cycles, and secretive aesthetics), as well as to elucidate ways in which this is effectively interrupted.

This "symmetrizing" move has been influenced by a broader theoretical tradition, one that on the one hand, expanded the political sphere to the most ordinary locations while also, most famously, acknowledging that thing–human and thing–thing interactions can shape politics as much as human–human ones. I am referring broadly to the work that has emerged out of nonlinear thinking, or henceforward *assemblage thinking,* that has successfully brought bacteria, metronomes, and logos into political analyses with much resonance in recent decades, in spite of their explicitly philosophical temperament.

The term *assemblage* was first used by Gilles Deleuze and Felix Guattari in the 1970s and refined in their book *A Thousand Plateaus* ([1980] 1987). The French term *agencement* indeed has at least two significations, which are somewhat merged in the English translation as "assemblage" (Müller 2015, 28). On the one hand, *agencement* points to a whole that is composed of heterogeneous parts that are in a relationship. On the other hand, it is itself an active term pointing to the fact that the relationships themselves are productive, thus implying that together these parts can do something different (as a whole, and to one another) than if they were alone. In other words, the properties of the assemblage are emergent, and thus exceed both the single parts and what they actualize, as well as the effects of the whole (Harman 2010, 184).

Thinking of social movements as assemblages thus allows us, for one thing, to move beyond the idea that they are made up of fixed components (a certain repertoire of action, for example) or that single elements that compose them are in a fixed relationship to the whole (a "failure" in internal communication could result in the establishment of entirely new networks and practices that were previously unrelated to the movement, as we saw with the accidental pun in chapter 3).

Although Deleuze and Guattari did not systematically elaborate a theory, this concept proved to be fruitful for many who were concerned with breaking modernist orders and hierarchies such as those discussed thus far. Assemblage theory has been revisited more recently by Manuel DeLanda (2006), who has made it his task to elaborate the term into a systematic theory that speaks (more) intelligibly to the social sciences. Though DeLanda has been called an "upside-down" version of Latour (Harman 2010, 176), and though ANT and assemblage theory have many points of divergence, the two approaches have some important nodes of convergence as well.

First, and most obviously, both embrace a flat ontology. This means, among many other things, that they interrupt the modern dualism that places the finite world of humans on one side and everything else on the other. Second, and more importantly, both are interested in understanding the relationships between things, without deciding in advance what their order of importance should be. Assemblage thinking thus disrupts the idea that the world is predetermined according to a specific order, be it Nature, God, Democracy, or Utility. Instead, it suggests that social order emerges from the specific arrangement of multiple objects (whether they be hashtags, kings, or icebergs) and that it is the *way* they relate to one another that gives rise to certain orders (e.g., collective actions and/or economies).

For instance, the law on the reutilization of mafia-confiscated assets contributed to the establishment of many anti-mafia economies. But so did the imprisonment of many bosses, activists' mimicking of mafia communication styles and channels, and the intimate testimonies given by individual family members of victims of mafia murders. In order to account for these elements, the micro and the macro should not be considered two fixed scales (i.e., individual subjectivity versus law enforcement, or the local versus the global), but rather should be used as categories that explain the relationship between concrete parts and an emergent whole *at any given scale* (DeLanda 2006, 32). This tradition enables us to move beyond the imaginative stagnation that comes from debating which order matters most in defining social life, be it a question of scale (i.e., state institutions versus grassroots formations, the IMF's monetary policies versus redistributive domestic practices) or of kind (i.e., culture, economy, or politics). It allows us instead to focus on what matters in and to the orders themselves.

In a nutshell, assemblage thinking has importantly suggested that, instead of defining categories in the absence of actors, and their relations a priori, research should focus more on how relationships between things are built and made either durable or precarious. This can be called a syntactical approach, that is, one that traces how things are related and ordered with regard to a given issue. For our purposes, this involves moving away from a definition of social movements as seamless wholes that define the *nature* of their component parts.[13] That is, we should grant the component parts of social movements (i.e., pamphlets, activists, slogans) the possibility of interacting with the dispositions of other entities (i.e., peach trees, cement, pop stars) and generating new alliances and collective formations, *without implying that these interactions change the very terms of association.* In this way, as Mellucci hoped (1996), studies of social movements may be oriented toward theorizing the *collective* dimension of social action.

An example: A group of people believes that rectangular doors are discriminatory. The group starts producing square doors and selling them, entering relationships of exchange with large corporations who join the campaign. This creates a new market and a new public sensibility, which eventually entails that other objects in households (frames, construction materials, furniture, accessories, etc.) become attuned to the novel square-door paradigm, spurring new relations of production, aesthetic sensibilities, and "door" ideologies. The fact that the door issue was not expressed through protest events, organized lobbying activities, and petitions to amend door legislation should not deprive this collective action of its status as a serious and valid form of contentious politics. Rather, it is the repeated, collectively orchestrated act (in whatever form) of being against rectangular doors (oppositional identity) and their disposition to invite other groups to do so (network formation) that should be of importance to the study of collective action. The relationships through which this is expressed are not central to the *nature* of the whole and should not be determined a priori.

This does not mean that one cannot classify different types

of collective action on the basis of *existing* empirical examples (ones that express themselves toward the state,[14] ones that express themselves through permaculture, etc.). Classification generates knowledge and allows for comparison. This does mean, however, that these distinct typologies should not *presume* the inherent nature of other such similar wholes, for these are the result of specific historical relationships between the individual parts that compose them. Categorizing different modes of contention as if they were made of different fixed *properties* or ingredients inevitably leads to a predefinition of how these may or may not develop, thereby making us blind to their actual and potential forms of development. This implies an ontological essentialism, and relatedly, an epistemology founded on sameness, rather than becoming. That is, other than being unfit to describe the unfolding of the world, this kind of organismic metaphor also limits the possibility for imagination, and thus represents a broader epistemic impasse. A syntactical approach, or a queering of social movements, on the other hand, not only allows diverse forms of contention to be taken seriously but also enlivens the organ of imagination.

Thinkers from different disciplines have fruitfully used assemblage thinking in relation to collective action that fractures a certain order. Unsurprisingly, one of the primary fields for this is geography (e.g., McFarlane 2009; Levkoe and Wakefield 2014; Turker and Murphy 2019; Sarmiento 2020). For instance, some studies have investigated how recycling and scavenging practices reconfigure power relations (Roelvink 2016), or how franking machines shape and spread social movements (Davies 2011). Geographers are in fact trained to think about the relationships between humans and nonhumans (water, borders, mountains, cargo ships), as well as mastering the art of situating them in extents of space and time (important dimensions of assemblages[15]) in a way that many other disciplines do not. Nonetheless contributions from other disciplines such as sociology (e.g., Chesters and Welsh 2006; Rodríguez-Giralt 2012), media and communication (e.g., Knudsen and Stage 2015; Micali 2015), and anthropology (e.g., Marrero-Guillamón 2013) have also deployed assemblage thinking to develop nuanced analyses of contentious politics.

In spite of this theoretical proliferation, the school where contention is most at home, social movement studies, remains grounded.[16] Although even some of the more prominent scholars have pushed for a more "relational" approach to social movements (McAdam et al. 2001), one that attempts to transcend these divergences and instead focuses on the *dynamics* of contention (not unlike assemblage thinking). Yet, it seems to me that these have remained recommendations, as the field has delayed in taking these seriously.[17] This is perhaps due to the origins of social movement studies, which, as we saw previously, emerged as a reaction to irrational streams of thought that saw collective action as a spontaneous reactive phenomenon (della Porta and Diani 2006; Borch 2012). It is thus hardly surprising that many social movement scholars have an intrinsic allergy to approaches that are amorphous, fluid, and speculative.

Also, a flat ontology and an unconditional love of relations—the two primary characteristics of what I am calling assemblage thinking—are difficult but very pressing concepts for the social sciences to promote. This approach in fact requires letting go of quick fixes and universally applicable categories, which makes ANT a "slowciology" (Latour 2005a, 165) that is "humble in its explanatory aspirations" (Rodríguez-Giralt et al. 2018, 262). At a time in which universities are under constant pressure to prove their societal relevance and to quantify their "impact," it is understandable why this might not be a popular path to choose.

The question of how to tackle this epistemological ethics is, of course, not an easy one. Latour suggests (2004a) that one basic starting point could be to shift attention from questions of "what is true" to questions of "what matters" for our well-being. Indeed, social movement studies have been criticized, from within as well as from the outside, as having become so professionalized and self-referential that they lose sight of what they originally intended to do: to help publics, and especially marginalized and disadvantaged groups, to understand better what power niches are available (Flacks 2003; Bevington and Dixon 2005). Shifting the gaze to "what matters" would, for instance, imply moving away from debating orders of importance like whether activists mobilize to maximize their personal interests or because they feel solidarity with others beyond themselves (i.e., does rationality or emotion order the world?). Are waves of protest the result of particular political opportunities, or of new values and collective identities (i.e., do institutions or cultures order the world)? Do internal organizational ties determine social movement outcomes or their relationship to external organizations (i.e., do micro or macro factors order the world)? Instead, syntactical approaches put these questions aside and focus rather on how specific combinations of how things form, potentiate, and collapse different movements. If we acknowledge that contentious issues come to life because they matter to a certain group, then our question, I will add, should be *how what matters comes to matter.*

Some Central Concepts

The nuanced analytical tools that social movement scholarship has provided is something we should work with, not against. The insights of this tradition can, and already have, helped us understand better the emergence, effects, and sustainability of certain types of contentious practices. One possible starting point to queer the gaze of this tradition of enquiry is to unpack some of the overlapping themes of interest in social movement studies and assemblage thinking.

Let me begin this exercise by using a definition of social movements that was originally proposed to synthesize divergent views on the concept:

> A social movement is a network of informal interactions between a plurality of individuals, groups and/or organisations, engaged in a political or cultural conflict, on the basis of a shared collective identity. (Diani 1992, 13)

I focus on three words in particular in this definition: network, conflict, and identity.[18]

Network

Networks have long played a central role in describing the formation, propagation, maintenance, and success rate of movements.

Authors have highlighted the coagulating role of preexisting relationships, common goals, ideologies and enemies, and strong leaders, as well as of certain media or organizational structures (e.g., Freeman 1972; Morris 1984; Polletta 1998). An assemblage analysis would not distinguish between these entry points a priori or choose one of the elements. For assemblage thinking, establishing and strengthening links between groups through the diffusion of resources, ideas, and information[19] could be achieved by high-speed trains as well as by skilled PR professionals or informal leaders. Likewise, a high level of resonance in interpretative frameworks[20] could explain the emergence of a movement, but so could a tsunami. Common goals could emerge from opposing a repressive regime, as well as from an aesthetic shock.[21] Not only would these factors not require different analyses, but they would also *in principle have to be* combinable in a single one, as a network is precisely the assemblage of all these things rather than just the result of them.

In line with what Bennett and Segerberg (2012) argue through Diani (2011), "networks are not just precursors or building blocks of collective action: they are in themselves organizational structures that can transcend the elemental units or organization and individuals." Yet, as Krinsky and Crossley (2014, 3) have remarked, analyses of social movements have often been focused on "certain types of tie and the strength of those ties, over questions of how these types of tie form." For instance, in social network analyses, networks are often seen as "*locations* where ideas, identities, and frames are shared and exchanged" (Levkoe and Wakefield 2014, 304, my emphasis) that can accordingly only be studied through specific types of interactions (i.e., "direct" ties: contact between activists/"indirect" ties: overlapping interests). In assemblage thinking, networks are not predefined by the actors that compose them (activists or for that matter, humans) nor by the types of ties between these (i.e., common ideology or participation in events). In this way, the analysis would insist precisely on what lies in between the ties, and also on the effects of the specific combination of elements on the ties themselves, as well as on other ties that go beyond the network (either in actuality or potentiality). Thus the focus would not be the network (a set structure that lives up to predefined properties), but the network's formation (patterns of association). Our peach jam assemblage in chapter 3 is an example of this: I used the jam to illustrate some of the complex patterns involved in associating against eco-mafias in Campania. Here activists worked by mimetically rearranging assemblages that are opportune for mafia investment and made them inopportune. Agricultural land, detainees who were prone to working for the Camorra, skilled marketing agents, and mozzarella desserts formed a hybrid network to prevent and interrupt toxic waste and cement cycles. In this sense, networks can be understood more as the "tools that help describe things out there, not what is being described" (Latour 2005a, 131).

Conflict

Social movements are generally thought of as being aimed at changing a situation or voicing an injustice, and in some way mobilizing others to do the same. Authors disagree on whether movements are opposed to large-scale "systemic" factors (Melucci 1984), or are rather just opposed to particular policies, codes of conduct, or specific malpractices (Turner and Killian 1957). Relatedly, they disagree on whether movements can be organized into face-to-face communities, looser networks that culminate in mass protests, or have little or no face-to-face interaction with others, operating, for instance, entirely on blogs. However, social movement scholars agree that a movement is in conflict or in opposition to something else.

As early as the 1930s, collective action was interpreted as a distinct social phenomenon, characterized by the participant's *will* to transform a certain order in society (Blumer 1939). As this was a reaction to streams of thought that saw collective action as slack, irrational, and feminine outbursts, the rational element became distinctive to collective behavior, and later to social movement thinking (Borch 2012), reducing will to rationality. Thus, in this tradition, conflict is strongly tied to intentionality.

While assemblage thinking does not equate opposition with intentionality, it also considers social action that matches means to ends and takes these seriously. Manuel DeLanda notes that rational activities, that is, those that match means to ends, entail carrying out a series of actions that involve complex interactions and assessments with the surrounding environment (2006, 22–25). Solving a means-to-end matching dilemma will involve the actor using a set of diverse skills to deal with the situations she encounters on her way to achieving her goal. These are thus not merely in the actor's head (Polletta 2004) but are the result of physical and linguistic interactions. Thus, the relationship between goal and action is neither linear nor abstracted from a context. Instead, it is embedded in a setting that requires the activist to evaluate her movement, speech, and behavior in relation to others *and* their ends. For instance, in chapter 3 we saw that upon realizing that there was a huge potential for the marketing of humor at the launch of the anti-Camorra box, Etiket rebranded their products and established new partnerships with different enterprises. In this process, they learned to mimic the Camorra's way of increasing its power, which also operates by gaining popular consensus via strategic communication. Today, Etiket's primary activity is to continuously reassess their target audience based on the surrounding milieu, and thereby use communication to strategically subvert the Camorra. The success of these enterprises has in turn led other activists to imitate their oppositional work, and anti-mafia communication has spread as a genre in its own right.

Luke Yates (2015b) has also worked to highlight the nuanced nature of prefiguration, a term most commonly used to describe activities that match means to ends. Yates argued that the term should not be used as an empty descriptor that assesses the level of homology between the movement's goals and ends, but as an analytical tool that investigates the practices, interactions, and expressions involved in the *process* of matching means to ends. This implies not treating a movement's intention as a seamless and transcendent whole, but rather highlighting the material and expressive components that participate in the achievement of a set of goals. Similarly, an assemblage analysis might trace actions aimed at matching means to end without limiting itself to the meaning of the goals (the semantics of the conflict), instead tracing the way goals relate different things and people (the syntax of the conflict).

Identity

The concept of collective identity has been foundational in explaining what keeps a movement together and what defines its boundaries. Indeed, identity is a highly relational concept, as it always involves a counter-part (what we are not). Uses and views of what identity is differ greatly.[22] Some authors use it to describe how individuals connect with social movements (Polletta and Jasper 2001). Others prefer to use it to describe the identity of the movement from a bird's-eye view, namely how the whole relates to the outside (Snow 2001).

Identity has become a particularly relevant concept for scholars who oppose the more "rational" views, which, for instance, attribute an individual's adherence to a movement to his personal cost-benefit calculations (Fominaya 2010, 393). In opposition to this, these tend to focus on the emotions, symbols, and frames of meaning that unite adherents. For instance, more recently the increase in digital communication has revived the idea that identity construction is in itself a mode of struggle and becoming (McDonald 2015), rather than a precondition for collective action (della Porta and Diani 2006). This has drawn attention to the importance of the affects and intensities that are inherent in the experience of collective action and in the related processes of subject formation (McDonald 2006).

Assemblage thinking espouses all these views at once. The individual's propensity to identify with a collective is just as important as the group's inclination to relate to, and thereby identify with, other groups. Indeed, these two parameters are co-constitutive: a tiny individual shift in identification could have effects on the entire group's attitude toward other groups, and likewise, a general change in external coalitions could radically transform an individual's behavior. Furthermore, an assemblage's causal (rational) and catalytic (emotional) components are not in contrast but are complementary. Indeed, an assemblage is held together, and thus defined, by two distinct but overlapping tendencies, one material, the other expressive (DeLanda 2006, 12–14).

Components playing a material role involve bodies and their

disposition and ordering. These include, for instance, specific legislation that restricts movement or grants the right to vote. It also refers to certain types of media such as radio or other information technologies that facilitate communication between bodies, but also food shortages or available campaign funds that limit or increase the body's energy and movement. A great example of a material component of the anti-mafia movement is the 109/96 law, which licenses the social reutilization of confiscated mafia assets, and permits the commoning of public property. As we saw in previous chapters, this law profoundly transformed the anti-mafia repertoire of action, marking a shift in the identity of the movement.

Components that play an expressive role include linguistic and nonlinguistic elements. These could be shared discourses that resonate in the community, such as "Immigrants are stealing our jobs," but also shared norms that are embodied through self-regulatory practices, such as wearing different types of clothes for different occasions, or stopping in front of a red light. We saw this exemplified in chapter 2, where volunteers paid to become attuned to anti-mafia flavors and aesthetics, via the production and ingestion of wines and grains produced according to certain ethical principles. These expressive practices played an important role in enforcing the anti-mafia valuation cycle, both at collective and individual levels.

The way these components are expressed and mixed in an assemblage can either increase the internal homogeneity of the movement (territorialization) or destabilize its boundaries (deterritorialization). The identity of an assemblage is strongly tied to how *often* a certain association of ideas or materials is repeated. To repeat an association of ideas does not necessarily mean to consciously reflect on them: repetition is not the same as self-perception. If a movement taps into discourses that already resonate within the broader community, the identity of the group might spread more easily and homogenize. But the same could happen if a highly heterogeneous group of people continually lacks water and coalesces around the sensation of thirst or fear.

The habitual associations between things and ideas can of course be disrupted, and these instances would cause a loss of identity and stability. Indeed this is the very aim of the anti-mafia movement: to destabilize meanings, structures and affects that enforce mafia power. However, these processes are not rooted in one particular space: a group's identity may, for example, even be strengthened if its members disperse and flee the country. Indeed, following assemblage theory, identity is not necessarily tied to a sense of "we-ness" that is commonly associated with physically circumscribable communities that have a spokesman or collective representation (McDonald 2004). Rather, the movement's identity is more tied to the *way* certain material and expressive components are repeated, and these repetitions may well transcend the spoken word or actions directed at institutional bodies that represent power (McDonald 2004). For example, anti-mafia tourist designs work by exposing individuals to the pain of the relatives of mafia victims, via relics, images, and testimonies. The repeated act of staging these affective trajectories seeks to constitute anti-mafia subjects. Here, a sense of we-ness is founded on the act of mourning, which creates the experience of being outside of oneself. This is one of many instances in which an intimate process of subjectivation strengthens the movement's identity.

Using Symmetry and Asymmetry to Navigate Piles of Everything

Assemblage thinking and social movement studies share many interests, of which networks, identity, and conflict are but three central ones. After all, in their different ways they are both philosophies of association. However, running through these key terms in social movement scholarship shows that many of the conflicts in the literature revolve around the question of "Which principle orders the world?" (formal political systems, capitalism, class, culture, or personal gain). On the other hand, assemblage approaches do not provide a priori hierarchies and do not reduce reality to a single "category" of object. Up until now, the solution would seem simple: social movement scholarship might benefit from ontologically and epistemically democratizing its field of inquiry.

However, this democratization, or "dingpolitik" (Latour 2005b), poses challenges in terms of point of access. Thinking of any phenomenon as a pile of everything clearly requires different engagements with empirical material. Indeed, Deleuze and Guattari themselves noted how there is no beginning or end to rhizomatic[23] forms of research (such as assemblage thinking) and how instead, by definition, they lie "in the middle" of things (1987, 25). This is why, for instance, ANT has been criticized for its methodological poverty.

One of the most common questions is how one draws the boundaries of a field and expresses it in a form that somebody other than oneself can use and understand. (Inevitably, Deleuze and Guattari are not remembered for their clarity). For instance, mapping a network based on representations of the network (the shared values that organizations might share, or the connections activists might feel they have with other organizations) poses this challenge to an entirely different degree.

So why make life difficult when social movement studies has already developed nuanced and highly technical models of social reality? The entire point of rhizomatic thinking is not to reproduce an assemblage with fidelity to reality (How would one represent it?), nor to trace its lineage (Where and when would one begin?), but rather to dig out less visible connections between things. Why is this important? Because it allows to make difference, rather than sameness, visible (Sedgewick 2003; Roelvink 2016, 33; Gibson-Graham 2020). If knowledge is a productive and constitutive force, rather than a detached reflection of reality (Gibson-Graham 2000), then it matters what we ally ourselves to as researchers. This is not only the case for theory, but also for the material objects and informants we engage with. Assemblage thinking could help us move away from debating "matters of fact" to sharing solutions to common "matters of concern," as Latour elegantly put it (2004b). Then the entry point to analysis becomes a political choice.

What inspired me to write this book was to learn about practices that empower people, practices that make it possible to live without mafia. This means that this study's entry point is in fact dictated in *asymmetric* terms: in order to potentiate themselves, these collective actions have had to interrupt, challenge, and transform relationships where one part had the upper hand,

and the other part was struggling with issues of unwanted dependency and/or exploitation. Thus, despite being informed by an epistemology that asserts a principle of ontological symmetry, assemblage thinking also makes it possible to work with empirical questions of power and asymmetry. In other words, ontological democratization is not (or should not) be conflated with or imply an absolute symmetry of historically manifest *relations* (Harman 2016). While a syntactical approach to social movements implies tracing how different elements come together without predefining which order matters most, this does not entail a simultaneous *loss* of political realism, nor sensitivity to the *collective* orders that are stronger and those that are weaker.

The first step is thus to *deconstruct* the asymmetry and assess whether or not the domination is harmful or violent, and thus a matter of concern. For while most relations are asymmetrical, not all are harmful. To move beyond description and toward the prescription of practices that permit the liberation of subaltern forces, one also must perform a second step, that is, a different kind of ordering, an ethical *choice* to ally oneself with certain social practices. This is what I have tried to carry out throughout this ethnography, and what Britta Timm Knudsen, Dorthe Refslund Christensen and Per Blenker (2015, 10) have called a work of *reconstruction,* that is, to prioritize (through text or other action) the collective orders (here anti-mafia) that matter to the prospect of building more livable worlds.

Goodbye Revolution

In this chapter, this operation has first meant deconstructing a series of conceptual tendencies that enforce essentialist visions of both politics and economy within social movement theories. As I have argued, the very terms *economy* and *politics* have often been employed to signify complete, already-realized systems with no outside, or at least with little recognition of the diversity of their empirical manifestations. If collective action is situated in this vocabulary, then the possibility of recognizing the existing and potential multiplicity and heterogeneity of grassroots politics is hampered. This leads to a crisis of imagination of the kind planted in Touraine's postsocial world with which I opened this chapter, and the same kind Franco Berardi describes as characteristic of our time in his book *Futurability: The Age of Impotence and the Horizon of Possibility* (2017). In his words:

> Future is not prescribed but inscribed, so it must be selected and extracted through a process of interpretation. The process of interpretation of the inscribed possibilities is enabled and shaped by concepts. The dominant code (the gestalt) forbids the vision and makes what is possible unconceivable. (Berardi 2017, 236)

To address this matter of concern, I have reconstructed queer approaches to collective action that operate beyond preestablished hierarchies or binaries and suggested some meeting points with dominant conceptions of social movements. To this purpose, I used the analytical concepts of network, conflict, and identity (shared reference points to most social movement theories) to reflect on some of the differing epistemological approaches to these terms, and connectedly, their broader ethical implications. It is my hope that this generative exercise can support a way of thinking and practicing collective action that can help heal the political imaginary of hopelessness and lassitude, of waiting for an event, an external eruption of vitality, a revolution.

The very term *revolution* indeed implies a pivotal motion, a total rotation around a central axis. This is commonly associated with a national government. A *coup,* for instance, would imply the overthrow of an institutional regime and its replacement by a different type of the same (i.e., another institutional regime). A more generative term for radical contention is *hack*. The verb *to hack* denotes the forceful cutting up of a large object into smaller bits. Colloquially it relates to the positive idea of quick, fast, innovative tricks, or negatively to some sort of misplaced object that does not work in a certain configuration (i.e., a charlatan). Essentially, it entails bringing elements of one assemblage into another assemblage, thereby unleashing new possibilities that were not present in the former configuration. Hacking is "a creative disruption, a form of applied knowledge to a material 'tinkering' capable of pushing existing boundaries beyond their singular actuality" (Micali 2015, 18)—in other words, an "abstractive potency" (Wark 2004). In this sense, hacking does not denote a predisposed arrangement of power, but instead challenges us to consider where it might lie.

If the term *revolution* speaks more to actualized powers, the term *hacking* speaks to potential powers. And imagination thrives in potential.

As we have seen, so does crime prevention.

Conclusion

The Shadow Economy

I will conclude by reflecting on a paradox.[1]

Italy has never had such a strong, vast, and diffused anti-mafia movement before. The last two decades have radically transformed the scope of the awareness, strategies, and tools available to fight mafias. After twenty-two years of annual requests, on March 1, 2017, the Chamber of Deputies unanimously voted for March 21 as a national day "of memory and commitment to commemorate victims of the mafias." Considering that only a few years ago the public press denied that mafia was a reality, this is an incredible achievement. In just under three decades 36,616 mafia assets (villas, castles, cars, supermarkets, pools, clinics, etc.) have been frozen or confiscated and are now state property.

Of these assets, 50 percent have been reallocated to collectives (Fattiperbene 2024). These assets are now sites that generate all sorts of community economies. The anti-mafia discourse has also increasingly spread beyond Italy. Many communities worldwide are carrying out collective actions that are similar to the ones described in this book, challenging other forms of organized crime and, more broadly, violent forms of exploitation that in many ways resemble mafia-type relations.

At the same time, mafias are finding new strategies and are far from weak. It seems that the Cosa Nostra is regaining force in the province of Trapani, where freemasonry and clans are forming strong alliances. At a national level, politicians, entrepreneurs, magistrates, and police forces continue to carry out corrupt exchanges, permitting the infiltration of criminal logics in institutional settings. As I type, I can see hectares of protected forest in flames. The perverse logic of destroying natural resources to obtain funding to requalify them continues, feeding into an intricate patron–client web that often serves mafias. At the same time, money-laundering activities continue to prosper, forging intricate international alliances that operate across class and sectors. The traffic of organs, drugs, and human beings proliferates as conflicts deepen and populations are desperate to survive. Banks, trucks, public tenders, shipping containers, and deep-web indexing move these exchanges. The paradox lies here: anti-mafia is stronger both on a grassroots and at an institutional level, but so are mafias. So, what challenges lie ahead?

A good starting point is to return to this quote from an activist that I already discussed in a previous chapter:

> When I go to the Zen[2] and talk to kids about the Mafia as something horrible, and I tell them the story of the heroes who have stood up to it and been murdered, they look at me and think: "Great. My father is in jail and my mother is a whore." What do they care about [Judge] Falcone? That's why we have to show them that the anti-mafia is a concrete alternative, that it works, that it employs people. (Libera activist, personal interview, July 10, 2014)

Judge Falcone is revered as a national paladin of legality and anti-mafia, because he was assassinated for his extraordinary work against the Cosa Nostra. One of the primary values that are upheld by the more formal and institutionalized parts of this movement is in fact legality. Yet legality paradoxically also poses many obstacles to the development of anti-mafia economies.

To begin with, it is onerous to formulate a legal vocabulary that accommodates the multiple facets of the mafia phenomenon (operating across class, nation-state, formal and informal sectors etc.). Not only because the anti-mafias' conceptions of mafia have amplified, but also because the mafias themselves are increasingly multicultural and diverse. Although Italy has developed some of the most nuanced and intellectually profound juridical anti-mafia corpora in the world, the task of rendering these legal instruments onto a global scale becomes more difficult as the number of conflicting political interests and cultural understandings of mafias continue to proliferate. But this is the easier bit.

In my view, an even greater challenge lies in the practical manifestations of the law. Because the law is generative technology, its empirical actualizations are often times divergent, if not in direct contradiction, from its intended content. The law in fact also functions as an empowering vector for many types of opportunists. A common and licit example is auditing companies or wealth managers hired to shield private interests from taxation and legal obligations, making international regulations actual instruments for lucrative investments (Harrington 2016). As we have seen this also applies to illicit actors such as mafia groups, whose *characteristic* is their capacity to navigate and parasitically exploit legitimate forms of power, such as the law and state institutions, to their own advantage.

The mafia's conception of power is in fact absolutist: it considers itself to be above any forms of liability (Jerne 2024). The anti-mafia instead strives for legitimacy and thus enforces its own norms by seeking (rather than commanding) social consensus. There are many, and oftentimes contrasting, views of the moral grounds of this legitimacy. While many collective actions are characterized by a drive for legality, on many occasions I have witnessed that anti-mafia forces are confronted with the limits of legality. The reasons for this are multiple and complex, as we have seen, but most of these relate back to the nature of the very object they are contesting. Since mafia is a paralegal force, it operates both by negating the rule of law and by asserting it. Countering such a paradoxical phenomenon thus requires solutions that exceed law enforcement, such as the development of nuanced tactics that mimic the mafias' hybrid nodes of power and modes of action.

Many of my interlocutors inevitably expressed their frustration with legality, some by attributing the insufficiency of the law to systemic flaws (government corruption, EU regulations, international trade agreements, etc.), others by defying the rules through creative forms of organization (e.g., illegally occupying mafia property to circumvent the slowness of bureaucracy). But the great majority prefers to deny the source of this frustration, because it would mean acknowledging the fragility of their struggle. Saying that a legal approach is simply insufficient would in fact mean embracing an overwhelming truth: opposing the mafia via mimetic action implies operating across the legal and illicit, the formal and informal, because mafia power is resilient precisely due to its composite, hybrid nature. And this is an admission that requires an openness and dexterity in navigating unchartered moral waters. Not exactly a position that easily wins social consensus.

To frame anti-mafia as a fight for legality is an ideally admirable project, one that many activists carry out and one that has certainly had numerous and vital results in hindering mafia power. However, to *reduce* it to a struggle for legality is both diminutive and counterproductive.

First, because informal, unregulated, and sometimes even illegal activities are valuable to enforcing anti-mafia economies. But importantly, also because one of the social strata that the mafias build their force on lives in contexts where the law is, as the activist noted in the quote above, simply irrelevant.[3] I am referring to marginalized milieus, which are one of many sites of mafia power. Here the very term *legality* actually often limits the field of attention of the people who are most susceptible and therefore most important to work with, because the law has a limited *resonance* in these kinds of environments (Hodder 2012, 125–32).

If we expand this consideration beyond Italy, and particularly to contexts with marked postcolonial relations, this is more a rule than an exception. As many have argued before me, violence and the law, "the legal and the lethal" as Jean and John Comaroff have nicely put it (Comaroff and Comaroff 2006, viii), are constitutive of one another. In other terms, the fact that the global rise in violent crime coincides with processes of state formation, and in particular, democratization, is no coincidence. It suffices to return to what I illustrated in chapter 1: mafia has its birthplace with the formalization of the rule of law and modern state institutions (Lupo 2009). Therefore, *it is paramount that anti-mafia forces also think and act beyond values of legality.*

Second, criminal organizations such as mafias take advantage of divisions. Many countries still ignore, remit, or deny their own relations to organized crime, and have yet to elaborate collective definitions of crime or social harm. In some cases, it is relegated to the Global South or "elsewhere." Spatial imaginaries in fact play a significant role in determining how criminalization practices are enforced and distributed. These geographic distinctions inevitably reproduce problematic moral, ethnic, and political hierarchies.

In others, organized crime is understood in classist terms, as some form of petty street disorder rather than a phenomenon that also, and perhaps even prevalently, occurs in large corporations, banks, and town halls. Jackie Wang (2018) proficiently illustrated this hierarchy in relation to predictive policing practices and their programmed emphasis on racialized neighborhoods rather than white-collar sectors in the United States. Although many efforts are underway, still no international policies sufficiently take into account the hybridity and diversity of organized crime.

We live in a tense moment where borders are expanding and livable space is contracting. As ecological uncertainty and organized violence push masses to move, mafias and organized crime groups capitalize on people's need to live safe from harm. Mafias thrive on border closures and lack of cooperation between states, corporations, and grassroots organizations. Mafias also thrive on war. Weapons and desperate human beings are the currency of transnational organized crime. They take advantage of power gaps, bureaucratic loopholes, as well as the ignorance and fear of the Other that is amplified by infodemics.

Neither grassroots actors nor individual national states can tackle issues of this scale independently. Certainly, institutions cannot operate at the same speed of organized crime. Slowness is not merely a disposition, but a property of institutions. However, if mafias weave themselves in and out of heavy institutional machines, then anti-mafia efforts must also mimic their flexibility.

International awareness and action are a prerequisite to even begin to move faster. But to do this, *anti-mafia needs to think and act flexibly and cooperatively, that is, beyond national borders, across scales and sectors.*

Third, in the past years the importance and prevalence of informal economies worldwide has become ever apparent. Not that this is a new phenomenon. The global pandemic has simply led to a widespread and repeated series of *breakdowns.* Martin Heidegger ([1927] 2008) gives us the famous example of the hammer, which remains invisible (*vorhanden*, ready-at-hand) until it breaks. Once we lose our reliance on it, we become aware of the hammer as it *is*, as a distinct composition of parts (*zuhanden*, being-at-hand). Similarly to the hammer, the construction of "the economy" is made visible in these moments of collapse, revealing all its stretch marks, component parts, and tempers. It is no longer credible to speak of "the economy" in purely formal terms, as a unified and singular "thing" operating in a pure vacuum of self-regulating laws. Its multiple, composite reality is revealed as operating in shifting *interdependence* with other objects. Thus, the dependencies and linkages of formal markets and GDPs, and informal, illicit, and illegal economies are no longer deniable.

What this implies is that there are informal as well as formal power structures that influence and shape these economies.[4] Some of these operate to distribute power and surplus in ways that is life affirming. Think of the renewed importance granted to families, religious communities, and neighbors in official political speeches. Previously these were discussed as subordinate rather than essential economic realities. When founded on ethics of care and fair redistribution, they provide relief, support, and access to vital means of survival in far more nuanced ways than the mere exchange of labor for a wage, which has long been seen as one of the primary activities that constitutes the economic subject (Ferguson 2015). Others, like mafias, are extractive of surplus, exploitative, and life draining. These forms of economies exert power using violence and by capitalizing on the urgencies of coping and the needs to survive. These are not exceptional or minoritarian social formations, but forces that constitute a hefty portion of the politics of distribution worldwide.

In order to spread and have effect globally, anti-mafia must increasingly learn from this diversity of economies that exist in the world.

Much of the Italian anti-mafia language—including collective action that is explicitly internationally aimed—is still inevitably based on ideas of mafias and politics that are culturally rooted in Italy. Moving forward, activists, researchers, and policy makers need to diversify and amplify their knowledge of how mafias and other forms of organized crime operate in different global contexts, and how different cultures understand them. Indeed one important starting point might be to work with diverse forms of governance and government, which mafias are an example of. This entails deessentializing the concepts of both state and civil society. That is, to move away from ideas of power that are rooted in Enlightenment ideals of state and government, and that see resistance as primarily located in the visible opposition to "the" social contract. A queering of social movements I have already proposed.

Of equal importance is the acknowledgment of the affective resonance carried by the very term *mafia,* and all the (mis)understandings this may imply when trying to communicate with other cultures. This could facilitate the location and deconstruction of similar systems of violence and power in different contexts.

Identifying the specific relationships that enforce harmful political economies is a prerequisite step to finding ways to reformulate their ethics. This may be a future research agenda for diverse economy scholars, who have for a long time focused on exploring activities that bring more livable worlds and that are life affirming. Another path to supporting these is to further expand the focus to the diversity of life-negating and violent economies, to gain more knowledge of the challenges and difficulties for the constitution of community economies (Gibson-Graham and Dombroski 2020, 18).

Although this book has shown different manners to prevent, oppose, and interrupt exploitative economic relations in the context of mafias in Italy, several of these strategies may be of use to collective actions in other contexts. One in particular lies at the heart of all others mentioned thus far.

Anti-mafia are shadow economies. The most obvious meaning of this is that they represent a minoritarian way of doing economy; they stand "in the shadow" of more dominant economic forms. But what I have sought to highlight throughout this book is the verbal form of the term *shadow*: when they work best, that is, when they effectively manage to break violent relations and sustain healthy livelihoods, they do so by mimicking the spheres of activity and types of relations that are central to mafia power. When they *shadow* mafia economies and reformulate their ethics and aesthetics.

Some form of shadowing is also at play in law enforcement

strategies. Judge Giovanni Falcone is, for instance, most famous for this tactic of "following the money": of tracing the movement of mafia capital and imagining what the next investment might be in order to stop it. In this case, shadowing implies following and tracing in order to prohibit, prevent, and punish. Contrarily, in the grassroots cases we have discussed, mimicry also implies an oppositional *reformulation* of that which grants power to that which is mimicked. In the case of mafias, it is the sources of their social control. This is thereby a collective and distributed exercise of crime prevention, which implies recognizing *oneself* as an integral and powerful part of the very same culture.

Accordingly, crime prevention must necessarily exceed the denial of a given action performed by a group or an individual, as criminal actions are, in themselves, an excessive imitative manifestation of a given cultural setting. Anticriminal culture is thereby not external or parallel to criminal culture, but simply one direction of the same social field. And the direction set by these imitative events, or anti-mafia inventions, as Tarde might call them, is rooted in the ethical and political choice of subverting commonly accepted norms (Tarde 2000, 86); to reshuffle the social bases of mafia power.

As we have seen throughout the book, this collective work of rearrangement occurs at semantic, syntactical, and affective levels. Purposely, resignifying, restructuring, and reframing have a common feature: the prefix *re-*. All these modes of collective actions indeed involve a tactic of oppositional mimicry, of citation; one that is, however, not reducible to language and semantics, but that also relates all the other nonrepresentational objects that constitute mafias. This form of politics can hardly be described in the classical language of social movements, which often, due to its epistemological premises, predetermines where and how collective action takes place. This is a far more imaginative exercise.

I have learned that mafia economies are both incredibly diverse and tremendously inventive. It is through the continuous and dedicated work of collective experimentation, of patient observation and learning that anti-mafia activists learn to locate mafia power and develop strategies. Their oppositional actions cannot rotate around a unified actor. Rather, it is the configuration and expression of diverse elements that increase mafia movement and influence. "They" cannot simply be jailed. Rather, "they," the hybrid configurations that enforce mafia relations, can be rearranged into non-mafia relationships.

This also infers that economic life is composed of many subjects who have agency, challenging the all too present idea that economy is "one unified (neoliberal) system" that must simply be "opposed." The protagonists of this book populate and, to the extent that they can, take part in shaping their own economic lives.

These collective experimentations also speak to a more general social unease and increasingly widespread critique of dominant economic practices that disconnect humans from themselves, from one another and their environments. These forms of opposition seek to operate at livable speeds: livable for the individual but also for the nonhuman collective. They strive to recognize interdependence rather than foster a race over self-realization. They prioritize collective well-being over output and individual performance. Here, work ethic does not mean sacrificing one's free time to produce more, but rather sacrificing individual profit to diminish social harm.

These forms of activism in fact tap into something broader than the specifics of mafia economies. They represent an indirect critique to the life conditions that have led to the rise of the exhausted and individualized *Homo computans*: a human subject who is constantly pushed to measure, extract meaning, and provide feedback on any lived experience in order to optimize it. This push for self-betterment and the pressure to produce reflexive signification coincides with constant reminders of crisis, imminent collapse, and disaster, creating a culture of anxiety. While many people are reacting by disinvesting desire and deserting society (Berardi 2024), others, like the activists here described, seek intense meaning-making experiences that bring hope. This is thus a fertile ground for an oppositional mimicry that also operates on the self but reformulates it via decompression. For example, as we saw in chapters 2 and 4, by exposing it to poetry,[5] new foods, people, landscapes, music, but also live human suffering—to ways of being that inevitably escape signification. One may say that these cultivations of economic subjectivity operate by creating the possibility of experiencing what Hartmut Rosa has called "resonance" (2016).[6] Resonance is the opposite of alienation; it reinscribes the subject into her world. Grants her the time to breathe. Feel. Relate. Think. Absorb. Simply, be.

These actions subvert the idea that the economic subject is fully realized and driven mainly by rational, profit-oriented, opportunistic drives. Economic life is here reenchanted, granted the possibility of being a space for wonder, knowledge generation, unsettlement, moral questioning, grief, and pleasure; in essence a site of connection with the world around us.

In an incitement to "stay with the trouble," I invite you to ask yourself: Which oppressive economic practices touch your life? Which role do you play in them? And what might happen if you shadow them?

Notes

Introduction

1. I am grateful for the anonymous reviewer for bringing the Habermasian influence to my attention. Here I am referring to the opposition he makes between the system (economy) and the lifeworld (culture, here also including political culture) in his theory of the colonization of the lifeworld (1987).

2. One of the first uses of the term *political economy* can, however, be traced back to 1615, when Antonie de Montchrétien wrote his *Treatise on Political Economy* that criticized the Aristotelian idea that politics was a separate realm of life to, among others, economy (Maucourant 2011). However, the concept did not gather momentum or theoretical attention until the middle of the eighteenth century, with Rousseau's 1758 essay *Discourse on Political Economy,* and then in 1763, with Quesnay and de Riquieti's *Rural Philosophy,* a founding work for physiocratic thought (Von Eggers 2015, 2016).

3. Because the discipline has forged the backbone of political science and sociological understandings of economy, these views also influence social movement studies.

4. This line of thought is generally referred to as being *substantivist. Formalist* approaches instead take their analytical departure from market equilibriums (i.e., prices in the case of neoclassical theories) rather than relating them to the historical conditions from which they arise. Formalist approaches thus view the market "as an object of its own with firm boundaries" that is dominated by pure rationality (Staheli 2011, 270).

5. This is why, for instance, the title of chapter 10 of Polanyi's work (1957) is called "Political Economy and the *Discovery* of Society" (my emphasis).

6. "Purely" calculative matters, those that did not take moral questions into account, were instead reserved for a different discipline, namely, chrematistics (Konings 2015, 43).

7. This does not imply that all economic actions are necessarily concerned with *questioning* the distribution and exercise of power.

In fact, most economic actions do not have political intent, despite inadvertently having political effects. All I am suggesting is that they do have the possibility of being sites of political action.

8. The Italian mafias can be divided into the following categories: Cosa Nostra (Sicily), Camorra (Campania), 'Ndrangheta (Calabria), Sacra Corona Unita (Apulia), Basilischi (Basilicata), and Banda della Magliana (Lazio). For in-depth accounts on these, see respectively Apollonio 2016; Barbagallo 2010; Camuso 2012; Lupo 2009; Nicasio 2007; and Sergi 2003.

9. Historian Salvatore Lupo sharply criticizes his work for trying to draw the roots of a common ethnic Sicilian "mafia" heritage, ignoring the empirical fact that the mafia did not develop everywhere in Sicily but only in a few specific areas (Lupo 2004, 22).

10. For a detailed and brilliant analysis of Putnam's dichotomous division between a civic and an uncivic Italy, see Lupo's article in *Meridiana,* a southern Italian journal born with the mission of countering such cultural determinisms (Lupo 1993).

11. See also dalla Chiesa (2017) for more discussions on the mafia as a form of power.

12. Both direct and indirect forms of violence (i.e., personal, cultural, and structural violence as in Johan Galtung's understanding [1969]).

13. See dalla Chiesa and Jerne (2024) for a historical review.

14. E.g. Tarde (1886, 1890); Sutherland (1937); Sutherland and Cressey (1978); Becker (1963); Katz (1988).

15. It seems to me that when Tarde speaks of the social sciences, he indeed uses repetition as a synonym of imitation.

16. Further, it is important to note that these rearticulations are not to be confused with role reversals or acts of what Gabriel Tarde calls "counter-imitation." The latter, which simply imply doing the exact opposite of what is being imitated, could not lead to an invention (1962, xviii). And inventions are the kind of differential imitation that we are interested in, for these are the motors of societal progress, as "every invention, like every discovery, is a solution to a problem" (Tarde 1962, 45).

17. Including criminal life. Tardean criminology in fact views crime as an *invention,* which is a new combination of imitative flows and which produces new desires and beliefs (Tarde 1902a). Once again, this stresses his profoundly social view on crime, and the refusal of the illusion that crime is an individual possession, which was a view shared by the philosophy of natural law, utilitarian political economy, and criminological positivism (Tonkonoff 2014a).

18. There are some interesting parallels here with the Hobbesian state of nature. Despite being founded on two very different teleological premises, both Girard and Hobbes see society, and in particular the

political (intended here as the governing of a collective via prohibitions and norms) moment, as founded on the distancing of humanity from its rivalrous and enthropic gestures. While the Hobbesian solution is a social contract founded on reason, Girardian chaos is regulated by a surrogate: the plastic figure of the victim, which is celebrated in two opposing ways: negation (prohibition) and affirmation (ritual).

1. Anti-Mafia

1. Although the issue is acknowledged in these terms, a common European definition of this type of criminal activity is still lacking (Directive 2014/42/EU of 3rd April).

2. Examples are the 1990 EU Convention on Laundering, Search, Seizure, and Confiscation of the Proceeds from Crime, the 2000 UN Convention on Transnational Organised Crime, and the 2010 OECD Financial Action Task Force's recommendations on Confiscation and Asset Recovery.

3. For instance, the Italian Penal Code has made a clear distinction between criminal associations and mafia associations. Mafia associations, according to the law (Article 416 bis, from 1982), use a particular form of intimidation where subjection is achieved by invoking omertà, a supposed code of behavior that implies virility and self-justice, a passive attitude of acceptance, an active choice not to collaborate with institutions, and noninterference in the activities (legal or illegal) of others.

4. For a gendered perspective, see Puglisi 1998; dalla Chiesa 2006; Abbate 2013. For an ethnography of commemorative practices, see Puccio Den 2008, 2011, and her most recent book (2021). The Schneiders' *Reversible Destiny* (Schneider and Schneider 2003) and a chapter in Jamieson's work (2000) on the role of civil society in Palermo are also valuable. Some authors have focused entirely on the theme of antiracket associations (Caradonna 2008; Conticello 2008; Grasso 1992; Gunnarson 2008, 2014; Marin and Russo 2015), others more broadly on the theme of critical consumption (Forno 2015, 2011; Forno and Garibaldi 2016) as an anti-mafia strategy. For the role of cooperatives in the anti-mafia, see Rakopoulous's ethnography (2017). Among exceptions to the otherwise predominant Sicilian focus of the struggle are Di Bella 1986; Armiero 2014; Armiero and D'Alisa 2012; and Caggiano and De Rosa 2015, and dalla Chiesa's attempts to reconstruct the movement's expansion into the north of Italy (2010b, 2014c).

5. Which takes its inspiration from dalla Chiesa 2010a.

6. Some exponents of the movement were even destined to become mafia bosses, and there were cases in which the leagues incorporated mafia elements in their regulations (such as killing dissidents who

202 Notes to Chapter 1

refused to strike, drawing out the names of members who should carry out thefts of wheat, and blood-sealing the promise of denying in the case of being caught) (Ganci 1977, 341).

7. Some of the leagues (Santo Stefano Quisquina, Santa Caterina Vilarmosa, Paternó) explicitly addressed the mafia in their statutes by banning them from the joining the *fasci* (Renda 1977, 143).

8. So long, as previously specified, as these operate within a modern nation-state system, however it may be expressed across eras and places.

9. To this day, this remains a central composition of anti-mafia activists, namely, left-wing civic associations and Catholic groups.

10. The Giuliano Bandits were one of the most prominent bandit groups in Sicily. Numerous sources testify to their interaction with formal institutions (Casarubbea 1997, 1998; La Bella and Mecarolo 2003; Lupo 2009).

11. The Anti-Mafia Commission was established by parliament in 1963 as a reaction to a period of intense internal mafia wars (1961–1963). The creation of the commission had been proposed since 1948, and only produced a report in 1976, not achieving legislative or political results until 1982.

12. Between the 1970s and 1980s, the Sicilian mafias produced, refined, and shipped most of the heroin consumed in the United States and Europe (Falcone and Padovani 1991). In 1979, the FBI began a massive investigation of the phenomenon. The name of the complex operation derives from the fact that pizza parlors were used as fronts for this market. The Pizza Connection trial was the longest criminal jury trial in the history of U.S. federal courts.

13. Between 1978 and 1984, 332 mafia-related homicides, of which 203 were internal to these groups, and circa a thousand victims in total (including cases of "*lupara bianca*," or bodies that were never found) have been documented (Chinnici and Santino 1989).

14. With the exception of the 1971 assassination of Attorney General Pietro Scaglione.

15. The Circolo Societá Civile was founded in Milan in 1985 to spread critical knowledge about the mafias (Mattoni 2013, 340).

16. Even Pope John Paul II publicly called on the mafia to convert to Catholicism in May 1993. Consequently, the Cosa Nostra started attacking cultural heritage sites outside Sicily, in particular two churches in Rome: San Giorgio in Velabro and San Giovanni in Laterano (dalla Chiesa 2014a).

17. The region of Campania, for instance, had already witnessed the birth of an anti-usury foundation in 1997, named after a famous mafia victim, Don Peppe Diana.

18. This idea resonates with Alberto Melucci's general definition of a social movement as one that 'breaks the limits of compatibility with the system it can tolerate without altering its structure' (Melucci 1989, 29).

19. The term *desapariciòn* refers to the phenomenon of political kidnappings and torture of potentially insurrectionary individuals and the consequent elimination of all traces of them. While this was originally associated with military dictatorships (particularly Argentinian and Chilean), the anti-mafia denounces it as a form of *collective torture* perpetrated by "criminal groups, corrupt powers, international mafias, fierce dictatorships but also international corporations, large extraction companies and exploitative landholders" (Libera 2016).

20. Red RETOÑO, a Mexican NGO, was founded in 2015 with this aim, in collaboration with the local EU delegation.

21. For a collection and review of classic anti-mafia thought, see dalla Chiesa and Jerne 2024. For a more complete review of contemporary work on the anti-mafia movement, see Mazzeo 2014.

22. Several mafia-mapping apps have emerged in the past few years. NoMa is a historical map of the city of Palermo showing important mafia-related sites, while terradeifuochi is a whistle-blowing app, where one can geolocate and track illegal ecological crimes in Campania.

23. Legality and responsibility (*legalitá e responsibilitá*) are the words that appear most frequently in the entire corpus of data I have gathered from organization leaders and activists.

24. Daughter of a mafia victim and Libera activist, personal interview, July 25, 2014.

25. Today, about 70 percent of relatives do not know who stood behind these homicides (Ciotti 2015).

26. 1,055 is the current number of names that are known and commemorated (Libera 2023).

27. Zen is a particularly dangerous neighborhood in the North of Palermo. The area has experienced high crime rates and mafia infiltrations.

28. Law 381/91 defines social cooperatives as subjects pursuing "the general interest of the community to human promotion and social integration of citizens" through the management of either educational or health and social services (type A cooperative) or through other activities (type B)—agricultural, industrial, commercial, or service-oriented—aimed at employing socially disadvantaged subjects (mentally ill, drug/alcohol addicted, physically disabled, etc.). On the basis of this, another law was passed in 2006 (D. Lgs. 155/2006) that regulates social enterprises, which include but are not limited to cooperatives, testifying to an expansion in business models that are aimed at collective rather than private ends.

29. And that specifically adhere to Libera Terra. Not all cooperatives that produce food from confiscated assets choose to adhere to this network, as they prefer to have more independence in defining the terms of production and distribution.

30. I shall return to this network in chapter 4. For a detailed account, see Arcidiacono et al. 2016.

31. For a study that does constructively prioritize such contradictions see Rakopoulos (2017).

32. I am very grateful to Christoffer Kølvraa for pointing this out to me.

2. È Cosa Nostra

1. Significantly in the sociology of Gabriel Tarde (1898), repetition, *opposition,* and adaptation are the three foundational movements of all social (and universal) orders.

2. In 2023, 3,007 volunteers spent their summer on one of 143 camps present in 14 regions in Italy. Participants are primarily young: 77.5 percent of the volunteers are under 25, 50.4 percent of which are aged 14–17. And 65.1 percent of the adherents come from the north of the country (E!state Liberi! 2023).

3. Another example is the construction of the Jato dam, led by Danilo Dolci, which was aimed at interrupting mafia monopoly in water and labor in northwestern Sicily.

4. I refer to the secondary literature on the case of collective rentals in my comparison, in particular Renda 1972, 1977; Sturzo 1974; and Santino 2009.

5. In 2024, 1065 (+7,4% compared to 2023) distinct actors managed confiscated assets. The largest proportion of these are associations (563) and social and worker cooperatives (237). Other types of actors include church groups, temporary associations or networks of associations, sports associations, public institutions, private and community funds, schools, and scout groups (Libera 2024).

6. The National Agency for Confiscated Assets, established in 2010, has the duty to allocate the assets to appropriate subjects that have "social" ends to their projects, but also to monitor the correct use of these (Forno 2011, 104).

7. In February 2024, the number of confiscated assets was 36,616 (4,384 of these are enterprises) (Fattiperbene 2024).

8. In the worst cases, confiscated businesses have been administered directly by state representatives who mismanaged them and led them into bankruptcy, as occurred to the Cavallotti family (Viviani 2014).

9. In many cases, associations that want to engage with confiscated

assets become cooperatives in order to ensure their productivity and sustainability.

10. These are banks that prioritize the financing of "social economies," that have very low interest rates, and for instance have lower guarantee requirements for borrowers.

11. Libera and Gruppo Abele have also made declarations on unemployment in campaigns such as Miseria Ladra (2014), focusing on the Great Recession and the consequent impoverishment of many citizens who are prone to collaborate with the mafia.

12. Commoning the access, use, benefit, care, and responsibility of an asset have been identified as fundamental actions in the construction of a community economy. For a detailed account see Gibson-Graham et al. 2013, 125–58.

13. A more fitting term for these types of activities in Italian is *esperienze formative,* literally "formative experience." This refers to the important fact that these experiences *shape* those who take part in them in the sense that they orient their bodies in a certain direction. The adjective "educational" misses the embodied element of knowledge making that is so present in this context, and arguably in any context where information is made and shared.

14. A fee that, although small (approximately €20 a day), makes this type of voluntarism more popular with members of the middle class who have a generally high level of education, which corresponds to the general social extraction of today's anti-mafia movement overall (Gunnarson 2014; Forno 2011; Santino 2009).

15. For example, on March 1, 2017, the Chamber of Deputies unanimously voted to make March 21 a national day "of memory and commitment to commemorate victims of the mafias."

16. *Encoding* refers to the process by which producers of media content imbue their texts with intended meanings, messages, and ideological positions. *Decoding,* in contrast, refers to the process by which audiences or consumers of media content interpret and make sense of these encoded meanings. The relationship between the encoded and decoded meaning can be more or less oppositional and is thus not necessarily political in an antagonistic sense. While Stuart Hall originally developed these terms for television studies, they have become hallmark terms for the study of communication and culture, more broadly intended. Moreover, these terms are not to be confused with Deleuze and Guattari's similar bionomial, *coding and decoding,* as Ceren Özselçuk kindly brought to my attention. Although these terms share many traits with Hall's interpretation, the former are more directly concerned with the relationship between power, desire and social organization. It is Stuart Hall's sense that I use here.

17. Here I intend "negative" in an ethical sense, rather than in its constrictive connotation (i.e., to negate).

18. Here I am referring to the first international volunteer camp held in San Giuseppe Jato, Sicily, June 28–July 12, 2014.

19. The Brusca family was an important branch of the Cosa Nostra in San Giuseppe Jato. Giovanni Brusca, owner of the asset, was also known as "lu scannacristiani" or "lu verru" (Sicilian for respectively "the people-slayer" or "the swine") because of his ruthless manners and innumerable murders.

20. *Pentiti* are those who have "repented" their affiliation with mafia groups and collaborated with justice. According to the farmer, San Giuseppe Jato is full of *pentiti,* while the Corleone clans were "true men of honor" who stubbornly refused to speak even under interrogation.

21. Throughout our stay, and particularly when we were in town, we took note of houses that looked particularly "clean" and discussed whether they were acquired through criminal activity.

22. In Italian *cosa nostra* literally means "our thing" or "our asset." The pun makes reference to the Sicilian mafia syndicate Cosa Nostra.

23. Acts of menace, such as vandalization of property, are extremely common in the first years of management of a confiscated asset.

24. In general, the control and management of hydrological resources has been historically important to the Cosa Nostra's power in Sicily.

25. Law 381/91.

26. Caritas is a Catholic humanitarian organization. In Rignano I observed a high density of representatives of similar NGOs, as well as trade unions.

27. This is a rough estimate of the number of workers employed in peak season (June–September 2014) provided by a trade unionist working in the area.

28. The main nationalities of the inhabitants were identified as Malian, Senegalese, Ghanaian, and Romanian.

29. A term used to define temporary housing made of tents, usually in the context of natural disasters such as earthquakes.

30. No. 604/2013.

31. Drawing on psychoanalytic theory, Stephen Healy similarly points to the importance that "voids" have for processes (economic) resubjectification (Healy 2015).

32. This is a genuine example of what Michel Foucault might call desubjugation, where the subject discerns the limits of a certain regime of truth, thereby recognizing its transformability (Foucault 1997; Butler 2002).

3. Disrupting Structures of Mafia Dependency

1. Including, but this time not prevalently, their expressive and semantic components.

2. When I use the term *objects,* I mean to include both humans and nonhumans. I prefer this to the terms *actors* or *agents* because I do not believe that objects are only interesting when they "act" or change something in the world. For most of the time they do not (Harman 2016).

3. Puissance, a Spinozian inspired concept of power (Deleuze and Guattari [1980] 1987, xvii).

4. Omertà, as I discussed in chapter 1, is a particular cultural code that is often associated to mafia. It implies a passive, tacit behavior that refuses interference with the legal or illegal activities of others.

5. Art. 416 bis. of the penal code, 3rd comma, my emphasis.

6. According to some studies (Transcrime 2014), the Camorra and the 'Ndrangheta make 70 percent of all criminal proceeds in Italy, which sum up to an annual €7.2 billion.

7. For in-depth accounts see Barbagallo et al (1989); Armiero (2008); Armiero and D'Alisa (2012); Caggiano and De Rosa (2015); Cantoni (2016).

8. See Saveria Antiochia Omicron association's well-documented executive summary on eco-mafias for a more detailed account (n.d.).

9. This is the recent case of the Sant'Anna hospital in Como that was constructed by Peregro Holding, an enterprise that collaborated with the 'Ndrangheta and buried asbestos in the foundations of the health facility.

10. The unfortunate Italian term is the *eco-balle,* which also means "eco-bullshit."

11. The name derives from the landscape given by the practice of burning domestic and industrial waste. It was coined by Giuseppe Ruggiero and popularized by Saviano in *Gomorra* (Saviano [2006] 2016, 309–36).

12. As a result of this, the association witnessed some conflicts with the previous owners (as well as with the municipality). The owners of the land came with lorries and uprooted fifty cherry trees. The second form of menace came from the nephew of the boss, Angelo Simeoli, after the association had hosted five hundred people on the terrain for Easter Monday. Another threat came after they had made a press release about their project, when three graves were dug out onto the land, with crosses drawn into the soil.

13. The Community Economies Collective (2001) calls this the "trauma of exploitation." "Restricted to the necessary labor that sustains you, separated from the surplus that sustains the larger society, you are constituted as an 'individual' bereft of a possible community and

communal subjectivity." See also Madra (2006) for an in-depth review of Marxian debates on the themes of exploitation and subjectivity.

14. In the cosmology of Gabriel Tarde, three fundamental categories govern all phenomena: repetition, opposition and adaptation (Tarde 1897). Of the three, it is repetition that enables true difference, or "that difference which opposes nothing and which serves no purpose" (L'opposition Universelle, 445, cited in Deleuze [1968] 2014, 164).

15. An assemblage is held together, and thus defined, by two distinct but overlapping tendencies: one material, the other expressive (DeLanda 2006, 12–14). Components playing a material role involve bodies and their disposition and ordering. Components playing an expressive role include linguistic and nonlinguistic elements. The way these components are expressed and mixed in an assemblage can either increase the internal homogeneity of the movement (territorialization) or destabilize its boundaries (deterritorialization). I shall return to this in more detail in chapter 5.

16. Etiket is also a word play between etico (ethical) and etichetta (label).

17. Casal di Principe has historically been a Camorra stronghold, as it was home to the Casalesi clan. The Casalesi clan distinguishes itself in its miscellaneous enterprises that range from drugs, weapons, real estate, aggregates, and dairy products. One of its strategies has been to collaborate with Albanian and Nigerian syndicates, distributing the direct management of the drug market and spreading the risk (Saviano [2006] 2016, 209).

18. In Lacan's terms, "mimicry reveals something in so far as it is distinct from what might be called an itself that is behind" (1977, 99). There is no original in the Lacanian world; it is the very act of imitation that becomes the focus of the communicative process.

19. The term pacco has (at least) a triple meaning in this context. The first, most obvious and originally intended meaning is "package," and more specifically, a package that contains books. The second, as translated here, is "to blow someone off," or better, "to stand someone up," "to bail on someone." It refers to the act of making plans with someone and then not showing up or canceling at the last minute, leaving the other person disappointed or let down. Here the activists (accidentally) say that their literary package (meaning 1) is, in truth "blowing off the Camorra" (meaning 2). So, they embraced the pun by renaming the package "un pacco alla Camorra." There is then a third meaning, which renders the whole phrase even more ridiculous, and that is that pacco also translates to "disappointment" or "dud." This connotation is more informal and slang. A pacco letterario (literary dud), in this case, would not refer to the fact that the literary content of the works in the package

were disappointing, but to the very fact that the box contains books (the books themselves are boring content). This last layer reinforces a sense of absurdity in using something as highbrowed as literature (intellectual and frail) to fight something like the mafia (ignorant and brutally strong).

20. This in many ways resonates with the frame alignment literature that has long argued that social movements diffuse better if they tap into shared meanings and discourses (i.e., Snow et al. 1986; Mooney and Hunt 1996).

4. Mobilizing Mafia Heritage

1. I am aware that affects and emotions are not the same, and that there is a great deal of literature within affect studies that is interested in exploring the distinction between these. My position in this debate is that affects precede emotions and are thus an alternation in a mode of being (Spinoza [1677] 2001; Jerne 2022), which does not necessarily translate emotionally. However, when emotions do manifest as a result of material/semiotic shifts, they always follow affective occurrences. Thereby both affects and emotions are examples of affective processes, which is why I include both instances under the framework of affective reframing.

2. The turn to tourism as a form of mobilization is a broader trend that is picking up among associations working with confiscated assets, either in connection with Libera (E!state Liberi!—the volunteering program or their own tour operator, Il Giusto di Viaggare), but also in the form of smaller independent initiatives. In one of the preparation meetings I attended for the 2016 season of E!state Liberi!, the organizers even addressed the issue of how to maintain their own integrity and attractiveness in the gradually more competitive anti-mafia market.

3. The members of the Addiopizzo committee accordingly refer to themselves as *attacchini,* or stickers (the ones who stick).

4. These types of services are provided by a parallel association, Libero Futuro, which emerged in 2007 and is the more technical branch of the movement. According to an Addiopizzo activist, branding the movement has made it particularly visible and appealing to young entrepreneurs who contact them in their start-up phase. Addiopizzo then redirects them to Libero Futuro who has pragmatic know-how.

5. "Facemu troppu scrusciu" (We are too loud now). During my fieldwork, Addiopizzo entrepreneurs and activists used this phrasing on various occasions.

6. A further development of this has been the launch of an official Addiopizzo card in 2014, which consumers can use when purchasing a good or service from the network of affiliated businesses. It gives

the consumer an "ethical discount," the sum of which the enterprises transfer into a common account. The aim of the pool is to realize a "collective investment"—a project that aims at requalifying Palermo. The decision of what to invest the money in is taken collectively through a democratic voting system. In 2016, the first project was the realization of a playground in Piazza Magione, which was "degraded and underutilised, . . . where illegality often reigns and where the value of public good is lost" (Addiopizzo 2017b).

7. A recent study study by Davide Beraldo (2017) for instance demonstrates how the social movement Anonymous operates through brand-making logics, a phenomenon that he describes with the notion of *contentious branding.*

8. These numbers refer to 2019.

9. In 2016, the cost per person was €335 for five days and four nights, including transportation, guided tours, access to museums, sleeping, and three meals per day.

10. The restaurant where we ate, supplied by Addiopizzo food chains, was filled with other groups of students, primarily in middle school, who were also there to perform anti-mafia tourism. The transportation was also provided by anti-mafia bus companies, which took us to different important heritage sights.

11. Recently, they have also made it possible for consumers to send fabric from abroad that then becomes the building block for the hat. This was framed as an attempt to imitate mafias' expansion into the recycling business.

12. For instance, anti-mafia rhetoric is deeply linked to ideas of beauty. Many (slightly distorted) references to anti-mafia activists such as Giuseppe Impastato or Giovanni Falcone speak of educating people to beauty as a means to fight mafia. *Educare alla bellezza* (educating to appreciate beauty) is, for example, one of the most popular slogans that activists write on the facades of confiscated assets. It is often used as a hashtag on Instagram activist channels.

13. One of Addiopizzo's tours is called "Palermo Theatre of noir: The spectacle of death." Interestingly, the tour is not mafia related, but refers to a much more distant history, that of the Catholic Inquisition. I borrow the term "spectacle of noir" precisely to highlight the (moral) tension of the experiential use of sensitive material.

14. Literally: "the clay-footed" or "the ones with dirty feet." This refers to the character of the social extraction of this clan (farmers), which was lower than the other clans of the territory of Palermo.

15. Indeed, this is precisely what he critiqued: that there ought to be more possibility to elaborate.

16. This visit was not organized by Addiopizzo, but by E!state Liberi!

in 2014. The tourists (in this case also volunteers) were, similarly to the previous case, not Italian. Thus, both cases share the challenge of transmitting the heritage to a group with a different cultural background.

17. As Jason Read reminds us, Baruch Spinoza in fact theorized that negative passions, emotional states that are externally triggered, do not necessarily have to bring about a diminishing of one's bodily capacities. They can indeed be empowering by preparing us for active joys: joys that we can act upon (similarly, excessive joys can be destructive) (Read 2016, 109).

18. Other than the more obvious fact that these tours are increasingly popular, that is, that this type of engagement with the past is in itself a development.

5. Queering Social Movements

1. Because collective action is commonly categorized as belonging to a specific subset of the "social system," that is, the "political system," this discussion will more specifically revolve around the relationship between politics and economy. For a similar discussion of the "social" see Miller (2019).

2. The first sociological example of this line of thought is Gabriel Tarde's work, on which these two authors strongly draw from.

3. I am grateful to Britta Timm Knudsen for introducing me to DeLanda before I was ready to appreciate him. It is thanks to his style of writing that I have become sensible to assemblage thinking, which is why I use his version of it, rather than the style of Deleuze and Guattari, which I often find abstruse.

4. For a review of some of the core differences between assemblages and actor networks, see Müller (2015).

5. I am grateful to Lea Muldtofte for introducing me to the work of Blanchot.

6. I am aware that these forms of contention did exist in the past, but were simply not as dominant, in the context of the anti-mafia at least.

7. For instance, in the works of Turner and Killian (1957), Smelser (1962) and particularly Berk (1974).

8. North American constructivist approaches, on the other hand, seem to be more of a reaction to institutional approaches and thus often look at movements that are not directed at institutions but that challenge symbols, identities, and cultural norms (Goodwin and Jasper 2004). Again there is a dichotomy similar to that between politics and the economy: social movements are either looked at as prosthetic to state politics or as outside state politics.

9. See Borch (2012) for a rigorous historical analysis.

10. The ontological separation between the economy and other areas of life, such as society or nature, can be traced further back to the birth of the social sciences in the nineteenth century. For an articulate study of this conceptual divorce and its consequences for the collective, see the work of Ethan Miller (2019).

11. In other words, meaning and culture have often been conflated with "agency" in opposition to other factors, such as novel governments, economic hardship, or highly contested laws, which are seen as "structural" constraints or opportunities for social movements. In other versions, meaning has been interpreted as "subjective" and malleable, while broader political or economic systems are "objective" factors that are firm and either constrain or enable protest from the "outside."

12. Moreover, the political process model (the social movement approach most commonly associated with "structuralism") has been criticized for prioritizing the role of one particular type of structure, that is, the state (Kurzman 2004, 112).

13. "There is a broad understanding . . . that recognizes social movements as essentially reticulate in structure, and therefore amenable to analysis through metaphors and formal operations that capture the properties of their networks" (Krinsky and Crossley 2014, 1). This is a common example of this type of thinking, where the whole cannot have emergent properties because its parts are defined by their properties rather than their dispositions.

14. Social movements are commonly referred to as being a particular form of contentious politics. The field of contentious politics was most influentially mapped by Charles Tilly, who defines social movements as characterized by "a sustained series of interactions between national authorities and persons successfully claiming to speak on behalf of a constituency lacking formal representation, in the course of which those persons make publicly visible demands for changes in the distribution or exercise of power, and back those demands with public demonstrations of support" (1981, 6). While this definition implies a relationship with representative politics, the term *social movement* is now commonly used to refer to various kinds of collective actions that are not necessarily directed toward the state. My intention is neither to critique this "incorrect" usage nor to undermine the validity of this definition, for this is a very useful classification. What I do find problematic is that there is a tendency to assume that this is the fixed or best matrix against which all collective actions should be compared or imagined.

15. Deleuze and Guattari distinguish between two axes of assemblages, one vertical, the other horizontal. While the two are interlinked, the former has a temporal dimension, while the latter is concerned with

how things come together (territorialization) and fall apart (deterritorialization) in space (Kennedy et al. 2013, 28).

16. Other than Graeme Chesters and Ian Welsh's (2006) engagement with complexity theory, the first systematic dialogue between the sociology of social movements and assemblage thinking occurred with the publication of a special issue of *Social Movement Studies* in 2018 (Rodríguez-Giralt et al. 2018).

17. More than two decades ago, Jeff Goodwin and James Jasper produced a platform to bridge theoretical divisions (2004). They brought together some of the "titans" of social movement thinking in an anthology named *Rethinking Social Movements: Structure, Meaning, and Emotion*. Uncoincidentally, this book is structured along the same concepts. Indeed, our intention is very similar. However, their strategy has been to bring diverse positions within the field in dialogue, which gave rise to a witty but rather belligerent book. This, in my view, ended up further highlighting the divisions. Rather than asking which paradigm is the best, my strategy has instead been to ask what it is that these separations enforce and why these matter.

18. As will soon become clearer, the three modes of collective action that I have already traced in the previous chapters—meaning, structure, and feeling—are transversal to these concepts. For instance, these modes can all territorialize a given network. Indeed, as I have shown thus far, meaning, structure, and feeling are three modes of organization that take part in territorializing or reterritorializing networks and identities that are conflictually oriented against mafias. I have not chosen to prioritize them because they already act as *divisive* concepts within the tradition of social movement studies. Conversely, network, conflict, and identity are commonly understood as definitional elements of social movements.

19. In the social movements literature, this is often called a mechanism of "brokerage" (Gould and Fernandez 1989).

20. The successful alignment of interpretative frames of reference has been theorized as being important to the formation, duration, and force of social movements (Snow et al. 1986).

21. This has been proficiently analyzed by Chesters and Welsh through their term "reflexive framing" (2006: 9), which has been developed as a critique of approaches that see framing as a primarily rational activity, ignoring the important mimetic processes that are inherently *aesthetic* in nature.

22. See Fominaya (2010) for a thorough overview.

23. Deleuze and Guattari notably compare rhizomatic thinking, which has multiple entry and exit points for data representation and interpretation, to arborescent thinking, which follows linear, hierarchical, and binary paths of thought which have clear-cut beginnings and ends (Deleuze and Guattari 1987).

Conclusion

1. Nando dalla Chiesa drew my attention to this paradox at a seminar in Aarhus 2015.

2. Zen is a particularly difficult neighborhood in the north of Palermo. The area has experienced high crime rates and mafia infiltrations.

3. See also Napoleone Colajanni's historical reflections on the significance of social class for legality (Colajanni 1900:69).

4. In fact, Milton Friedman's (1962) idea of freedom in capitalism is flawed precisely because it presupposes that economic transactions are "impersonal," ahistorical, and substantially symmetrical. Markets are dense interpersonal and intersystemic relations. As long as there are nation-states, organizations, and people involved in markets, there can be no free market. There are always stronger and weaker parties involved in transactions simply because relations of exchange are *populated.*

5. Franco Berardi's antidote to the suffocating overload of human computation is in fact poetry, a form of excess in the field of signification (Berardi 2019).

6. I am grateful to the anonymous reviewer for pointing out this connection.

Bibliography

Abbate, Lirio. 2013. *Fimmine Ribelli: Come le donne salveranno il paese dalla 'ndrangheta.* Milan: Rizzoli.

Addiopizzo. 2017a. "Certificato Addiopizzo." http://www.addiopizzo.org /index.php/pago-chi-non-paga/certificato-addiopizzo/. Accessed June 1, 2017.

Addiopizzo. 2017b. "Investimento Collettivo." http://www.addiopizzo .org/index.php/investimento-collettivo-2. Accessed June 1, 2017.

Addiopizzo. 2023. "Pago chi non paga." https://addiopizzo.org/rete -imprese. Accessed March 17, 2023.

Agamben, Giorgio. 2009. *Il regno e la gloria: Per una genealogia teologica dell'economia e del governo.* Turin: Bollati Boringhieri.

Alongi, Giuseppe. 1886. *La maffia nei suoi fattori e nelle sue manifestazioni: Studio sulle classi pericolose della Sicilia.* Turin: Bocca.

Alvarez, Sonia E., Evelina Dagnino, and Arturo Escobar. 1998. "Introduction: The Cultural and the Political in Latin American Social Movements." In *Cultures of Politics/Politics of Cultures: Re-visioning Latin American Social Movements,* edited by Sonia E. Alvarez, Evelina Dagnino, and Arturo Escobar, 1–29. Boulder, Colo.: Westview.

Antal, Ariane B., Michael Hutter, and David Stark, eds. 2015. *Moments of Valuation: Exploring Sites of Dissonance.* Oxford: Oxford University Press.

Apollonio, Andrea. 2016. *Storia della Sacra Corona Unita.* Soveria Mannelli: Rubbettino.

Arcidiacono, C., M. Baldascino, A. De Rosa, et al. 2016. *Local Design Network: Rete di economia sociale nelle Terre di don Peppe Diana.* Rovereto: LISt lab.

Arcifa, Gabriella. 2014. "The New EU Directive on Confiscation: A Good (Even If Still Prudent) Starting Point for the Post-Lisbon EU Strategy on Tracking and Confiscating Illicit Money." (Working Paper No. 64). Università degli Studi di Catania and Centro di Documentazione Europeo.

Arlacchi, Pino. 1983. *La Mafia imprenditrice. L'Etica mafiosa e lo spirito del capitalismo.* Bologna: Il Mulino.

Armiero, Marco. 2008. "Seeing Like a Protester: Nature, Power, and Environmental Struggles." *Left History* 13 (1): 59–76.

Armiero, Marco. 2014. "Garbage Under the Volcano: The Waste Crisis in Campania and the Struggles for Environmental Justice." In *A History of Environmentalism: Local Struggles, Global Histories,* edited by Marco Armiero and Lise Sedrez, 167–83. London: Bloomsbury.

Armiero, Marco, and Giacomo D'Alisa. 2012. "Rights of Resistance: The Garbage Struggles for Environmental Justice in Campania, Italy." *Capitalism, Nature, Socialism* 23 (4): 52–68.

Arvidsson, Adam. 2006. *Brands: Meaning and Value in Media Culture.* London: Routledge.

Arvidsson, Adam, and Nicolai Peitersen. 2013. *The Ethical Economy: Rebuilding Value after the Crisis.* New York: Columbia University Press.

Banfield, Edward C. 1958. *The Moral Basis of a Backward Society.* New York: Free Press.

Barbagallo, Francesco. 2010. *Storia della Camorra.* Bari: Laterza.

Barbagallo, Francesco, Isaia Sales, and Ada C. Becchi, eds. 1989. *L'affare terremoto: libro bianco sulla ricostruzione.* Agri: Sciba.

Barnes, Nicholas. 2017. "Criminal Politics: An Integrated Approach to the Study of Organized Crime, Politics, and Violence." *Perspectives on Politics* 15 (4): 967–87.

Barnett, Clive, Paul Cloak, Nick Clarke, and Alice Malpass. 2010. *Globalising Responsibility: The Political Rationalities of Ethical Consumption.* Chichester, UK: Wiley Blackwell.

Barry, Andrew. 2002. "The Anti-Political Economy." *Economy and Society* 31 (2): 268–84.

Baudrillard, Jean. (1976) 1993. *Symbolic Exchange and Death.* Translated by Iain Hamilton Grant. London: Sage.

Becchi, Ada C. 1988. "Catastrofi, sviluppo e politiche del territorio: alcune riflessioni sull'esperienza italiana." *Archivio di studi urbani e regionali,* no. 31.

Becker, Howard. 1963. *Outsiders: Studies in the Sociology of Deviance.* New York: Free Press of Glencoe.

Bennett, Jane. 2010. *Vibrant Matter: A Political Ecology of Things.* Durham, N.C.: Duke University Press.

Bennett, Lance W., and Alexandra Segerberg. 2012. "The Logic of Connective Action." *Information, Communication and Society* 15 (5): 753.

Beraldo, Davide. 2017. "Contentious Branding: Reassembling Social Movements through Digital Mediators." PhD diss., University of Amsterdam.

Berardi, Franco. 2014. *And: Phenomenology of the End.* Helsinki: Alto University Press.

Berardi, Franco. 2017. *Futurability: The Age of Impotence and the Horizon of Possibility.* London: Verso.

Berardi, Franco. 2019. *Breathing: Chaos and Poetry.* Los Angeles: Semiotext(e).

Berardi, Franco. 2024. *Quit Everything: Interpreting Depression.* London: Repeater.

Berk, Richard A. 1974. *Collective Behavior.* Dubuque, Iowa: Wm. C. Brown.

Bevington, Douglas, and Chris Dixon. 2005. "Movement-Relevant Theory: Rethinking Social Movement Scholarship and Activism." *Social Movement Studies* 4 (3): 185–208.

Bhabha, Homi K. 1994. *The Location of Culture.* London: Routledge.

Blackman, Lisa. 2015. "Researching Affect and Embodied Hauntologies: Exploring an Analytics of Experimentation." In *Affective Methodologies. Developing Cultural Research Strategies for the Study of Affect,* edited by Britta Timm Knudsen and Carsten Stage, 25–44. Basingstoke, UK: Palgrave Macmillan.

Blanchot, Maurice. (1959) 1987. "Everyday Speech." Translated by Susan Hanson. *Yale French Studies* 73: 12–20.

Blok, Anton. 1974. *The Mafia of a Sicilian Village, 1860–1960: A Study of Violent Peasant Entrepreneurs.* New York: Harper Torchbooks.

Blumer, Herbert. 1939. "Collective Behavior." In *A New Outline of the Principles of Sociology,* edited by Robert E. Park, 165–222. New York: Barnes and Noble.

Blumer, Herbert. 1951. "Collective Behavior." In *Principles of Sociology,* edited by Alfred M. Lee, 67–121. New York: Barnes & Noble.

Boltanski, Luc. (1993) 1999. *Distant Suffering: Morality, Media, Politics.* Translated by Graham D. Burchell. Cambridge: Cambridge University Press.

Boorstin, Daniel. (1961) 1992. *The Image: A Guide to Pseudo-events in America.* New York: Vintage Books.

Borch, Christian. 2012. *The Politics of Crowds: An Alternative History of Sociology.* Cambridge University Press: New York.

Borch, Christian. 2015. *Foucault, Crime and Power: Problematisations of Crime in the Twentieth Century.* Oxon: Routledge.

Borowiak, Craig, Maliha Safri, Stephen Healy, and Marianna Pavlovskaya. 2018. "Navigating the Fault Lines: Race and Class in Philadelphia's Solidarity Economy." *Antipode* 50: 577–603.

Bosi, Lorenzo, and Lorenzo Zamponi. 2015. "Direct Social Actions and Economic Crises: The Relationship between Forms of Action and Socio-economic Context in Italy." *Partecipazione e Conflitto* 8 (2): 367–91.

Boswijk, Albert, Ed Peelen, and Stephen Olthof, 2012. *Economy of Meaningful Experiences Humanising Business.* Amsterdam: European Centre for the Experience Economy.

Boswijk, Albert, Thomas Thijssen, and Ed Peelen. 2007. *Experience Economy: A New Perspective.* Amsterdam: Pearson Education.

Bruns, Axel. 2008. *Blogs, Wikipedia, Second Life, and Beyond: From Production to Produsage.* New York: Peter Lang.

Butler, Judith. 1993. *Bodies That Matter: On the Discursive Limits of Sex.* New York: Routledge.

Butler, Judith. 1997. *Excitable Speech. A Politics of the Performative.* New York: Routledge.

Butler, Judith. 2002. "What Is Critique? An Essay on Foucault's Virtue." In *The Political: Blackwell Readings in Continental Philosophy,* edited by David Ingram, 212–26. Malden, Mass.: Blackwell.

Butler, Judith. 2004. *Undoing Gender.* New York: Routledge.

Butler, Judith. 2010. "Performative Agency." *Journal of Cultural Economy* 3 (2): 147–61.

Butler, Judith, and Athena Athanasiou. 2013. *Dispossession: The Performative in the Political.* Cambridge: Polity.

Caggiano, Monica, and Salvatore Paolo De Rosa. 2015. "Social Economy as Antidote to Criminal Economy: How Social Cooperation Is Reclaiming Commons in the Context of Campania's Environmental Conflicts." *Partecipazione e Conflitto* 8 (2): 530–54.

Calabria, Esmeralda, Andrea D'Ambrosio, and Peppe Ruggiero. 2007. *Biùtiful cauntri.* Indipendenti Regional.

Callon, Michel. 1986. "Some Elements of a Sociology of Translation: Domestication of the Scallops and the Fishermen of St Brieux Bay." In *Power, Action and Belief: A New Sociology of Knowledge?,* edited by John Law, 196–229. London: Routledge & Kegan Paul.

Callon, Michel, ed. 1998. *The Laws of the Markets.* London: Blackwell.

Camuso, Angela. 2012. *Mai ci fu pietá. La banda della Magliana dal 1977 a Mafia Capitale.* Rome: Castelvecchi RX.

Cantoni, Roberto. 2016. "The Waste Crisis in Campania, South Italy: A Historical Perspective on an Epidemiological Controversy." *Endeavour* 4 (2): 102–13.

Caradonna, Salvatore. 2008. "Le imprese e il movimento antiracket." In *I costi dell'illegalitá: Mafia ed estorisioni in Sicilia,* edited by Antonio La Spina. Bologna: Il Mulino.

Caruso, Loris, and Lorenzo Cini. 2020. "Rethinking the Link between Structure and Collective Action: Capitalism, Politics, and the Theory of Social Movements." *Critical Sociology* 46 (7–8): 1005–23.

Casarubbea, Giuseppe. 1997. *Portella della Ginestra: Microstoria di una strage di stato.* Milan: F. Angeli.

Casarubbea, Giuseppe. 1998. *"Fra'diavolo" e il governo nero. "Doppio tato" e stragi nella Sicilia del secondo dopoguerra.* Milan: F. Angeli.

Catanzaro, Raimondo. 1988. *Il delitto come impresa. Storia sociale della mafia.* Padua: Liviana Editrice.

Chesters, Graeme, and Ian Welsh. 2006. *Complexity and Social Movements: Multitudes at the Edge of Chaos.* London: Routledge.

Chinnici, Giorgio, and Umberto Santino. 1989. *La violenza programmata: omicidi e guerre di mafia a Palermo dagli anni '60 ad oggi.* Milan: FrancoAngeli.

Chouliaraki, Lilie. 2006. *The Spectatorship of Suffering.* New Delhi: Sage Publications.

Ciconte, Enzo. 2008. *Storia criminale: La resistibile ascesa di mafia, 'ndrangheta e camorra dall'Ottocento ai giorni nostri.* Soveria Mannelli: Rubbettino.

Ciotti, Luigi. 2011. *La speranza non è in vendita.* Turin: Giunti Editore-Gruppo Abele.

Ciotti, Luigi. 2015. "La Veritá Illumina La Giustizia" (interview by TG1). https://www.youtube.com/watch?v=Uh78WbkEYul. Accessed May 2015.

Clough, Patricia T., with Jean Halley, eds. 2007. *The Affective Turn: Theorizing the Social.* Durham, N.C.: Duke University Press.

Colajanni, Napoleone. (1900) 2024. "In the Mafia Kingdom." In *Against the Mafia: The Classic Italian Writings,* edited by Nando dalla Chiesa and Christina Jerne, translated by Christina Jerne. London: Palgrave Macmillan.

Colli, Francesca. 2020. "Indirect Consumer Activism and Politics in the Market." *Social Movement Studies* 19 (3): 249–67.

Comaroff, Jean, and John Comaroff, eds. 2006. *Law and Disorder in the Postcolony.* Chicago: University of Chicago Press.

Comba, Pietro, Fabrizio Bianchi, Lucia Fazzo, et al. 2006. "Cancer Mortality in an Area of Campania (Italy) Characterized by Multiple Toxic Dumping Sites." *Annals of the New York Academy of Sciences* 1076: 449–61.

Community Economies Collective. 2001. "Imagining and Enacting Noncapitalist Futures." *Socialist Review* 28 (3–4): 93–135.

Community Economies Collective. 2019. "Diverse Economies Iceberg." https://www.communityeconomies.org/index.php/resources/diverse-economies-iceberg. Accessed August 22, 2019.

Consiglio Nazionale dell'Economia e del Lavoro. 2007. "Liberalizzazioni e Privatizzazioni." http://www.cnel.it/53?shadow_documenti=8074. Accessed March 16, 2015.

Conticello, Filippo. 2008. *L'isola che c'è. La Sicilia che si ribella al pizzo.* Rome: Round Robin.

Cova, Bernard, Robert Kozinets, and Avi Shankar, eds. 2007. *Consumer Tribes.* Oxford: Butterworth-Heinemann.

Crouch, David, Lars Aronsson, and Lage Wahlström. 2001. "Tourist Encounters." *Tourist Studies* 1 (3): 253–70.

dalla Chiesa, Carlo Alberto. (1982) 2024. "How I Fight the Mafia." In *Against the Mafia: The Classic Italian Writings,* edited by Nando dalla Chiesa and Christina Jerne, translated by Christina Jerne. London: Palgrave Macmillan.

dalla Chiesa, Nando. 1983. "Gli Studenti Contro la Mafia: Note (di merito) per un movimento." *Quaderni Piacentini* 11: 39–60.

dalla Chiesa, Nando. 2006. *Le ribelli: Storie di donne che hanno sfidato la mafia per amore.* Milan: Melampo.

dalla Chiesa, Nando. 2010a. *Contro la mafia: I testi classici.* Turin: Einaudi.

dalla Chiesa, Nando. 2010b. "Una nuova stagione per il movimento anti-mafia." *Narcomafie,* no. 3.

dalla Chiesa, Nando, ed. 2014a. *La scelta Libera: Giovani nel movimento antimafia.* Turin: Edizioni Gruppo Abele.

dalla Chiesa, Nando. 2014b. *Manifesto dell'Antimafia.* Turin: Einaudi.

dalla Chiesa, Nando. 2014c. "The Antimafia Movement in Milan." *Dissent* (April).

dalla Chiesa, Nando. 2017. "Defining the Mafia: Between Sociology and Law." In *Redefining Organised Crime: A Challenge for the European Union?* edited by Stefania Carnevale, Serena Forlati, and Orsetta Giolo, 225–50. Oxford: Hart.

dalla Chiesa, Nando. 2024. "Introduction: Mafia and Anti-mafia: A History to Fill." In *Against the Mafia: The Classic Italian Writings,* edited by Nando dalla Chiesa and Christina Jerne, translated by Christina Jerne. London: Palgrave Macmillan.

dalla Chiesa, Nando, and Christina Jerne, eds. 2024. *Against the Mafia. The Classic Italian Writings.* Translated by Christina Jerne. London: Palgrave Macmillan.

Davies, Andrew D. 2011. "Assemblage and Social Movements: Tibet Support Groups and the Spatialities of Political Organisation." *Transactions of the Institutes of British Society* 37: 273–86.

DeLanda, Manuel. 2006. *A New Philosophy of Society: Assemblage Theory and Social Complexity.* London: Continuum.

Deleuze, Gilles. 1988. *Spinoza: Practical Philosophy.* Translated by Robert Hurley, San Francisco: City Light Books.

Deleuze, Gilles. (1968) 2014. *Difference and Repetition.* Translated by Paul Patton, London: Bloomsbury.

Deleuze, Gilles, and Felix Guattari. (1980) 1987. *One Thousand Plateaus.* Translated by Brian Massumi. Minneapolis: University of Minnesota Press.

della Porta, Donatella. 2015. *Social Movements in Times of Austerity: Bringing Capitalism Back into Protest Analysis.* Cambridge: Polity.

della Porta, Donatella, and Mario Diani, eds. 2006. *Social Movements: An Introduction.* 2nd ed. Oxford: Blackwell.

della Porta, Donatella, and Alberto Vannucci. 1999. *Corrupt Exchanges: Actors, Resources, and Mechanisms of Political Corruption.* New York: Aldine de Gruyter.

DeRosa, Antonio, and Mauro Baldascino. 2016. "La rete in construzione." In *Local Design Network: Rete di economia sociale nelle Terre di don Peppe Diana,* edited by Caterina Arcidiacono et al., 61–72. Rovereto, Italy: LISt lab.

Dewey, John. 1939. *Theory of Valuation.* Chicago: University of Chicago Press.

Dewey, John. (1927) 2012. *The Public and Its Problems: An Essay in Politics Inquiry.* University Park: Penn State University Press.

Diani, Mario. 1992. "The Concept of Social Movement." *Sociological Review* 40 (1): 5.

Diani, Mario. 2011. "The Cement of Civil Society: Civic Networks in Local Settings. Barcelona." Unpublished manuscript. Cited in Lance W. Bennett and Alexandra Segerberg. 2012. "The Logic of Connective Action." *Information, Communication and Society* 15 (5): 753.

Dickie, John. 2004. *Cosa Nostra: A History of the Sicilian Mafia.* London: Hodder & Stoughton.

Dickie, John. 2013. *Mafia Republic: Italy's Criminal Curse: Cosa Nostra, 'Ndrangheta and Camorra from 1946 to the Present.* London: Hodder & Stoughton.

Dilling-Hansen, Lise. 2015. "Affective Fan Experiences of Lady Gaga." *Transformative Works and Cultures,* no. 20.

Di Bella, Saverio. 1986. *Un popolo contro la mafia.* Soveria Mannelli: Rubbettino.

Diprose, Graham. 2016. "Negotiating Interdependence and Anxiety in Community Economies." *Environment and Planning A* 48 (7): 1411–27.

Dolci, Danilo. (1955) 2024. "Bandits in Partinico." In *Against the Mafia: The Classic Italian Writings,* edited by Nando dalla Chiesa and Christina Jerne, translated by Christina Jerne. London: Palgrave Macmillan.

Dolci, Danilo. 1960. *Spreco: Documenti e inchieste su alcuni aspetti dello spreco nella Sicilia occidentale.* Turin: Einaudi.

Dombroski, Kelly. 2018. "Thinking with, Dissenting within: Care-Full Critique for More-than-Human Worlds." *Journal of Cultural Economy* 11 (3): 261–64.

Duncombe, Stephen. 2007. "(From) Cultural Resistance to Community Development." *Community Development Journal* 42 (4): 490–500.

Durkheim, Émile. 1984. *The Division of Labor in Society.* New York: Free Press.

E!state Liberi!. 2023. "E!state Liberi! 2023. Campi di impegno e formazione sui beni confiscati alle mafie." https://www.libera.it/documenti/schede/scarica_il_rapporto_2023.pdf. Accessed November 2024.

Falcone, Giovanni. (1990) 2024. "The Italian Mafias Explained in Mexico." In *Against the Mafia: The Classic Italian Writings,* edited by Nando dalla Chiesa, and Christina Jerne, translated by Christina Jerne, London: Palgrave Macmillan.

Falcone, Giovanni. 1994. *La posta in gioco: Interventi e proposte per la lotta alla mafia.* Milan: Biblioteca Universitaria Rizzoli.

Falcone, Giovanni, and Marcelle Padovani. 1991. *Cose di Cosa Nostra.* Milan: Rizzoli.

Fattiperbene. 2024. "Libera News." https://www.libera.it/schede-1573-fattiperbene. Accessed February 19, 2024.

Federazione Lavoratori Agro Industria. 2017. "Caporalato." http://www.flai.it/osservatoriopr/. Accessed July 2017.

Fennel, David A. 2015. *Ecotourism.* 4th ed. New York: Routledge.

Ferguson, James. 2015. *Give a Man a Fish: Reflections on the New Politics of Distribution,* Durham, N.C.: Duke University Press.

Fisher, Mark. 2009. *Capitalist Realism: Is There No Alternative?* Winchester, UK: Zero Books.

Flacks, Richard. 2003. "Review: McAdam, D., Tarrow, S., Tilly, C. (2003) Dynamics of Contention." *Social Movement Studies* 2 (1): 99–102.

Fominaya, Cristina F. 2010. "Collective Identity in Social Movements: Central Concepts and Debates." *Sociology Compass* 4 (6): 393–404.

Fominaya, Cristina F., and Graeme Hayes. 2016. "Resisting Austerity: Collective Action in Europe in the Wake of the Global Financial Crisis." Special Issue, *Social Movement Studies* 16 (1).

Forno, Francesca. 2011. *La spesa a pizzo zero.* Milan: Altra Economia.

Forno, Francesca. 2015. "Bringing Together Scattered and Localized Actors: Political Consumerism as a Tool for Self-Organizing Anti-mafia Communities." *International Journal of Consumer Studies* 39: 535–43.

Forno, Francesca, and Roberta Garibaldi. 2016. "Ethical Travel: Holidaying to Fight the Italian Mafia." In *Reinventing the Local in Tourism: Producing, Consuming and Negotiating Place,* edited by Antonio Paolo Russo and Greg Richards, 50–64. Bristol: Channel View Publications.

Forno, Francesca, and Paolo Graziano. 2014. "Sustainable Community Movement Organisations." *Journal of Consumer Culture* 14 (2): 139–57.

Foucault, Michel. 1977. *Discipline and Punish: The Birth of the Prisons.* Translated by Alan Sheridan, London: Penguin.

Foucault, Michel. 1978. *The History of Sexuality,* vol. 1. New York: Random House.

Foucault, Michel. 1982. "The Subject and Power." *Critical Inquiry* 8 (4): 777–95.

Foucault, Michel. 1997. "What Is Critique?" In *The Politics of Truth,* edited by Sylvére Lotringer, translated by Lysa Hochroth and Catherine Porter, 41–81. New York: Semiotext(e).

Foucault, Michel. (1966) 2002. *The Order of Things.* Oxon: Routledge.

Foucault, Michel. 2008. *The Birth of Biopolitics.* New York: Palgrave.

Franchetti, Leopoldo. (1877) 2024. "Political and Administrative Conditions of Sicily." In *Against the Mafia: The Classic Italian Writings,* edited by Nando dalla Chiesa and Christina Jerne, translated by Christina Jerne. London: Palgrave Macmillan.

Freeman, Jo. 1972. "The Tyranny of Structurelessness." *Berkeley Journal of Sociology* 17: 151–65.

Friedman, Milton. 1962. *Capitalism and Freedom.* Chicago: University of Chicago Press.

Freud, Sigmund. 1922. *Group Psychology and the Analysis of the Ego.* London: International Psycho-analytical Press.

Galtung, Johan. 1969. "Violence, Peace, and Peace Research." *Journal of Peace Research* 6 (3): 167–91.

Gambetta, Diego. 1996. *The Sicilian Mafia. The Business of Private Protection.* Cambridge, Mass.: Harvard University Press.

Ganci, Massimo. 1977. *I fasci dei lavoratori,* Caltanissetta: S. Sciascia.

Garcia, Tristan. 2018. *The Life Intense: A Modern Obsession.* Translated by Abigail RayAlexander, Christopher RayAlexander, and Jon Cogburn. Edinburgh: Edinburgh University Press.

Gibson-Graham, J. K. 2000. "Post-structural Interventions." In *A Companion to Economic Geography,* edited by Eric Sheppard and Trevor J. Barnes, 95–110. Oxford: Blackwell.

Gibson-Graham, J. K. 2006a. *A Post-capitalist Politics.* Minneapolis: Minnesota University Press.

Gibson-Graham, J. K. (1996) 2006b. *The End of Capitalism (As We Knew It).* 2nd ed. Minneapolis: University of Minnesota Press.

Gibson-Graham, J. K. 2020. "Reading for Economic Difference." In *The Handbook of Diverse Economies,* edited by J. K. Gibson-Graham and Kelly Dombroski, 476–86. Cheltenham, UK: Edward Elgar.

Gibson-Graham, J. K., Jenny Cameron, Kelly Dombroski, Stephen Healy, and Ethan Miller. 2018. "Cultivating Community Economies." In *The Next System Project: Essays,* edited by M. Adams, J. K. Gibson-Graham, and K. Dombroski, 21–28. New York: Monthly Review.

Gibson-Graham, J. K., Jenny Cameron, and Stephen Healy. 2013. *Take*

Back the Economy: An Ethical Guide for Transforming Our Communities. Minneapolis: University of Minnesota Press.

Gibson-Graham, J. K., and Kelly Dombroski, eds. 2020. *The Handbook of Diverse Economies,* Cheltenham, UK: Edward Elgar.

Girard, René. 1987. *Things Hidden since the Foundation of the World.* Stanford, Calif.: Stanford University Press.

Gould, Roger, and Roberto J. Fernandez. 1989. "Structures of Mediation." *Sociological Methodology* 19: 89–126.

Granovetter, Mark. 1985. "Economic Action and Social Structure: The Problem of Embeddedness." *American Journal of Sociology* 91 (3): 481–510.

Grasso, Franco. 1956. *A Montelepre hanno piantato una Croce. Danilo Dolci missionario civile nella zona della mafia e del banditismo.* Milan: Edizioni Avanti!.

Grasso, Tano. 1992. *Contro il racket: Come opporsi al ricatto mafioso.* Bari: Laterza.

Goodwin, Jeffery, and James Jasper, eds. 2004. *Rethinking Social Movements: Structure, Meaning and Emotion.* Oxford: Rowman and Littlefield.

Guattari, Felix, and Éric Alliez. 1983. "Le Capital en fin de compte: Systèmes, structures et processus capitalistiques." *Change International* 1: 100–106.

Gunnarson, Carina. 2008. *Cultural Warfare and Trust: Fighting the Mafia in Palermo.* Manchester, UK: Manchester University Press.

Gunnarson, Carina. 2014. "Changing the Game: Addiopizzo's Mobilisation against Racketeering in Palermo." *European Review of Organized Crime* 1 (1): 39–77.

Habermas, Jürgen. 1987. *Theory of Communicative Action, Vol. 2: Lifeworld and System: A Critique of Functionalist Reason.* Cambridge: Polity.

Haenfler, Ross, Brett Johnson, and Ellis Jones. 2012. "Lifestyle Movements: Exploring the Intersection between Lifestyle and Social Movements." *Social Movement Studies* 11 (1): 1–20.

Haiven, Max. 2014. *Crises of Imagination, Crises of Power: Capitalism, Creativity and the Commons.* London: Zed Books.

Hall, Stuart. 1980. "Encoding/Decoding." In *Culture, Media, Language,* edited by Stuart Hall, Dorothy Hobson, Andrew Lowe, and Paul Willis, 128–38. London: Hutchinson.

Hall, Stuart. 1999. "Encoding, Decoding." In *The Cultural Studies Reader,* edited by Simon During, 507–17. London: Routledge.

Hall, Tim. 2018. *The Economic Geographies of Organized Crime.* New York: Guilford.

Hall, Tim, and Ray Hudson. 2021. "The Economic Geographies of Transnational Organized Crime." In *Routledge Handbook of Transnational*

Organized Crime, edited by Felia Allum and Stavros Gilmour, 11–25. London: Routledge.

Halliwell, Stephen. 2002. *The Aesthetics of Mimesis: Ancient Texts and Modern Problems.* Princeton, N.J.: Princeton University Press.

Hamilton, Kathy, and Paul Hewer. 2010. "Tribal Mattering Spaces: Social-Networking Sites, Celebrity Affiliations, and Tribal Innovations." *Journal of Marketing Management* 26 (3–4): 271–89.

Harman, Graham. 2010. *Towards Speculative Realism: Essays and Lectures.* Winchester, UK: Zero Books.

Harman, Graham. 2016. *Immaterialism. Objects and Social Theory.* Cambridge: Polity.

Harrington, Brooke. 2016. *Capital without Borders: Wealth Managers and the One Percent.* Cambridge, Mass.: Harvard University Press.

Hazen, Jennifer N., and Dennis Rodgers, eds. 2014. *Global Gangs: Street Violence Across the World.* Minneapolis: University of Minnesota Press.

Healy, Stephen. 2015. "Biofuels, Ex-felons, and Empower, a Worker Owned Cooperative. Performing Enterprises Differently." In *Making Other Worlds Possible. Performing Diverse Economies,* edited by Gerda Roelvink, Kevin St. Martin, and Julie and Katherine Gibson-Graham, 98–126. Minneapolis: University of Minnesota Press.

Heidegger, Martin. (1927) 2008. *Being and Time.* New York: Harper Perennial.

Hetland, Gabriel, and Jeffery Goodwin. 2013. "The Strange Disappearance of Capitalism from Social Movement Studies." In *Marxism and Social Movements,* edited by Colin Barker, Laurence Cox, John Krinsky and Alf Gunvald Nilsen, 83–102. Leiden: Brill.

Hersey, Tricia. 2022. *Rest Is Resistance: A Manifesto.* Little Brown Spark.

Hess, Henner. 1973. *Mafia and Mafiosi. The Structure of Power.* Westmead, U.K.: Saxon House.

Hirschfeld, Katherine. 2015. *Gangster States: Organized Crime, Kleptocracy and Political Collapse.* New York: Palgrave Macmillan.

Hodder, Ian. 2012. *Entangled: An Archaeology of the Relationships between Humans and Things.* Malden, Mass.: Wiley-Blackwell.

Holmes, Seth. 2013. *Fresh Fruit, Broken Bodies: Migrant Farmworkers in the United States.* Berkeley: University of California Press.

Hossein, Caroline S. 2016. *Politicized Microfinance: Money, Power and Violence in the Black Americas.* Toronto: University of Toronto Press.

Hossein, Caroline S., ed. 2018. *The Black Social Economy in the Americas: Exploring Diverse Community Based Markets.* New York: Palgrave Macmillan.

Inglehart, Ronald. 1977. *The Silent Revolution: Changing Values and Political Styles among Western Publics.* Princeton, N.J.: Princeton University Press.

Isomaa, Saija, Soile Kivistö, Pekka Lyytikäinen, Merja Polvinen, and Ralf Rossi, eds. 2012. *Rethinking Mimesis: Concepts and Practices of Literary Representation.* Newcastle upon Tyne, UK: Cambridge Scholars.

Jacobsen, Eivind, and Arne Dulsrud. 2007. "Will Consumers Save the World? The Framing of Political Consumerism." *Journal of Agricultural and Environmental Ethics* 20: 469–82.

Jameson, Fredric. 2003. "Future City." *New Left Review,* no. 21: 65–79.

Jamieson, Alison. 2000. *The Antimafia: Italy's Fight against Organized Crime.* London: Macmillan.

Jensen, Jakob Linaa, and Anne Marit Waade. 2009. *Medier og turisme.* Århus: Academica.

Jerne, Christina. 2015. "From Marching for Change to Producing the Change: Reconstructions of the Italian Anti-mafia Movement." *Interface* 7 (1): 185–214.

Jerne, Christina. 2017. "Event-Making the Past: Commemorations as Social Movement Catalysts," *Memory Studies* 13 (4): 486–501.

Jerne, Christina. 2020. "Anti-mafia Enterprise: Italian Strategies to Counter Violent Economies." In *The Handbook of Diverse Economies,* edited by J. K. Gibson-Graham and Kelly Dombroski, 82–89. Cheltenham, UK: Edward Elgar.

Jerne, Christina. 2022. "Activating Limit as Method. An Affective Experiment in Ethnographic Criminology." In *Methodologies of Affective Experimentation,* edited by Britta Timm Knudsen, Mads Krogh, and Carsten Stage, 287–306. Cham, Switzerland: Palgrave Macmillan.

Jerne, Christina. 2024. "Conclusion. Resilient Social Violence." In *Against the Mafia: The Classic Italian Writings,* edited by Nando dalla Chiesa and Christina Jerne, translated by Christina Jerne. London: Palgrave Macmillan.

Katz, Jack. 1988. *Seductions of Crime.* New York: Basic Books.

Kennedy, Rosanne, Jonathan Zapasnik, Hannah McCann, and Miranda Bruce. 2013. "All Those Little Machines: Assemblage as Transformative Theory." *Australian Humanities Review* 55: 45–66.

Knorr-Cetina, Karin. 1997. "Sociality with Objects: Social Relations in Postsocial Knowledge Societies." *Theory, Culture and Society* 14 (4): 1–30.

Knudsen, Britta Timm. 2011. "Thanatourism: Witnessing Difficult Pasts." *Tourist Studies* 11 (1): 55–72.

Knudsen, Britta Timm. 2018. "Reframing." ECHOES: European Colonial Heritage Modalities in Entangled Cities. https://keywordsechoes.com/. Accessed March 17, 2023.

Knudsen, Britta Timm, Dorthe Refslund Christensen, and Per Blenker, eds. 2015. *Enterprising Initiatives in the Experience Economy: Transforming Social Worlds.* London: Routledge.

Knudsen, Britta Timm, and Christina Jerne. 2019. "Oplevelsesøkonomi og begivenhedskultur." In *Ny Kulturteori*, edited by Birgit Eriksson and Bjørn Schiermer, 169–96. Copenhagen: Hans Reizels Forlag.

Knudsen, Britta Timm, and Carsten Stage. 2015. *Global Media, Biopolitics and Affect: Politicizing Bodily Vulnerability.* New York: Routledge.

Knudsen, Britta Timm, and Anne Marit Waade, eds. 2010. *Reinvesting Authenticity: Tourism, Place and Emotions.* Bristol: Channel View.

Konings, Martijn. 2015. *The Emotional Logic of Capitalism: What Progressives Have Missed.* Stanford, Calif.: Stanford University Press.

Krinsky, John, and Nick Crossley. 2014. "Social Movements and Social Networks: Introduction." *Social Movement Studies* 13 (1): 1–21.

Krippendorf, Jost. 1982. "Towards New Tourism Policies: The Importance of Environmental and Sociocultural Factors." *Tourism Management* 3 (3): 135–48.

Kurzman, Charles. 2004. "The Poststructuralist Consensus in Social Movement Theory." In *Rethinking Social Movements: Structure, Meaning and Emotion*, edited by Jeffery Goodwin and James Jasper, 111–20. Oxford: Rowman and Littlefield.

Kølvraa, Christoffer. 2015. "Affect, Provocation, and Far Right Rhetoric." In *Affective Methodologies*, edited by Britta Timm Knudsen and Carsten Stage. London: Palgrave Macmillan.

La Bella, Angelo, and Rosa Mecarolo. 2003. *Portella della Ginestra. La Strage che ha Cambiato L'Italia.* Rome: Teti Editore.

Laarman, Jan G., and Patrick B. Durst. 1987. "Nature Travel in the Tropics." *Journal of Forestry* 85 (5): 43–46.

La Loggia, Enrico. 1953. "Le affittanze collettive in Sicilia al Congresso di Roma del 1912." In *Autonomia e Rinascita della Sicilia*, Palermo: Ires.

Lacan, Jacques. 1977. *The Four Fundamental Concepts of Psycho-Analysis.* Edited by Jacques Alain Miller, London: Routledge.

Lash, Scott, and Celia Lury. 2007. *Global Culture Industry: The Mediation of Things.* Cambridge: Polity.

Latour, Bruno. 1988. *The Pasteurization of France.* Translated by Alan Sheridan and John Law. Cambridge, Mass.: Harvard University Press.

Latour, Bruno. 2004a. *The Politics of Nature. How to Bring the Sciences into Democracy*, Translated by Catherine Porter. Cambridge, Mass.: Harvard University Press.

Latour, Bruno. 2004b. "How to Talk about the Body? The Normative Dimension of Science Studies." *Body and Society* 10: 205–29.

Latour, Bruno. 2005a. *Reassembling the Social: An Introduction to Actor-Network Theory.* New York: Oxford University Press.

Latour, Bruno. 2005b. "From Realpolitik to Dingpolitik or How to Make Things Public." In *Making Things Public: Atmospheres of Democracy*, edited by Bruno Latour and Peter Weibel, 14–41. Cambridge, Mass.: MIT Press.

Latour, Bruno. 2007. "Turning Politics Around. A Note on Gerard de Vries' Paper." *Social Studies of Science* 37 (5): 811–20.

Latour, Bruno. 2013. *An Enquiry into Modes of Existence: An Anthropology of the Moderns.* Translated by Catherine Porter. Cambridge, Mass.: Harvard University Press.

Law, John. 1986. "On the Methods of Long-Distance Control: Vessels, Navigation and the Portuguese Route to India." In *Power, Action and Belief: A New Sociology of Knowledge?,* edited by John Law, 234–63. London: Routledge & Kegan Paul.

Le Bon, Gustave. (1895) 1960. *The Crowd: A Study of the Popular Mind.* New York: Viking.

Lessing, Benjamin. 2021. "Conceptualizing Criminal Governance." *Perspectives on Politics,* 19 (3): 854–73.

Levkoe, Charles Z., and Sarah Wakefield. 2014. "Understanding Contemporary Networks of Environmental and Social Change: Complex Assemblages within Canada's Food Movement." *Environmental Politics* 22 (2): 302–20.

Lewis, Tania, and Emily Potter, eds. 2011. *Ethical Consumption: A Critical Introduction.* New York: Routledge.

Libera. 2016. "Giornata mondiale dei desaparecidos." http://www.libera.it/flex/cm/pages/ServeBLOB.php/L/IT/IDPagina/12905. Accessed November 24, 2016.

Libera. 2023. "I numeri della memoria." https://vivi.libera.it/it-statistiche. Accessed March 6, 2023.

Libera. 2024. "Raccontiamo il bene 2024." https://www.libera.it/it-schede-2558-raccontiamo_il_bene. Accessed January 23, 2025.

Lippmann, Walter. (1927) 1993. *The Phantom Public.* New Brunswick: Transaction.

Lippmann, Walter. (1922) 1997. *Public Opinion.* New York: Free Press Paperbacks.

Lupo, Salvatore. 1987. "L'utopia totalitaria del fascismo." In *La Sicilia,* edited by Maurice Aymard and Giuseppe Giarrizzo, 376. Turin: Einaudi.

Lupo, Salvatore. 1993. "Usi e abusi del passato. Le radici dell'Italia di Putnam." *Meridiana* 18: 151–68.

Lupo, Salvatore. 2004. *Storia della mafia.* 3rd ed. Rome: Donzelli.

Lupo, Salvatore. 2007. *Che cos'è la mafia?* Rome: Donzelli.

Lupo, Salvatore.2009. *History of the Mafia.* Translated by Anthony Shugaar. New York: Columbia University Press.

Lury, Celia. 2004. *Brands: The Logos of the Global Economy.* London: Routledge.

Lury, Celia. 2009. "Brands as Assemblage." *Journal of Cultural Economy* 2 (2): 67–82.

MacCannell, Dean. 1973. "Staged Authenticity: Arrangements of Social Space in Tourist Settings." *American Journal of Sociology* 79 (3): 589–603.

Macdonald, Sharon. 2006. "Undesirable Heritage: Fascist Material Culture and Historical Consciousness in Nuremberg." *Journal of Heritage Studies* 12 (1): 9–28.

Madra, Yahya. 2006. "Questions of Communism: Ethics, Ontology, Subjectivity." *Rethinking Marxism* 18 (2): 205–24.

Maheu, Louis. 1996. "The Sociology of Alain Touraine: A Modernist Look at Post-industrialization and the Ambivalence of Social Movements." In *Alain Touraine*, edited by Jon Clark and Marco Diani, 93–111. London: Falmer.

Manjoo, Fahrad. 2008. *True Enough: Learning to Live in a Post-fact Society.* Hoboken, N.J.: John Wiley & Sons.

Marin, Laura E. M., and Vincenzo Russo. 2015. "Re-localizing 'Legal' Food: A Social Psychology Perspective on Community Resilience, Individual Empowerment and Citizen Adaptations in Food Consumption in Southern Italy." *Agriculture and Human Values* 33 (1): 179–90.

Marrero-Guillamón, Isaac. 2013. "Actor-Network Theory, Gabriel Tarde and the Study of an Urban Social Movement: The Case of Can Ricart, Barcelona." *Qualitative Sociology* 36 (4): 403–42.

Marres, Noortje. 2005. "No Issue, No Public: Democratic Deficits after the Displacement of Politics." PhD diss., University of Amsterdam.

Marres, Noortje. 2012. *Material Participation. Technology, the Environment and Everyday Publics.* Basingstoke, UK: Palgrave Macmillan.

Marx, Karl. (1844) 1959. *Economic and Philosophic Manuscripts of 1844.* Translated by Martin Milligan. Moscow: Progress.

Mattoni, Alice. 2013. "I movimenti antimafie in Italia." In *Atlante delle mafie: storia, economia, società, cultura, vol. II,* edited by Enzo Ciconte, Franceso Forgione, and Isaia Sales, 323–37. Soveria Mannelli: Rubbettino Editori.

Maucourant, Jérôme. 2011. "The Ambiguous Birth of Political Economy: Montchrestien vs. Cantillon." Paper presented at ESHET (European Society for the History of Economic Thought) 2011—Competition, Innovation and Rivalry, Boğaziçi University, Istanbul, March 20.

Mazzeo, Martina. 2014. "Il movimento antimafia contemporaneo: una bibliografia ragionata." In *La scelta Libera: giovani nel movimento antimafia,* edited by Nando dalla Chiesa. Turin: Gruppo Abele.

McAdam, Doug. 1982. *Political Process and the Development of Black Insurgency, 1930–1970.* Chicago: University of Chicago Press.

McAdam, Doug, and Ronnelle Poulsen. 1993. "Specifying the Relationship between Social Ties and Activism." *American Journal of Sociology* 99 (3): 640–67.

McAdam, Doug, Sidney Tarrow, and Charles Tilly. 2001. *Dynamics of Contention.* New York: Cambridge University Press.

McCarthy, John D. and Mayer N. Zald. 1977. "Resource Mobilization and Social Movements: A Partial Theory." *American Journal of Sociology* 82 (6): 1212–41.

McDonald, Kevin. 2004. "Oneself as Another: From Social Movement to Experience Movement." *Current Sociology* 52 (4): 575–93.

McDonald, Kevin. 2006. *Global Movements: Action and Culture.* Malden, Mass.: Blackwell.

McDonald, Kevin. 2015. "From Indymedia to Anonymous: Rethinking Action and Identity in Digital Cultures." *Information, Communication & Society* 18 (8): 968–82.

McFarlane, Collin. 2009. "Translocal Assemblages: Space, Power and Social Movements." *Geoforum* 40 (4): 561–67.

McKinnon, Katharine, Kelly Dombroski, and Oona Morrow. 2018. "The Diverse Economy: Feminism, Capitalocentrism and Postcapitalist Futures." In *The Handbook of International Political Economy of Gender,* edited by Juanita Elias and Adrienne Roberts, 335–52. Cheltenham, UK: Edward Elgar.

Melucci, Alberto. 1984. "Movimenti in un mondo di segni." In *Altri codici. Aree di movimento nella metropoli,* edited by Alberto Melucci. Bologna: Il Mulino.

Melucci, Alberto. 1985. "The Symbolic Challenge of Contemporary Movements." *Social Research* 52 (4): 789–816.

Melucci, Alberto. 1989. *Nomads of the Present: Social Movements and Individual Needs in Contemporary Society.* London: Century Hutchinson.

Melucci, Alberto. 1996. *Challenging Codes: Collective Action in the Information Age.* Cambridge: Cambridge University Press.

Melucci, Alberto. 2000. *Culture in gioco: Differenze per convivere.* Milan: Saggiatore.

Meyer, David S. 1995. "The Challenge of Cultural Elites: Celebrities and Social Movements." *Sociological Inquiry* 65 (2): 181–206.

Micali, Alberto. 2015. "Notes for an Ecological Archaeology of Imaginary Media Hacking." *Journal of Contemporary Archaeology* 2 (1): 15–23.

Micheletti, Michele. 2003. *Political Virtue and Shopping: Individuals, Consumerism, and Collective Action.* New York: Palgrave Macmillan.

Miller, Ethan. 2019. *Reimagining Livelihoods: Life beyond Economy, Society and Environment.* Minneapolis: University of Minnesota Press.

Miseria Ladra. 2014. "Le proposte a livello locale, nazionale ed europeo." http://www.miserialadra.it/le-proposte-a-livello-locale-nazionale-ed-europeo. Accessed October 2014.

Moebius, Stephan. 2004. "Imitation, Repetition and Iterability." *Distinktion: Scandinavian Journal of Social Theory* 5 (2): 55–69.

Mooney, Patrick H., and Scott A. Hunt (1996). "A Repertoire of Interpretations: Master Frames and Ideological Continuity in U.S. Agrarian Mobilization." *The Sociological Quarterly*, 37 (1): 177–97.

Morris, Aldon. 1984. *The Origin of the Civil Rights Movement*. New York: Free Press.

Mosca, Gaetano. (1900) 2024. "What Is the Mafia?" In *Against the Mafia: The Classic Italian Writings*, edited by Nando dalla Chiesa and Christina Jerne, translated by Christina Jerne. London: Palgrave Macmillan.

Mouffe, Chantal. 2005. *On the Political*. London: Routledge.

Müller, Martin. 2015. "Assemblages and Actor-Networks: Rethinking Socio-material Power, Politics and Space." *Geography Compass* 9 (1): 27–41.

Muniesa, Fabian. 2012. "A Flank Movement in the Understanding of Valuation." *Sociological Review* 59 (2): 24–38.

Muniesa, Fabian. 2014. *The Provoked Economy: Economic Reality and the Performative Turn*. Oxon: Routledge.

Nancy, Jean Luc. 1991. *The Inoperative Community*. Edited by Peter Connor, translated by Peter Connor, Lisa Garbus, Michael Holland, and Simona Sawhney. Minneapolis: University of Minnesota Press.

Nancy, Jean Luc. 2000. *Being Singular Plural*. Translated by Robert Richardson and Anne O'Byrne. Stanford, Calif.: Sanford University Press.

Naylor, Lindsay. 2019. *Fair Trade Rebels: Coffee Production and Struggles for Autonomy in Chiapas*. Minneapolis: University of Minnesota Press.

Nelson, Lise. 2003. "Decentering the Movement: Collective Action, Place, and the 'Sedimentation' of Radical Political Discourses." *Environment and Planning D: Society and Space* 21: 559–81.

Nicasio, Antonio. 2007. *'Ndrangheta. Le radici dell'odio*. Reggio Emilia: Aliberti.

Nordstrom, Carolyn. 2007. *Global Outlaws: Crime, Money and Power in the Contemporary World*. Berkeley: University of California Press.

Nünning, Ansgar. 2010. "Making Events—Making Stories—Making Worlds: Ways of Worldmaking from a Narratological Point of View." In *Cultural Ways of Worldmaking: Media and Narratives*, edited by Vera Nünning, Ansgar Nünning, and Birgit Neuman, 191–214. New York: De Gruyter.

Offe, Claus. 1985. "New Social Movements: Challenging the Boundaries of Institutional Politics." *Social Research* 52 (4): 817–68.

Olson, Mancur. 1965. *The Logic of Collective Action*. Cambridge: Harvard University Press.

Park, Robert E., and Ernest W. Burgess. 1921. *Introduction to the Science of Sociology*. Chicago: University of Chicago Press.

Partridge, Henry. 2012. "The Determinants of and Barrier to Critical Consumption: A Study of Addiopizzo." *Modern Italy* 17 (3): 343–63.

Pine, Joseph B., and James H. Gilmore. 2011. *The Experience Economy.* Boston: Harvard Business Review.

Pitré, Giuseppe. (1889) 1978. *Usi e costumi, credenze e pregiudizi del popolo Siciliano.* Vol. 2. Palermo: I Vespri.

Polanyi, Karl. 1957. *The Great Transformation: The Political and Economic Origins of Our Time.* London: Beacon.

Polletta, Francesca. 1998. "It Was Like a Fever." *Social Problems* 45: 137–59.

Polletta, Francesca. 2004. "Culture Is Not Just in Your Head." In *Rethinking Social Movements: Structure, Meaning and Emotion,* edited by Jeffery Goodwin and James Jasper, 97–110. Oxford: Rowman and Littlefield.

Polletta, F., and J. Jasper. 2001. "Collective Identity and Social Movements." *Annual Review of Sociology* 27 (1): 283–305.

Pollichieni, Luciano, Sandro Ruotolo, Fabrizio Valletti, Ciro Corona, and Isaia Sales. 2016. "Come Scampia è diventata Scampia e come può risorgere." *Limes,* May 4, 2016. http://www.limesonline.com/come-scampia-e-diventata-scampia-e-come-puo-risorgere/91259. Accessed March 14, 2023.

Portwood-Stacer, Laura. 2012. "Anticonsumption as Tactical Resistance: Anarchists, Subculture, and Activist Strategy." *Journal of Consumer Culture* 12 (1): 87–105.

Puccio-Den, Deborah. 2008. "The Anti-mafia Movement as Religion? The Pilgrimage to Falcone's Tree." In *Shrines and Pilgrimage in the Modern World,* edited by Peter Jan Margry, 49–70. Amsterdam: Amsterdam University Press.

Puccio-Den, Deborah. 2011. "Difficult Remembrance: Memorializing Mafia Victims in Palermo." In *Grass-Root Memorials: The Politics of Memorializing Traumatic Death,* edited by Peter Jan Margry and Cristina Sánchez-Carettero, 51–70. New York: Berghahn Books.

Puccio-Den, Deborah. 2021. *Mafiacraft: An Ethnography of Deadly Silence.* Chicago: University of Chicago Press.

Puglisi, Anna. 1998. *Donne, mafia, antimafia.* Palermo: Centro di Documentazione Giuseppe Impastato.

Putnam, Robert D. 1993. *Making Democracy Work: Civic Traditions in Modern Italy.* Princeton, N.J.: Princeton University Press.

Rakopoulos, Theodoros. 2017. *From Clans to Co-ops: Confiscated Mafia Land in Sicily.* New York: Berghahn Books.

Ramella, Francesco, and Carlo Trigilia. 1997. "Associazionismo e mobilitazione contro la criminalità organizzata nel Mezzogiorno." In *Mafia e società Italiana. Rapporto '97,* edited by Luciano Violante, Livia Minervini and Emmanuel Barbe. Roma-Bari: Laterza.

Read, Jason. 2016. "The Affective Economy: Producing and Consuming in Affects in Deleuze and Guattari." In *Deleuze and the Passions*, edited by Ceciel Meiborg and Sjoerd van Tuinen, 103–24. New York: Punctum.

Renda, Francesco. 1972. *Socialisti e cattolici in Sicilia: 1900–1904. Le lotte agrarie.* Caltanissetta-Rome: Salvatore Sciascia Editore.

Renda, Francesco. 1977. *I Fasci Siciliani: 1892–1894.* Turin: Einaudi.

Renda, Francesco. 1984. *Storia della Sicilia dal 1860 al 1970 (Vol. 1–3).* Palermo: Sellerio.

Renda, Francesco. 1993. *Resistenza alla mafia come resistenza nazionale.* Soveria Mannelli: Rubbettino.

Renda, Francesco. 1997. *Storia della mafia: Come, dove, quando.* Palermo: Sigma Edizioni.

Renda, Francesco. 2003. *Storia della Sicilia dal 1860 al 1970.* Palermo: Sellerio.

Reuter, Peter. 1983. *Disorganized Crime: The Economics of the Visible Hand.* Cambridge, Mass.: MIT Press.

Resnick, Stephen A., and Richard D. Wolff. 1987. *Knowledge and Class: A Marxian Critique of Political Economy.* Chicago: University of Chicago Press.

Ricoeur, Paul. 1972. "L'herméneutique du témoignage." *Archivio di Filosofia* 42 (1–2): 35–61.

Ricoeur, Paul. 2004. *Memory, History, Forgetting.* Chicago: University of Chicago Press.

Rodgers, Dennis. 2022. "(Il)legal Aspirations: Of Legitimate Crime and Illegitimate Entrepreneurship in Nicaragua." *Latin American Politics and Society* 64 (4): 48–69.

Rodríguez-Giralt, Israel. 2012. "Social Movements as Actor-Networks: Prospects for a Symmetrical Approach to Doñana's Environmental Protests." *Convergencia, Revista de Ciencias Sociales* 18 (56): 13–35.

Rodríguez-Giralt, Israel, Isaac Marrero-Guillamón, and Denise Milstein. 2018. "Reassembling Activism, Activating Assemblages: An Introduction." *Social Movement Studies* 17 (3): 257–68.

Roelvink, Gerda. 2010. "Collective Action and the Politics of Affect." *Emotion, Space and Society* 3: 111–18.

Roelvink, Gerda. 2016. *Building Dignified Worlds: Geographies of Collective Action.* Minneapolis: University of Minnesota Press.

Roelvink, Gerda, Kevin St. Martin, and J. K. Gibson-Graham, eds. 2015. *Making Other Worlds Possible: Performing Diverse Economies.* Minneapolis: University of Minnesota Press.

Romano, Salvatore F. 1963. *Storia della mafia.* Milan: Sugar.

Rosa, Hartmut. 2016. *Resonance: A Sociology of Our Relationship to the World.* Translated by Jonathan Trejo-Mathys. Cambridge: Polity.

Rossi, Adolfo. (1894) 1988. *L'agitazione in Sicilia. Inchiesta sui Fasci dei lavoratori.* Palermo: La Zisa.

Rossi, Federico. 2022. "Capitalism and Social Movements." In *The Wiley-Blackwell Encyclopedia of Social and Political Movements,* edited by David Snow, Donatella della Porta, Bert Klandermans, and Doug McAdam. Oxford: Wiley.

Santino, Umberto. 2006, *Dalla mafia alle mafie: scienze sociali e crimine organizzato.* Soveria Mannelli, Italy: Rubbettino.

Santino, Umberto. 2007. *Mafie e globalizzazione.* Trapani, Italy: Di Girolamo Crispino.

Santino, Umberto. 2009. *Storia del movimento antimafia: Dalla lotta di classe all'impegno civile.* (2nd ed.). Rome: Editori Riuniti.

Sarmiento, Eric. 2020. "Field Methods for Assemblage Analysis: Tracing Relations between Difference and Dominance." In *The Handbook of Diverse Economies,* edited by J. K. Gibson-Graham and Kelly Dombroski, 486–93. Cheltenham, UK: Edward Elgar.

Sausdal, David, and Henrik Vigh. 2019. "Anthropological Criminology 2.0: Ethnographies of Global Crime and Criminalization." *Focaal: Journal of Global and Historical Anthropology* 85: 1–14.

Saveria Antiochia Omicron. n.d. "Ecomafie in Italia: Una Panoramica." http://www.filcacisl.it/sindacato/wp-content/uploads/2012/07/SINTESI-20_-Ecomafie.docx. Accessed March 14, 2023.

Saviano, Roberto. (2006) 2016. *Gomorra. Viaggio nell'impero economico e nel sogno di dominio della camorra.* Milan: Mondadori.

Savona, Ernesto. 2014. "Organised Crime Numbers." *Global Crime* 15 (1–2): 1–9.

Savona, Ernesto, and Francesco Calderoni, eds. 2015. *Criminal Markets and Mafia Proceeds.* London: Routledge.

Savona, Ernesto U., Michele Riccardi, and Giulia Berlusconi, eds. 2016. *Organised Crime in European Businesses.* Abingdon, UK: Routledge.

Schlosberg, David, and Luke Craven. 2019. *Sustainable Materialism: Environmental Movements and the Politics of Everyday Life.* Oxford: Oxford University Press.

Schneider, Jane, and Peter Schneider. 1976. *Culture and Political Economy in Western Sicily.* New York: Academic Press.

Schneider, Jane, and Peter Schneider. 2003. *Reversible Destiny: Mafia, Antimafia and the Struggle for Palermo.* Berkeley: University of California Press.

Schram, Sanford, F., and Marianna Pavlovskaya, eds. 2017. *Rethinking Neoliberalism: Resisting the Disciplinary Regime.* London: Routledge.

Sciascia, Leonardo. 1961. *Il giorno della civetta.* Turin: Einaudi.

Seaton, Anthony V. 1996. "Guided by the Dark: From Thanatopsis to Thanatourism." *International Journal of Heritage Studies* 2 (4): 234–44.

Sedgewick, Eve. 2003. *Touching Feeling: Affect, Pedagogy, Performativity.* Durham, N.C.: Duke University Press.

Senior, Katryn, and Alfredo Mazza. 2004. "Italian 'Triangle of Death' Linked to Waste Crisis." *The Lancet Oncology* 5: 525–27.

Sergi, Pantaleone. 2003. *Gli anni dei Basilischi. Mafia, istituzioni e società in Basilicata.* Milan: Angeli.

Smelser, Neil J. 1962. *Theory of Collective Behavior.* New York: Free Press.

Smith, Dwight C. 1980. "Paragons, Pariahs and Pirates: A Spectrum Based Theory of Enterprise." *Crime and Delinquency* 26 (3): 358–86.

Snow, David. 2001. "Collective Identity and Expressive Forms." University of California, Irvine eScholarship Repository. http://escholarship.org/uc/item/2zn1t7bj#page-2. Accessed March 20, 2023.

Snow, David A. 2004. "Social Movements as Challenges to Authority: Resistance to an Emerging Conceptual Hegemony." In *Authority in Contention,* edited by Daniel J. Myers, Daniel M. Cress and Patrick Coy, 3–25. New York: Elsevier.

Snow, David, E. Burke Rochford, Stephen K. Worden, and Robert D. Benford. 1986. "Frame Alignment Processes, Micromobilization, and Movement Participation." *American Sociological Review* 51 (4): 464–81.

Sontag, Susan. 2003. *Regarding the Pain of Others.* New York: Farrar, Straus and Giroux.

Spinosa, Charles, Fernando Flores, and Hubert L. Dreyfus. 1997. *Disclosing New Worlds: Entrepreneurship, Democratic Action, and the Cultivation of Solidarity.* Cambridge, Mass.: MIT Press.

Spinoza, Baruch. (1677) 2001. *Ethics.* Translated by William Hale White, and Amelia Hutchison Stirling. London: Wordsworth.

Staggenborg, Suzanne. 1998. "Social Movement Communities and Cycles of Protest: The Emergence and Maintenance of a Local Women's Movement." *Social Problems* 45 (2): 180–204.

Staggenborg, Suzanne, and Verta Taylor. 2005. "Whatever Happened to the Women's Movement?" *Mobilization: An International Journal* 10 (1): 37–52.

Staheli, Ürs. 2011. "Decentering the Economy: Governmentality Studies and Beyond?" In *The Government of Life: Foucault, Biopolitics, and Neoliberalism,* edited by Ulrich Bröckling, Susanne Krasmann, and Thomas Lemke, 269–85. London: Routledge.

Sturzo, Luigi. 1974. *Scritti inedita, vol. 1: 1890–1924.* Rome: Cinque Lune.

Sutherland, Edwin. 1937. *The Professional Thief.* Chicago: University of Chicago Press.

Sutherland, Edwin, and Donald Cressey. 1978. *Principles of Criminology.* Philadelphia: Lippincott.

Tarde, Gabriel. 1886. *La Criminalité Comparée* [Crime, compared]. Paris: Félix Alcan.

Tarde, Gabriel. 1895. *La logique sociale.* Paris: Félix Alcan.

Tarde, Gabriel. 1897. *L'opposition universelle.* Paris: Félix Alcan.

Tarde, Gabriel. 1898. *Les lois sociales: Esquisse d'une sociologie* [Social laws: An outline of sociology]. Paris: Félix Alcan.

Tarde, Gabriel. 1902a. "L'Invention Considérée Comme Moteur de l'Évolution Sociale." *Revue Internationale de Sociologie* 7: 561–74.

Tarde, Gabriel. 1902b. *Psychologie économique.* Paris: Félix Alcan.

Tarde, Gabriel. (1890) 1903. *The Laws of Imitation.* Translated by Elsie C. Parsons. New York: Henry Holt.

Tarde, Gabriel. 1962. *The Laws of Imitation.* Translated by Elsie C. Parsons, from the Second French Edition. New York: Henry Holt.

Tarde, Gabriel. (1901) 1989. *L'opinion et la foule.* Paris: Presses Universitaires de France.

Tarde, Gabriel. 2000. *Social Laws: An Outline of Sociology.* Kitchener: Batoche Books. Cited in Stephan Moebius. 2004. "Imitation, Repetition and Iterability." *Distinktion: Scandinavian Journal of Social Theory* 5 (2): 62.

Tarde, Gabriel. (1890) 2001. *Penal Philosophy.* Translated by R. Howell. New Brunswick, N.J.: Transaction.

Tarrow, Sidney. 1989. *Democracy and Disorder: Social Conflict, Political Protest and Democracy in Italy, 1965–1975.* New York: Oxford University Press.

Taussig, Michael. 1993. *Mimesis and Alterity: A Particular History of the Senses.* London: Routledge.

Thrift, Nigel. 2008. "The Material Practices of Glamour." *Journal of Cultural Economy* 1 (1): 9–23.

Tilly, Charles. 1977. "From Mobilization to Revolution." Working Paper no. 156. Center for Research on Social Organization, University of Michigan.

Tilly, Charles. 1981. "Britain Creates the Social Movement." Working Paper no. 232. Centre for Research on Social Organization, University of Michigan.

Tilly, Charles. 1985. "War Making and State Making as Organised Crime." In *Bringing the State Back in,* edited by Peter B. Evans, Dietrich Rueschemeyer, and Theda Skocpol. Cambridge: Cambridge University Press.

Tilly, Charles, and Sidney Tarrow. 2006. *Contentious Politics.* Boulder, Colo.: Paradigm.

Toews, David. 2003. "The New Tarde: Sociology after the End of the Social." *Theory, Culture & Society* 20 (5): 81–98.

Tomasi di Lampedusa, Giuseppe. 1958. *Il gattopardo.* Milan: Feltrinelli.

Tonkonoff, Sergio. 2014a. "Crime as the Limit of Culture." *Human Studies* 37: 529–44.

Tonkonoff, Sergio. 2014b. "Crime as Social Excess: Reconstructing Gabriel Tarde's Criminal Sociology." *History of the Human Sciences* 27 (2): 60–74.

Tormey, Simon. 2006. "'Not in My Name': Deleuze, Zapatismo and the Critique of Representation." *Parliamentary Affairs* 59 (1): 138–54.

Tormey, Simon. 2015. *The End of Representative Politics.* London: Polity.

Touraine, Alain. 1981. *The Voice and the Eye: An Analysis of Social Movements.* Translated by Alan Duff. Cambridge: Cambridge University Press.

Touraine, Alain. 2014. *After the Crisis.* Cambridge: Polity.

Transcrime. 2014. Executive Summary. http://www.transcrime.it/wp -content/uploads/2014/02/PON-Executive.pdf. Accessed March 14, 2023.

Tridico, Pasquale. 2013. *Italy: From Economic Decline to Current Crisis,* Rome: Dipartimento di Economia Università degli Studi Roma Tre.

Turker, Kaner A., and James T. Murphy. 2019. "Assembling Community Economies." *Progress in Human Geography* 45 (1): 49–69.

Turner, Ralph H., and Lewis M. Killian. 1957. *Collective Behavior.* Englewood Cliffs, N.J.: Prentice-Hall.

United Nations Office on Drugs and Crime. 2011. "Estimating Illicit Financial Flows Resulting from Drug Trafficking and Other Transnational Organized Crimes." http://www.unodc.org/documents /data-and-analysis/Studies/Illicit_financial_flows_2011_web.pdf. Accessed March 3, 2023.

Urry, John. 1990. *The Tourist Gaze.* New Delhi: Sage.

Varese, Federico. 2010. "What Is Organised Crime?" In *Organized Crime,* vol. 1, edited by Federico Varese, 1–33. London: Routledge.

Varese, Federico. 2011. *Mafias on the Move: How Organized Crime Conquers New Territories.* Princeton, N.J.: Princeton University Press.

Vegas Mob Tour. 2023. https://vegasmobtour.com/. Accessed March 17, 2023.

Viriasova, Inna. 2011. "Politics and the Political: Correlation and the Question of the Unpolitical." *Peninsula: A Journal of Relational Politics* 1 (18).

Viviani, Matteo. 2014. "Mafia, antimafia e aziende che affondano." *Le Iene.* http://www.video.mediaset.it/video/iene/puntata/510828 /viviani-mafia-antimafia-e-aziende-che-affondano.html. Accessed March 10, 2023.

Von Eggers, Nicolai. 2015. "Genealogies of Political Economy as Government." In *Challenging Ideas: Theory and Empirical Research in Social Sciences and Humanities,* edited by Marit Lytje, Torben K. Nielsen, and Martin Ottovay Jørgensen, 109–26. Newcastle upon Tyne: Cambridge Scholar.

Von Eggers, Nicolai. 2016. "The Emergence of the Concept 'Political Economy.'" In *Intellectual History of Economic Normativities,* edited by Mikkel Thorup, 73–89. New York: Palgrave Macmillan.

Wahlen, Stefan, and Mikko Laamanen. 2015. "Consumption, Lifestyle and Social Movements." *International Journal of Consumer Studies* 39 (5): 397–403.

Wang, Jackie. 2018. *Carceral Capitalism.* South Pasadena, Calif.: Semiotext(e).

Wang, Ning. 1999. "Rethinking Authenticity in Tourism Experience." *Annals of Tourism Research* 26 (2): 349–370.

Wark, McKenzie. 2004. *A Hacker Manifesto.* Cambridge Mass.: Harvard University Press.

Weaver, David B. 2013. *Sustainable Tourism: Theory and Practice,* 2nd ed. London: Routledge.

Wolcott, Harry F. 1995. *The Art of Fieldwork.* Walnut Creek, Calif.: Altamira.

World Tourism Organization. 2015. "About UNWTO." http://cf.cdn .unwto.org/sites/all/files/docpdf/130718basicdocumentsenweb.pdf. Accessed March 20, 2023.

Yates, Luke. 2015a. "Everyday Politics, Social Practices and Movement Networks: Daily Life in Barcelona's Social Centres." *British Journal of Sociology* 66 (2): 236–58.

Yates, Luke. 2015b. "Rethinking Prefiguration: Alternatives, Micropolitics and Goals in Social Movements." *Social Movement Studies* 14 (1): 1–21.

Young, Iris M. 1989. "Polity and Group Difference: A Critique of the Ideal of Universal Citizenship." *Ethics* 99 (2): 250–74.

Zald, Mayer N. 2000. "Ideologically Structured Action: An Enlarged Agenda for Social Movement Research." *Mobilization* 5 (1): 1–16.

Index

Christina Jerne is assistant professor in the Department of Anthropology, University of Copenhagen, Denmark. She is the coeditor and translator of *Against the Mafia: The Classic Italian Writings.*